Study Guide

for use with

Macroeconomics

Fourth Edition

David C. Colander
Middlebury College

Prepared by
David C. Colander
Middlebury College

Douglas Copeland
Johnson County Community College

Jenifer Gamber

**McGraw-Hill
Irwin**

Boston   Burr Ridge, IL   Dubuque, IA   Madison, WI   New York   San Francisco   St. Louis
Bangkok   Bogotá   Caracas   Lisbon   London   Madrid
Mexico City   Milan   New Delhi   Seoul   Singapore   Sydney   Taipei   Toronto

Study Guide for use with
MACROECONOMICS
David C. Colander

3 4 5 6 7 8 9 0 MCG/MCG 0 9 8 7 6 5 4 3 2

ISBN 0-07-236639-7

www.mhhe.com

Contents

Preface

We wrote this study guide to help you do well in your economics courses. Even using a great book like the Colander textbook, we know that studying is not all fun. The reality is: most studying is hard work and a study guide won't change that. Your text and lectures will give you the foundation for doing well. So the first advice we will give you is:

1. Read the textbook.
2. Attend class.

We cannot emphasize that enough. Working through the study guide will not replace the text or lectures; this study guide is designed to help you retain the knowledge from the text and classroom by practicing the tools of economics. It is not an alternative to the book and class; it is **in addition to them**.

Having said that, we should point out that buying this guide isn't enough. You have to *use* it. Really, if it sits on your desk, or even under your pillow, it won't do you any good. Osmosis only works with plants. This study guide should be well worn by the end of the semester — dog-eared pages, scribbles beneath questions, some pages even torn out. It should look used.

WHAT CAN YOU EXPECT FROM THIS BOOK?

This study guide concentrates on the terminology and models in your text. It does not expand upon the material in the textbook; it reinforces it. It primarily serves to give you a good foundation to understanding principles of economics. Your professor has chosen this study guide for you, suggesting that your economics exams are going to focus on this kind of foundational understanding. You should be sure of this: if your professor is going to give you mainly essay exams, or complex questions about applying the foundations (like the more difficult end-of-chapter questions in your textbook) this study guide will not be enough to ace that exam.

To get an idea of what your exams will be like, ask your professor to take a look at these questions and tell the class whether they are representative of the type of questions that will be on the exam. And if they will differ, how.

HOW SHOULD YOU USE THIS STUDY GUIDE?

As we stated above, this book works best if you have attended class and read the book. Ideally, you were awake during class and took notes, you have read the textbook chapters more than once, and have worked through some of the questions at the end of the chapter. (So, we're optimists.)

Just in case the material in the book isn't fresh in your mind, before turning to this study guide it is a good idea to refresh your memory about the material in the text. To do so:

1. Read through the margin comments in the text; they highlight the main concepts in each chapter.
2. Turn to the last few pages of the chapter and reread the chapter summary.
3. Look through the key terms, making sure they are familiar. (O.K., we're not only optimists, we're wild optimists.)

Even if you do not do the above, working though the questions in the study guide will help to tell you whether you really do know the material in the textbook chapters.

STRUCTURE OF THE STUDY GUIDE

This study guide has two main components: (1) a chapter-by-chapter review and (2) pretests based upon groups of chapters.

Chapter-by-chapter review
Each chapter has eight elements:

1. A chapter at a glance: A brief exposition and discussion of the learning objectives for the chapter.
2. Short-answer questions keyed to the learning objectives.

3. A test of matching the terms to their definitions.
4. Problems and applications.
5. A brain teaser
6. Multiple choice questions.
7. Potential essay questions
8. Answers to all questions.

Each chapter presents the sections in the order that we believe they can be most beneficial to you. Here is how we suggest you use them:

Chapter at a Glance: These should jog your memory about the text and lecture. If you don't remember ever seeing the material before, you should go back and reread the textbook chapter. The numbers in parentheses following each learning objective refer to the page in the text that covers that objective. Remember, reading a chapter when you are thinking about a fantasy date is almost the same as not having read the chapter at all.

Short-Answer Questions: The short-answer questions will tell you if you are familiar with the learning objectives. Try to answer each within the space below each question. Don't just read the questions and assume you can write an answer. Actually writing an answer will reveal your weaknesses. If you can answer them all perfectly, great. But, quite honestly, we don't expect you to be able to answer them all perfectly. We only expect you to be able to sketch out an answer.

Of course, some other questions are important to know. For example, if there is a question about the economic decision rule and you don't remember that it excludes past costs and benefits, you need more studying. So the rule is: Know the central ideas of the chapter; be less concerned about the specific presentation of those central ideas.

After you have sketched out all your answers, check them with those at the end of the chapter and review those that you didn't get right. Since each question is based upon a specific learning objective in the text, for those you didn't get right, you may want to return to the textbook to review the material covering that learning objective.

Match the Terms and Concepts to Their Definitions: Since the definitions are listed, you should get most of these right. The best way to match these is to read the definition first, and then find the term on the left that it defines. If you are not sure of the matching term, circle that definition and move on

to the next one. At the end return to the remaining definitions and look at the remaining terms to complete the matches. After completing this part, check your answers with those in the back of the chapter and figure our what percent you got right. If that percent is below the grade you want to get on your exam, try to see why you missed the ones you did and review those terms and concepts in the textbook.

Problems and Applications: Now it's time to take on any problems in the chapter. These problems are generally more difficult than the short-answer questions. These problems focus on numerical and graphical aspects of the chapter.

Working through problems is perhaps one of the best ways to practice your understanding of economic principles. Even if you are expecting a multiple choice exam, working through these problems will give you a good handle on using the concepts in each chapter.

If you expect a multiple choice exam with no problems, you can work through these fairly quickly, making sure you understand the concepts being tested. If you will have a test with problems and exercises, make sure you can answer each of these questions accurately.

Work out the answers to all the problems in the space provided before checking them against the answers in the back of the chapter. Where our answers differ from yours, check to find out why. The answers refer to specific pages in the textbook so you can review the text again too.

Most of the problems are objective and have only one answer. A few are interpretative and have many answers. We recognize that some questions can be answered in different ways than we did. If you cannot reconcile your answer with ours, check with your professor. Once you are at this stage — worrying about different interpretations — you're ahead of most students and, most likely, prepared for the exam.

A Brain Teaser: This section consists of one problem that is generally one step up in the level of difficulty from the "Problems and Applications" exercises or is a critical thought question. It is designed to provide a challenge to those few students who have studied the way we have suggested.

Multiple Choice Questions: The next exercise in each chapter is the multiple choice test. It serves to test the breadth of your knowledge of the text material. Multiple choice questions are not the final arbiters of your understanding. They are, instead, a way of determining whether you have read the book and generally understood the material.

Take this test after having worked through the other questions. Give the answer that most closely corresponds to the answer presented in your text. If you can answer these questions you should be ready for the multiple choice part of your exam.

Work through all the questions in the test before grading yourself. Looking up the answer before you try to answer the questions is a poor way to study. For a multiple choice exam, the percent you answer correctly will be a good predictor of how well you will do on the test.

You can foul up on multiple choice questions in two ways—you can know too little and you can know too much. The answer to knowing too little is obvious: Study more—that is, read the chapters more carefully (and maybe more often). The answer to knowing too much is more complicated. Our suggestions for students who know too much is not to ask themselves "What is the answer?" but instead to ask "What is the answer the person writing the question wants?" Since, with these multiple choice questions, the writer of many of the questions is the textbook author, ask yourself: "What answer would the textbook author want me to give?" Answering the questions in this way will stop you from going too deeply into them and trying to see nuances that aren't supposed to be there.

For the most part questions in this study guide are meant to be straightforward. There may be deeper levels at which other answers could be relevant, but searching for those deeper answers will generally get you in trouble and not be worth the cost.

If you are having difficulty answering a multiple choice question, make your best guess. Once you are familiar with the material, even if you don't know the answer to a question you can generally make a reasonable guess. What point do you think the writer of the question wanted to make with the question? Figuring out that point and then thinking of incorrect answers may be a way for you to eliminate wrong answers and then choose among the remaining options.

Notice that the answers at the end of the chapter are not just the lettered answers. We have provided an explanation for each answer — why the right one is right and why some of the other choices are wrong. If you miss a question, read that rationale carefully. If you are not convinced, or do not follow the reasoning, go to the page in the text referred to in the answer and reread the material. If you are still not convinced, see the caveat on the next page.

Potential Essay Questions: These questions provide yet another opportunity to test your understanding of what you have learned. Answering these questions will be especially helpful if you expect these types of questions on the exams. We have only sketched the beginning to an answer to these. This beginning should give you a good sense of the direction to go in your answer, but be aware that on exam a more complete answer will be required.

Questions on Appendices: In the chapters we have included a number of questions on the text appendices. To separate these questions from the others, the letter A precedes the question number. They are for students who have been assigned the appendices. If you have not been assigned them (and you have not read them on your own out of your great interest in economics) you can skip these.

Answers to All Questions: The answers to all questions appear at the end of each chapter. They begin on a new page so that you can tear out the answers and more easily check your answers against ours. We cannot emphasize enough that the best way to study is to answer the questions yourself first, and then check out our answers. Just looking at the questions and our answers may tell you what the answers are but will not give you the chance to see where your knowledge of the material is weak.

Pretests

Most class exams cover more than one chapter. To prepare you for such an exam, we provide multiple choice pretests for groups of chapters. These pretests consist of 25-40 multiple choice questions from the selected group of chapters. These questions are identical to earlier questions so if you have done the work, you should do well on these. We suggest you complete the entire exam before grading yourself.

We also suggest taking these under test conditions. Specifically,

Use a set time period to complete the exam.
Sit at a hard chair at a desk with good lighting.

Each answer will tell you the chapter on which the question is based, so if you did not cover one of the chapters in the text for your class, don't worry if you get that question wrong. If you get a number of questions wrong from the chapters your class has covered, worry.

There is another way to use these pretests which we hesitate to mention, but we're realists so we will. That way is to forget doing the chapter-by-chapter work and simply take the pretests. Go back and review the material you get wrong.

However you use the pretests, if it turns out that you consistently miss questions from the same chapter, return to your notes from the lecture and reread your textbook chapters.

A FINAL WORD OF ADVICE

That's about it. If you use it, this study guide can help you do better on the exam by giving you the opportunity to use the terms and models of economics. However, we reiterate one last time: The best way to do well in a class is to attend every class and read every chapter in the text as well as work through the chapters in this study guide. Start early and work consistently. Do not do all your studying the night before the exam.

THANKS AND A CAVEAT

We and our friends went through this book more times than we want to remember. All the authors proofed the entire book, as did our good friends, Jim Craven, Pam Bodenhorn and Elizabeth DeVault. We also had some superb students, Kaia Laursen, Jana Prodanova, Usman El Haque, Saad Rasool, and Mashrib Zahid, go through it. (Our sincere thanks go to them for doing so.) Despite our best efforts, there is always a chance that there's a correct answer other than the one the book tells you is the correct answer, or even that the answer the book gives is wrong. If you find a mistake, and it is a small problem about a number of an obvious mistake, assume the error is typographical. If that is not the case, and you still think another answer is the correct one, write up an alternative rationale and e-mail Professor Colander the question and the alternative rationale. Professor Colander's e-mail is:

colander@middlebury.edu.

When he gets it he will either send you a note thanking you immensely for finding another example of his fallibility, or explaining why we disagree with you. If you're the first one to have pointed out an error he will also send you a copy of an honors companion for economics—just what you always wanted, right?

David Colander
Douglas Copeland
Jenifer Gamber

ECONOMICS AND ECONOMIC REASONING

CHAPTER AT A GLANCE

This review is based upon the learning objectives that open the chapter.

1. Three central coordination problems any economy must solve are: (5)
    *   What to produce.
    *   How to produce it.
    *   For whom to produce it.

    Most economic coordination problems involve scarcity.

2. If the marginal benefits of doing something exceed the marginal costs, do it. If the marginal costs of doing something exceed the marginal benefits, don't do it. This is known as the economic decision rule. (7)

    You really need to think in terms of the marginal, or "extra" benefits (MB) and marginal, or "extra" costs (MC) of a course of action.

    ### Economic decision rule:
    If MB>MC $\Rightarrow$ *Do more of it because "it's worth it."*

    If MB<MC $\Rightarrow$ *Do less of it because "it's not worth it."*

    NOTE: The symbol " $\Rightarrow$ *" means "implies" or "logically follows."*

3. Opportunity cost is the basis of cost/benefit economic reasoning; it is the benefit forgone, or the cost of the next-best alternative to the activity you've chosen. In economic reasoning, that cost is less than the benefit of what you've chosen. (8)

    Opportunity cost $\Rightarrow$ *"What must be given up in order to get something else." Opportunity costs are often "hidden." You need to take into consideration all costs when making a decision.*

4. Economic reality is controlled by economic forces, social forces and political forces: (9-11)

    What happens in a society can be seen as the reaction and interaction of these 3 forces.

    *   Economic forces;
        These are the market forces of demand, supply, and prices, etc.

    *   Social and historical forces;
        Social forces can prevent economic forces from becoming market forces.

    *   Political and legal forces.
        Political and legal forces affect decisions too.

5. Microeconomics considers economic reasoning from the viewpoint of individuals and builds up; macroeconomics considers economic reasoning from the aggregate and builds down. (14)

    Microeconomics (micro) $\Rightarrow$ *concerned with some particular segment of the economy. Macroeconomics (macro)* $\Rightarrow$ *concerned with the entire economy.*

6a. *Positive economics* is the study of what is, and how the economy works. (16)

    Deals with "what is" (objective analysis).

6b. *Normative economics* is the study of what the goals of the economy should be. (16)

    Deals with "what ought to be" (subjective analysis).

6c. The *art of economics* is the application of the knowledge learned in positive economics to the achievement of the goals determined in normative economics. (16)

The art of economics is sometimes referred to as "policy economics."

"Good" policy tries to be objective. It tries to weigh all the benefits and costs associated with all policy options and chooses that option in which the benefits outweigh the costs to the greatest degree.

See also, Appendix A: "Graphish: The Language of Graphs"

In Appendix A, remember 2 types of relationships:

- *Direct (Positive) Relationship: expressed as an upward sloping curve.*

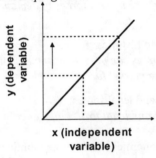

Note: as x increases, y increases; as x decreases, y decreases.

- Inverse (Negative) Relationship: expressed as a downward sloping curve.

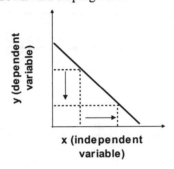

Note: as x increases, y decreases; as x decreases, y increases.

● SHORT-ANSWER QUESTIONS

1. What are the three central problems that every economy must solve?

   - what to Produce
   - how to Produce
   - whom to Produce

2. What is scarcity? What are two elements that comprise scarcity? How do they affect relative scarcity? *→ The goods available are too few to satisfy individuals' desires*

   2 Elements are:
   ① Our wants
   ② Our means of fulfiling those wants

3. State the economic decision rule.

   - If marginal benefits of doing something exceed the marginal cost. Do it
   MB > MC - ✓
   - If marginal cost of doing something exceeds marginal benefit - Don't Do it
   MC > MB - ✗

4. Define opportunity cost.

   Cost/ Benefit economic reasoning.

   - undertaking an activity is the benefit forgone by undertaking that activity

5. What is the importance of opportunity cost to economic reasoning?

   Economic reasoning → that cost is less than the Benefit

6. What is an economic force? What are the forces that can keep an economic force from becoming a market force?

   EF → necessary reactions to scarcity → are always operating

7. How does microeconomics differ from macroeconomics? Give an example of a macroeconomic issue and a microeconomic issue.

8. Define positive economics, normative economics, and the art of economics. How do they relate to one another?

MATCHING THE TERMS
Match the terms to their definitions

_l_	1.	art of economics	a. Additional benefit above what you've already derived.
_c_	2.	economic decision rule	b. Additional cost above what you've already incurred.
_e_	3.	economic forces	c. If benefits exceed costs, do it. If costs exceed benefits, don't.
_o_	4.	economic model	d. The study of individual choice, and how that choice is influenced
_r_	5.	economic policies	by economic forces.
_p_	6.	economic principle	e. Necessary reactions to scarcity.
_j_	7.	economics	f. The benefit forgone, or the cost, of the best alternative to the activity
_q_	8.	efficiency	ity you've chosen.
_n_	9.	invisible hand	g. The study of what is, and how the economy works.
_h_	10.	invisible hand theory	h. The insight that a market economy, through the price mechanism,
_i_	11.	macroeconomics	will allocate resources efficiently.
_a_	12.	marginal benefit	i. The study of the economy as a whole, which includes inflation,
_b_	13.	marginal cost	unemployment, business cycles, and growth.
_m_	14.	market force	j. The study of how human beings coordinate their wants.
_d_	15.	microeconomics	k. Goods available are too few to satisfy individuals' desires.
_s_	16.	normative economics	l. The application of the knowledge learned in positive economics
_f_	17.	opportunity cost	to the achievement of the goals determined in normative econom-
_g_	18.	positive economics	ics.
_k_	19.	scarcity	m. An economic force that is given relatively free rein by society to
_t_	20.	sunk costs	work through the market.
			n. The price mechanism.

o. A framework that places the generalized insights of theory in a more specific contextual setting.

p. A commonly-held economic insight stated as a law or general assumption.

q. Achieving a goal as cheaply as possible.

r. Actions taken by government to influence economic actions.

s. Study of what the goals of the economy should be.

t. Costs that have already been incurred and cannot be recovered.

● PROBLEMS AND APPLICATIONS

1. State what happens to scarcity for each good in the following situations:

   a. New storage technology allows college dining services to keep peaches from rotting for a longer time. (Good: peaches).

      scarcity will fall because fewer peaches will rot

   b. More students desire to live in single-sex dormitories. No new single-sex dormitories are established. (Good: single-sex dormitory rooms).

      scarcity will rise

2. State as best you can:

   a. The opportunity cost of going out on a date tonight with the date you made last Wednesday.

   Benefit forgone of best alternative

   b. The opportunity cost of breaking the date for tonight you made last Wednesday.

   c. The opportunity cost of working through this study guide.

   d. The opportunity cost of buying this study guide.

3. Assume you have purchased a $15,000 car. The salesperson has offered you a maintenance contract covering all major repairs for the next 3 years, with some exclusions, for $750.

   a. What is the opportunity cost of purchasing that maintenance contract?

   b. What information would you need to make a decision based on the economic decision rule?

   c. Based upon that information how would you make your decision?

4. State for each of the following whether it is an example of political forces, social forces or economic forces at work:

   a. Warm weather arrives and more people take Sunday afternoon drives. As a result, the price of gasoline rises.

   b. In some states, liquor cannot be sold before noon on Sunday.

   c. Minors cannot purchase cigarettes.

   d. Many parents will send money to their children in college without the expectation of being repaid.

A BRAIN TEASER

1. Suppose you are a producer of handcrafted picture frames. The going market price for your frames is $250 a piece. No matter how many frames you sell your revenue per unit (equal to the selling price per unit) is constant at $250 per frame. However, your per unit costs of producing each additional picture frame are not constant. Suppose the following table summarizes your costs of producing picture frames. Use benefit/cost analysis to determine the most economical (profit maximizing) number of frames to produce given the price per unit and the cost schedule shown below. What are your total profits per week?

# of Frames	Price	Total Cost
0	$250	$0
1	$250	$25
2	$250	$75
3	$250	$150
4	$250	$300
5	$250	$560

● MULTIPLE CHOICE

Circle the one best answer for each of the following questions:

1. Economic reasoning
   a. provides a framework with which to approach questions.
   b. provides correct answers to just about every question.
   c. is only used by economists.
   d. should only be applied to economic business matters.

2. Scarcity could be reduced if
   a. individuals work less and want fewer consumption goods.
   b. individuals work more and want fewer consumption goods.
   c. world population grows and world production remains the same.
   d. innovation comes to a halt.

3. In the textbook, the author focuses on coordination rather than scarcity as the central point of the definition of economics because
   a. economics is not really about scarcity.
   b. scarcity involves coercion, and the author doesn't like coercion.
   c. the author wants to emphasize that the quantity of goods and services depends upon human action and the ability to coordinate that human action.
   d. the concept "scarcity" does not fit within the institutional structure of the economy.

4. In the U.S. economy, who is in charge of organizing and coordinating overall economic activities?
   a. Government.
   b. Corporations.
   c. No one.
   d. Consumers.

5. You bought stock A for $10 and stock B for $50. The price of each is currently $20. Assuming no tax issues, which should you sell if you need money?
   a. Stock A.
   b. Stock B.
   c. It doesn't matter which.
   d. You should sell an equal amount of both.

6. In deciding whether to go to lectures in the middle of the semester, you should
   a. include tuition as part of the cost of that decision.
   b. not include tuition as part of the cost of that decision.
   c. include a portion of tuition as part of the cost of that decision.
   d. only include tuition if you paid it rather than your parents.

7. In making economic decisions you should consider
   a. marginal costs and marginal benefits.
   b. marginal costs and average benefits.
   c. average costs and average benefits.
   d. total costs and total benefits, including past costs and benefits.

8. In arriving at a decision, a good economist would say that
   a. one should consider only total costs and total benefits.
   b. one should consider only marginal costs and marginal benefits.
   c. after one has considered marginal costs and benefits, one should integrate the social and moral implications and reconsider those costs and benefits.
   d. after considering the marginal costs and benefits, one should make the decision on social and moral grounds.

9. In making decisions economists primarily use
   a. monetary costs.
   b. opportunity costs.
   c. benefit costs.
   d. dollar costs.

10. The opportunity cost of reading Chapter 1 of the text
   a. is about 1/20 of the price you paid for the book because the chapter is about one twentieth of the price of the book.
   b. zero since you have already paid for the book
   c. has nothing to do with the price you paid for the book.
   d. is 1/20 the price of the book plus 1/20 the price of the tuition.

11. Rationing devices that our society uses include
   a. the invisible hand only.
   b. the invisible hand and social forces only.
   c. the invisible hand and political forces only.
   d. the invisible hand, the social forces, and political forces.

12. If at Female College there are significantly more females than males (and there are not a significant number of gays) economic forces
   a. will be pushing for females to pay on dates.
   b. will be pushing for males to pay on dates.
   c. will be pushing for neither to pay on dates.
   d. are irrelevant to this issue. Everyone knows that the males always should pay.

13. Individuals are prohibited from practicing medicine without a license. This is an example of
   a. the invisible hand.
   b. social forces.
   c. political forces.
   d. market forces.

14. Which of the following is most likely an example of a microeconomic topic?
   a. The effect of a flood in the Midwest on the price of bottled water.
   b. How a government policy will affect inflation.
   c. The relationship between unemployment and inflation.
   d. Why an economy goes into a recession.

15. Which of the following is an example of a macroeconomic topic?
   a. The effect of a frost on the Florida orange crop.
   b. Wages of cross-country truckers.
   c. How the unemployment and inflation rates are related.
   d. How income is distributed in the United States.

16. The statement, "The distribution of income should be left to the market," is
   a. a positive statement.
   b. a normative statement.
   c. an art-of-economics statement
   d. an objective statement.

17. "Given certain conditions, the market achieves efficient results" is an example of a
   a. positive statement.
   b. normative statement.
   c. art-of-economics statement.
   d. subjective statement.

A1. In the graph below, the point A represents

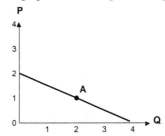

   a. a price of 1 and a quantity of 2.
   b. a price of 2 and a quantity of 2.
   c. a price of 2 and a quantity of 1.
   d. a price of 1 and a quantity of 1.

A2. The slope of the line in the graph below is
   a. 1/2.
   b. 2.
   c. minus 1/2.
   d. minus 2.

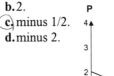

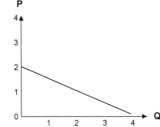

A3. At the maximum and minimum points of a nonlinear curve, the value of the slope is equal to

    a. 1.
    b. zero.
    c. minus 1.
    d. indeterminate.

A4. Which of the four lines in the graphs below has the larger slope?

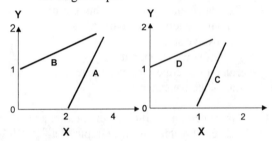

    a. A.
    b. B.
    c. C.
    d. A and C.

● POTENTIAL ESSAY QUESTIONS

You may also see essay questions similar to the "Problems & Applications" and "Brain Teasers" exercises.

1. Respond to the following statement: "Theories are of no use to me because they are not very practical. All I need is the facts because they speak for themselves."

2. The United States is one of the wealthiest nations on earth, yet our fundamental economic problem is scarcity. How can this be?

3. Does economics help teach us how to approach problems, or does it give us a set of answers to problems?

4. Can we say that what is true for the part (micro) is necessarily true for the whole (macro)?

ANSWERS

SHORT-ANSWER QUESTIONS

1. The three central problems that every economy must solve are (1) what to produce, (2) how to produce it, and (3) for whom to produce it. (5)

2. Scarcity occurs when there are not enough goods available to satisfy individuals' desires. Scarcity has two elements, our wants and our means of fulfilling those wants. Since each of these two elements can change, relative scarcity can also change. If we can reduce our wants, scarcity will fall. Likewise if we can increase our efforts to produce more goods or if technological changes allow people to produce more using the same resources, scarcity will fall. (5)

3. If the marginal benefits of doing something exceed the marginal costs, do it. If the marginal costs of doing something exceed the marginal benefits, don't do it. (7)

4. Opportunity cost is the benefit forgone by undertaking an activity. It is the benefit forgone of the next best alternative to the activity you have chosen. Otherwise stated, it is what must be given up in order to get something else. (8-9)

5. Opportunity cost is the basis of cost/benefit economic reasoning. In economic reasoning, opportunity cost is less than the benefit of what you have chosen. (8-9)

6. An economic force is the necessary reaction to scarcity. All scarce goods must be rationed in some way. If an economic force is allowed to work through the market, that economic force becomes a market force. The invisible hand is the price mechanism, the rise and fall of prices that guides our actions in a market. Social and political forces can keep economic forces from becoming market forces. (9)

7. Microeconomic theory considers economic reasoning from the viewpoint of individuals and builds up while macroeconomics considers economic reasoning from the aggregate and builds down. Microeconomics studies things like household buying decisions such as how much of one's income to save and how much to consume. Macroeconomics studies things like the unemployment rate. (14-15)

8. Positive economics is the study of what is and how the economy works. Normative economics is the study of what the goals of the economy should be. The art of economics is the application of the knowledge learned in positive economics to the achievement of the goals one has determined in normative economics. (16)

ANSWERS

MATCHING

1-l; 2-c; 3-e; 4-o; 5-r; 6-p; 7-j; 8-q; 9-n; 10-h; 11-i; 12-a; 13-b; 14-m; 15-d; 16-s; 17-f; 18-g; 19-k; 20-t.

ANSWERS

PROBLEMS AND APPLICATIONS

1. a. Scarcity will fall because fewer peaches will rot. (10)
    b. Scarcity of single-sex dorm rooms will rise since the number of students desiring single-sex dorm rooms has risen, but the number available has not. (10)

2. a. The opportunity cost of going out on a date tonight that I made last Wednesday is the benefit forgone of the best alternative. If my best alternative was to study for an economics exam, it would be the increase in my exam grade that I would have gotten had I studied. Many answers are possible. (8-9)
    b. The opportunity cost of breaking the date for tonight that I made last Wednesday is the benefit forgone of going out on that date. It would be all the fun I would have had on that date. Other answers are possible. (8-9)
    c. The opportunity cost of working through this study guide is the benefit forgone of the next-best alternative to studying. It could be the increase in the grade I would have received by studying for another exam, or the money I could have earned if I were working at the library. Many answers are possible. (8-9)

d. The opportunity cost of buying this study guide is the benefit forgone of spending that money on the next-best alternative. Perhaps it is the enjoyment forgone of eating two pizzas. Other answers are possible. (8-9)

3. a. The opportunity cost of purchasing the maintenance contract is the benefit I could receive by spending that $750 on something else like a moon roof. (8-9)

b. I would need to know the benefit of the maintenance contract to assess whether the cost of $750 is worthwhile. (8-9)

c. For me the benefit of the maintenance contract is the expected cost of future repairs that would be covered and the peace of mind of knowing that future repairs are covered by the contract. The cost is the opportunity cost of using the $750 in another way. If the benefit exceeds the cost, do it. If the cost exceeds the benefit, do not do it. (8-9)

4. a. This is an example of an economic force. (9)

b. This is an example of legal forces. Some states have laws, called blue laws, against selling liquor on Sundays altogether or selling it before noon. (11)

c. This is an example of a legal force. This is a federal law. (11)

d. This is an example of a social force. (11)

ANSWERS

A BRAIN TEASER

1. The most economical (profit-maximizing) quantity of frames to produce is 4 frames. This is because the marginal benefit of producing frames (the revenue per unit–equal to the price per unit of $250)–exceeds the marginal (extra) cost of producing frames through the first 4 frames produced. The 5th frame should not be produced because the marginal benefit (the price received) is less than the marginal (extra) cost of production. You would be adding more to your costs than to your revenues and thereby reducing your profits. Your profit would total $700 per week.

Price (P) Marginal (Q) Benefit	Total Cost (TC)	Marginal Cost	Total Revenue (TR=PQ)	Profit TR−TC
0 $250	$0	—	$0	$0
1 $250	$25	$25	$250	$225
2 $250	$75	$50	$500	$425
3 $250	$150	$75	$750	$600
4 $250	$300	$150	$1000	$700
5 $250	$560	$260	$1250	$690

ANSWERS

MULTIPLE CHOICE

1. a As discussed on page 6, the textbook author clearly believes that economic reasoning applies to just about everything. This eliminates c and d. He also carefully points out that it is not the only reasoning that can be used; hence b does not fit. So the correct answer must be a.

2. b On page 5 of the textbook, the author states that the problem of scarcity depends upon our wants and our means of fulfilling those wants. An implication of this is that scarcity could be reduced if individuals worked more and wanted less.

3. c On page 5 of the book the author emphasizes the human action reason for focusing on coordination. He explicitly points out that scarcity is important, but that the concept of coordination is broader.

4. c As discussed on page 8, the invisible hand of the market coordinates the activities and is a composite of many individuals rather than just any one individual. If you were tempted to say b, corporations, your instincts are right, but the "overall" eliminated that as a possible answer.

5. c As is discussed on pages 10 and 11 of the book, in making economic decisions you consider that only costs from this point on are relevant; historical costs have no relevance. Since the prices of the stocks are currently the same, it doesn't matter which you sell.

6. b As discussed on pages 6 and 7, in economic decisions, you only look at costs from this point on; sunk costs are sunk costs, so tuition can be forgotten. Economic decisions focus on forward-looking marginal costs and marginal benefits.

7. a The economic decision rule is "If benefits exceed costs, do it." As is discussed on page 6 of the text, however, the relevant benefits and relevant costs to be considered are marginal (additional) costs and marginal benefits. The answer d is definitely ruled out by the qualifying phrase referring to past benefits and costs. Thus, only a is correct.

8. c As the textbook points out on page 7, economists use a framework of costs and benefits initially, but then later they add the social and moral implications to their conclusions. Adding these can change the estimates of costs and benefits, and in doing so can change the result of economic analysis, so there is an integration between the two. (This was a hard question which required careful reading of the text to answer correctly.)

9. b As discussed on page 8 of the text, opportunity costs include measures of nonmonetary costs. The other answers either do not include all the costs that an economist would consider, or are simply two words put together. The opportunity costs include the benefit forgone by undertaking an activity.

10. c As discussed on pages 8-9, the correct answer is that it has nothing to do with the price you paid since that is already paid, so a and d are wrong. The opportunity cost is not zero, however, since there are costs of reading the book. The primary opportunity cost of reading the book is the value of the time you're spending on it which is determined by what you could be doing with that time otherwise.

11. d As discussed on pages 8 and 9 of the text, all of these are rationing devices. The invisible hand works through the market and thus is focused on in economics. However the others also play a role in determining what people want, either through legal means or through social control.

12. a As discussed on pages 9 and 10 of the text, if there are significantly more of one gender than another, dates with that group must be rationed out among the other group. Economic forces will be pushing for the group in excess quantity supplied (in this case women) to pay. Economic forces may be pushing in that direction even though historical forces may push us in the opposite direction. Thus, even if males pay because of social forces, economic forces will be pushing for females to pay.

13. c Laws are legal forces.

14. a As discussed on pages 14 and 15, macroeconomics is concerned with inflation, unemployment, business cycles and growth. Microeconomics is the study of individuals and individual markets.

15. c As discussed on pages 14 and 15, macroeconomics is concerned with inflation, unemployment, business cycles and growth. Microeconomics is the study of individuals. The distribution of income is a micro topic because it is concerned with the distribution of income among individuals.

16. b As discussed on pages 16 and 17, this could be either a normative or an art-of-economics statement, depending on whether there is an implicit "given the way the real-world economy operates to best achieve the growth rate you desire." Since these qualifiers are not there, "normative" is the preferable answer.

17. a As discussed on page 16 this is a positive statement. It is a statement about *what is,* not about what should be.

A1. a   As discussed in Appendix A, page 21 and 24, a point represents the corresponding numbers on the horizontal and vertical number lines.

A2. c   As discussed on page 23 of Appendix A, the slope of a line is defined as rise over run. Since the rise is -2 and the run is 4, the slope of the above line is minus 1/2.

A3. b   As discussed on page 24 of Appendix A, at the maximum and minimum points of a curve the slope is zero.

A4. c   As discussed in Appendix A, page 24, the slope is defined as rise over run. Line C has the largest rise for a given run so c is the answer. Even though, visually, line A seems to have the same slope as line C, it has a different coordinate system. Line A has a slope of 1 whereas line B has a slope of 1/4. Always be careful about checking coordinate systems when visually interpreting a graph.

ANSWERS

POTENTIAL ESSAY QUESTIONS

The following are annotated answers. They indicate the general idea behind the answer.

1. Theories are practical because they are generalizations based on real world observations or facts. They enable us to predict and to explain real-world economic behavior. Because they are generalizations, they enable us to avoid unnecessary details or facts. The drawback, however, is that because they are generalizations, at times there will be exceptions to the prediction we would generally expect to observe.

Facts, on the other hand, do not always speak for themselves. One can often be overwhelmed by a large set of data or facts. Not until one systematically arranges, interprets and generalizes upon facts, tying them together, and distilling out a theory (general statement) related to those facts, do they take on any real meaning. In short, theory and facts are inseparable in the scientific process because theory gives meaning to facts and facts check the validity of theory.

2. The United States is still faced with scarcity because we are unable to have as much as we would like to have. Our resources (as vast as they are) are still scarce relative to the amount of goods and services we would like to have (indeed, our wants appear to be unlimited).

3. Economics is a methodology, or an approach to how we think about the world. It does not come to us equipped with a whole set of solutions to complex real-world problems. However, it may help shed some light on the complexities of real world issues helping us to find solutions.

4. No, not necessarily. For example, if one farmer has a "bumper-crop" year, an unusually large harvest, he will be better off. But, if all farmers experience the same thing, then the increased supply of the crop made available in the market will drive its price down and all farmers will be worse off.

THE ECONOMIC ORGANIZATION OF SOCIETY

CHAPTER AT A GLANCE

This review is based upon the learning objectives that open the chapter.

1. <u>Capitalism</u> is an economic system based on private property and the market. It gives private property rights to individuals, and relies on market forces to coordinate economic activity. (28)

   Capitalism ("market-oriented economy") is characterized by:
   (I) mainly private ownership of resources
   (II) market system solves the What? How? and For whom? problems.

   <u>*Capitalism's solutions*</u> *to the central economic problems:*

   ● *What to produce: what businesses believe people want, and what is profitable.*
   ● *How to produce: businesses decide how to produce efficiently, guided by their desire to make a profit.*
   ● *For whom to produce: distribution according to individuals' ability and/or inherited wealth.*

2. <u>Socialism</u> is, in theory, an economic system that tries to organize society in the same way as most families are organized—all people should contribute what they can, and get what they need. (29-30)

   Socialism ("government-controlled economy") is characterized by:

   (I) government control over resources
   (II) government solves the What? How? and For whom? problems.

   <u>*Soviet-style socialism's*</u> *solutions to the three problems:*

   ● *What to produce: what central planners believe is socially beneficial.*
   ● *How to produce: central planners decide, based on what they think is good for the country.*
   ● *For whom to produce: central planners distribute goods based on what they determine are individuals' needs.*

3. Capitalism and socialism haven't existed forever. (30-31)

   ● *In the eighth century, feudalism—an economic system based upon tradition—dominated.*
   ● *In the fifteenth century, feudalism gave way to mercantilism—an economic system in which government doles out the right to undertake certain economic activities.*
   ● *In the eighteenth century, mercantilism gave way to capitalism.*

4. Remember this graph:

   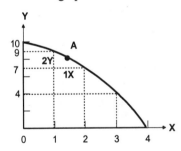

   <u>*Production Possibilities Curve*</u>
   Shows the trade-off (or opportunity cost) between two things.

   The slope tells you the opportunity cost of good X in terms of good Y. In this particular graph you have to give up 2 Y to get 1 X when you're around point A. (35-36)

5. The principle of increasing marginal opportunity cost states that opportunity costs increase the more you concentrate on the activity. In order to get more of something, one must give up ever-increasing quantities of something else. (37)

The following production possibility curve and table demonstrate the principle of increasing marginal opportunity cost.

<u>*Production Possibility Curve*</u>

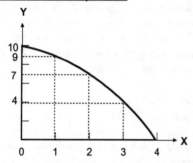

<u>*Production Possibility Table*</u>

Opportunity cost of X

<u>X</u> <u>Y</u> <u>(amount of Y which must be foregone)</u>

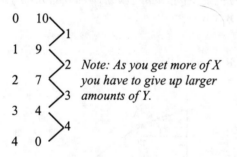

Note: As you get more of X you have to give up larger amounts of Y.

6. Because decisions are contextual, what the production possibility curve for a particular decision looks like depends upon the existing institutions, and the analysis can be applied only in that institutional and historical context. (40-41)

The production possibility curve is an engine of analysis to make contextual choices, not a definitive tool to decide what one should do in all cases.

7. When individuals trade, using their comparative advantages, their combined production possibility curve shifts out. (36-37)

Specialization and trade based on comparative advantage is mutually beneficial to all involved.

Markets and trading make people better off.

To find the curve that shows the combined production possibilities for two people (assuming constant opportunity cost), do the following: (1) Find the amount of good A that can be produced if both produce good A. This is the A-axis intercept. (2) Find the amount of good B that can be produced if both produce good B. This is the B-axis intercept. (3) Determine the amount of each good A and B that can be produced if each person specializes and takes advantage of his or her comparative advantage. (4) Connect these three points and you've got it. As long as one person has a comparative advantage in one good, this curve will be bowed out.

See also, Appendix A: "The History of Economic Systems."

SHORT-ANSWER QUESTIONS

1. What is capitalism? How does it solve the three central economic problems?

2. What is socialism? In practice, how has it solved the three central economic problems?

3. Name the economic systems that have evolved from the eighth century to today in the order that they occurred.

4. How can markets coordinate economic decisions without the active involvement of government?

5. Design a grade production possibility curve of studying economics and English, and show how it demonstrates the concept of opportunity cost.

6. State the principle of increasing marginal opportunity cost.

7. What would the production possibility curve look like if opportunity cost were constant?

8. What happens to the production possibility curve with trade? Why does trade make individuals better off?

9. Why is the production possibility curve more useful in discussing small changes than in discussing changes in entire economic systems?

A2. Why did mercantilism evolve into capitalism?

A1. Why did feudalism evolve into mercantilism?

A3. Explain what is meant by the statement that capitalism has evolved into welfare capitalism.

MATCHING THE TERMS
Match the terms to their definitions

_l_ 1. capitalism
_h_ 2. comparative advantage
_n_ 3. decision tree
_g_ 4. feudalism
_b_ 5. Industrial Revolution
_f_ 6. NIMBY
_i_ 7. principle of increasing marginal opportunity cost
_k_ 8. productive efficiency
_j_ 9. production possibility curve
_m_ 10. production possibility table
_a_ 11. private property rights
_d_ 12. socialism
_e_ 13. Soviet-style socialism
_c_ 14. welfare capitalism

a. Control a private individual or firm has over an asset or right.

b. Period when technology and machines rapidly modernized industrial production and mass produced goods replaced handmade goods.

c. Economic system in which the market operates but government regulates markets significantly.

d. Economic system that tries to organize society in the same way that families do — people contribute what they can and get what they need.

e. Economic system that uses administrative control or central planning to answer the questions what to produce, how to produce it, and for whom to produce it.

f. Represents <u>N</u>ot <u>I</u>n <u>M</u>y <u>B</u>ack <u>Y</u>ard; a phrase used by people who may approve of a project, but don't want it to be near them.

g. Economic system in which tradition rules.

h. The advantage that attaches to a resource when that resource is better suited to the production of one good than to the production of another good.

i. In order to get more of something, one must give up ever-increasing quantities of something else.

j. A curve measuring the maximum combination of outputs that can be obtained from a given number of inputs.

k. Achieving as much output as possible from a given amount of inputs or resources.

l. An economic system based on private property and the market in which, in principle, individuals decide how, what, and for whom to produce.

m. Table that lists a choice's opportunity cost by summarizing alternative outputs that can be achieved with your inputs.

n. Visual description of sequential choices demonstrating that the cost of reversing your path rise the further one is along the path.

● PROBLEMS AND APPLICATIONS

1. Suppose a restaurant has the following production possibility table:

Resources devoted to pizza in % of total	Output of pizza in pies per week	Resources devoted to spaghetti in % of total	Output of spaghetti in bowls per week
100	50	0	0
80	40	20	10
60	30	40	17
40	20	60	22
20	10	80	25
0	0	100	27

a. Plot the restaurant's production possibility curve. Put output of pizza in pies on the horizontal axis.

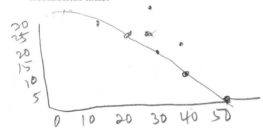

b. What happens to the marginal opportunity cost as the output of bowls of spaghetti increases?

marginal OC increases

c. What would happen to the production possibility curve if the restaurant found a way to toss and cook pizzas faster?

d. What would happen to the production possibility curve if the restaurant bought new stoves and ovens that cooked both pizzas and spaghetti faster?

2. Suppose Ecoland has the following production possibilities table:

% resources devoted to production of guns	Number of guns	% resources devoted to production of butter	Pounds of butter
100	50	0	0
80	40	20	5
60	30	40	10
40	20	60	15
20	10	80	20
0	0	100	25

a. Plot the production possibility curve for the production of guns and butter. Put the number of guns on the horizontal axis.

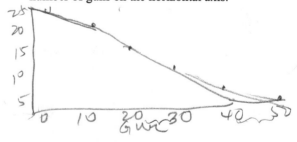

b. What is the per unit opportunity cost of increasing the production of guns from 20 to 30? From 40 to 50?

c. What happens to the opportunity cost of producing guns as the production of guns increases?

d. What is the per unit opportunity cost of increasing the production of butter from 10 to 15? From 20 to 25?

e. What happens to the opportunity cost of producing butter as the production of butter increases?

f. Given this production possibility curve, is producing 26 guns and 13 pounds of butter possible?

g. Is producing 34 guns and 7 pounds of butter possible? Is it efficient?

3. Using the following production possibility tables and using production possibility curves, show how the United States and Japan would be better off specializing in the production of either food or machinery and then trading rather than producing both food and machinery themselves and not trading.

United States Production per year		Japan Production per year	
Tons food	1000 units machinery	Tons food	1000 units machinery
10	0	12.5	0
8	5	10	1
6	10	7.5	2
4	15	5	3
2	20	2.5	4
0	25	0	5

4. Assume that France can produce wine at 25 francs per bottle and can produce butter at 5 francs per pound. Assume that Italy can produce wine at 16,000 lire per bottle and butter at 10,000 lire per pound.

a. In terms of pounds of butter, what is the opportunity cost of producing wine in each country?

b. Who has the comparative advantage in producing butter?

c. Which country should most likely specialize in wine and which should specialized in butter?

● A BRAIN TEASER

1. Consider the production possibilities for an entire nation. Within any national economy there are only two general kinds of products that can be produced–consumer products and capital products. Consumer products (e.g. food, clothes, medical services, etc ...) satisfy our wants directly when we use them and while we consume them. Capital products (e.g. machines, and other plant and equipment) satisfy our wants indirectly and in the future because they increase our productivity and help us produce even more products over time. Answer the following questions based on the production possibilities of consumer and capital products for a national economy shown in the graph below.

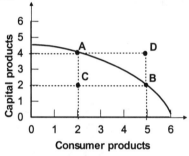

a. Between the production possibilities A and B, which would provide the greatest amount of current satisfaction? Why?

b. What is the opportunity cost of moving from point B to A?

c. Consider the choice of currently producing a relatively large amount of consumer products shown at point B (which means, given limited resources, relatively few capital products can be produced), compared to producing a relatively large amount of capital products now, shown at point A (which means relatively few consumer

products can be produced). Which of these two points (or combinations of consumer and capital goods production) do you think will increase the production possibilities (shift the curve to the right) the most over time giving rise to the greatest rate of economic growth? Why? *(Hint: Whenever workers have more capital, like factories and machinery to work with, then they become more productive.)*

● MULTIPLE CHOICE

1. For a market to exist, you have to have
    a. public property rights.
    b. private property rights.
    c. a combination of public and private property rights.
    d. coordination rights.

2. The concept of fairness embodied in a pure capitalist system can be stated as:
    a. to each according to their needs; from each according to their ability.
    b. to each according to their ability; from each according to their needs.
    c. them that works, gets; them that don't, starve.
    d. everyone gets enough, but those who work harder get more.

3. In theory socialism is an economic system
    a. that tries to organize society in the same ways as most families organize, striving to see that individuals get what they need.
    b. based on central planning and government ownership of the means of production.
    c. based on private property rights.
    d. based on markets.

4. Soviet-style socialism is an economic system:
    a. that tries to organize society in the same ways as most families organize, striving to see that individuals get what they need.
    b. based on central planning and government ownership of the means of production.
    c. based on private property rights.
    d. based on markets.

5. In capitalism, the "what to produce" decision is made by
    a. consumers.
    b. the market.
    c. government.
    d. firms.

6. In Soviet-style socialism, the "what to produce" decision is supposed to be made by
    a. what people want.
    b. what firms believe people want and will make a profit for firms.
    c. what government believes people want and what will make a profit for government.
    d. what central planners want or what they believe is socially beneficial.

7. The U.S. economy today can best be described as
    a. socialist.
    b. pure capitalist.
    c. welfare capitalist.
    d. state socialist.

8. If the opportunity cost of good X in terms of good Y is 2Y, so you'll have to give up 2Y to get one X, the production possibility curve would look like
    a. a.
    b. b.
    c. c.
    d. a, b and c.

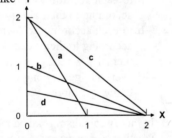

9. If the opportunity cost of good X in terms of good Y is 2Y, so you'll have to give up 2Y to get one X, the production possibility curve would look like
    a. a.
    b. b.
    c. c.
    d. d.

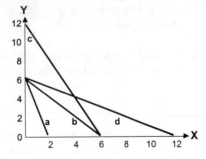

10. If the opportunity cost of good X in terms of good Y is 2Y, so you'll have to give up 2Y to get one X, the production possibility curve would look like
    a. a.
    b. b.
    c. c.
    d. a, b and c.

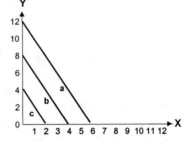

11. If the opportunity cost is constant for all combinations, the production possibility frontier will look like
    a. a.
    b. b.
    c. c.
    d. d.

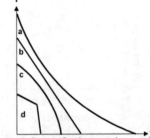

12. If the principle of increasing marginal opportunity cost applies at all points, the production possibility curve looks like
    a. a.
    b. b.
    c. c.
    d. d.

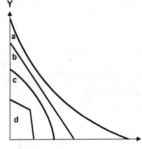

13. Given the accompanying production possibility curve, when you're moving from point C to B the opportunity cost of butter in terms of guns is
    a. 1/3.
    b. 1.
    c. 2.
    d. 3/2.

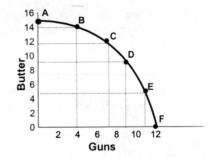

14. In the graph for question 14, in the range of points between A and B there is
a. a high opportunity cost of guns in terms of butter.
b. a low opportunity cost of guns in terms of butter.
c. no opportunity cost of guns in terms of butter.
d. a high monetary cost of guns in terms of butter.

15. In the accompanying production possibility diagram, point A would be

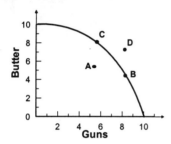

a. an efficient point.
b. a super-efficient point.
c. an inefficient point.
d. a non-attainable point.

16. A law about the growth of efficiency of computers states that computer chip technology doubles the efficiency of computers each year. If that holds true, which of the four arrows would demonstrate the appropriate shifting of the production possibility curve?

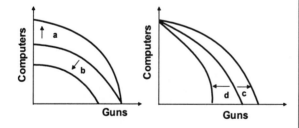

a. a.
b. b.
c. c.
d. d.

17. Say that methods of production are tied to particular income distributions, so that choosing one method will help some people but hurt others. Say also that method A produces significantly more total output than method B. In this case
a. method A is more efficient than method B.
b. method B is more efficient than method A.
c. if method A produces more and gives more to the poor people, method A is more efficient.
d. one can't say whether A or B is more efficient.

18. If the United States and Japan have production possibility curves as shown in the diagram below, at what point would they most likely be after trade?
a. A
b. B
c. C
d. D

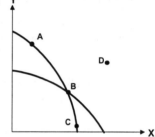

A1. In feudalism the most important force was
a. the price mechanism.
b. cultural force.
c. legal force.
d. anarchy.

A2. In mercantilism, the guiding force is
a. the price mechanism.
b. legal force.
c. cultural force.
d. anarchy.

A3. Mercantilism evolved into capitalism because
a. government investments did not pan out.
b. the Industrial Revolution undermined the craft guilds' mercantilist method of production.
c. the guilds wanted more freedom.
d. serfs wanted more freedom.

A4. Marx saw the strongest tension between
a. rich capitalists and poor capitalists.
b. capitalists and government.
c. capitalists and the proletariat.
d. government and the proletariat.

A5. State socialism is an economic system in which
  a. business sees to it that people work for their own good until they can be relied upon to do that on their own.
  b. business sees to it that people work for the common good until they can be relied upon to do that on their own.
  c. government sees to it that people work for their own good until they can be relied upon to do so on their own.
  (d.) government sees to it that people work for the common good until they can be relied upon to do so on their own.

● POTENTIAL ESSAY QUESTIONS

You may also see essay questions similar to the "Problems & Applications" and "Brain Teasers" exercises.

1. There has always been much political debate between "conservatives" and "liberals" in this country, as well as in other countries, over what constitutes the "appropriate" role for government to play in correcting for the problems of a market-oriented, capitalist economy.

  a. Is this controversy ever likely to go away? Why or why not?

  b. Could greater reliance upon positive economic analysis of "what is" as opposed to normative economic analysis of "what ought to be" help reduce some of this controversy?

2. Contrast capitalism's and socialism's solutions to the three economic problems.

3. What is a decision tree? What is its significance?

ANSWERS

SHORT-ANSWER QUESTIONS

1. Capitalism is an economic system based on private property and the market. It gives private property rights to individuals, and relies on market forces to coordinate economic activity. In a capitalist economy businesses produce what they believe people want and think they can make a profit supplying. Businesses decide how to produce, guided by their desire to make a profit. Goods are distributed according to individuals' ability and/or inherited wealth. (28-29)

2. Socialism is an economic system that tries to organize society in the same way as do most families — all people should contribute what they can, and get what they need. A Soviet-style socialist economy solves the problem what to produce: what central planners believe is socially beneficial. It solves the problem how to produce: central planners decide, based, one hopes, on what they think is good for the country. It solves the problem for whom to produce: central planners distribute goods based on what they determine are individuals' needs. (29-30)

3. Economic systems have evolved from feudalism (from the 8th to the 15th centuries) to mercantilism (from the mid-15th to the 18th centuries) to capitalism (from the 18th century to today). Economic systems are constantly evolving. (30-31)

4. The invisible hand — the price mechanism — guides the actions of suppliers and consumers to the general good. That is, competition directs individuals pursuing profit to do what society needs to have done. Markets coordinate economic decisions by turning self-interest into social good. (32)

5. The production possibility curve shows the highest combination of grades you can get with 20 hours of studying economics and English. The grade received in economics is on the vertical axis and the grade received in English is on the horizontal axis. The graph tells us the opportunity cost of spending any combination of 20 hours on economics and English. For example, the opportunity cost of increasing your grade in economics by 6 points is decreasing your English grade by 4 points (2/3 grade point reduction in English for one grade point improvement in Economics). (34-36)

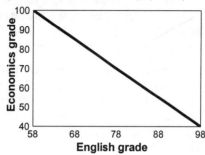

6. The principle of increasing marginal opportunity cost states that in order to get more of something, one must give up ever-increasing quantities of something else. (37)

7. Such a production possibility curve would be a straight line connecting the maximum number of units that could be produced of each product if all inputs were devoted to one or the other good. (35)

8. By comparing individual production possibility curves, one can determine those activities in which each has a comparative advantage. By concentrating on those activities for which one has a comparative advantage and trading those goods for goods for which others have a comparative advantage, individuals can end up with a combination of goods not attainable without trade. The production possibility curve shifts out with trade. (33-39)

9. The production possibility curve is best used when discussing small changes because the relationships between costs and production can be assumed to remain constant. Changes in economic systems can change the relationships that affect costs in everyday decisions and in production. The text's example of how changing from socialism to capitalism would affect the production possibility curve is a good example of how an analysis using just the production possibility curve can mask the probability that beneficial results of major structural changes may take many years. (40-41)

A1. Feudalism evolved into mercantilism as the development of money allowed trade to grow, undermining the traditional base of feudalism.

Politics rather than social forces came to control the central economic decisions. (50)

A2. Mercantilism evolved into capitalism because the Industrial Revolution shifted the economic power base away from craftsmen toward industrialists and toward an understanding that markets could coordinate the economy without the active involvement of the government. (50-51)

A3. Capitalism has evolved into welfare capitalism. That is, the human abuses marked by early capitalist developments led to a criticism of the market economic system. Political forces have changed government's role in the market, making government a key player in determining distribution and in making the what, how, and for whom decisions. This characterizes the U.S. economy today. (52-53)

ANSWERS

MATCHING

1-l; 2-h; 3-n; 4-g; 5-b; 6-f; 7-i; 8-k; 9-j; 10-m; 11-a; 12-d; 13-e; 14-c.

ANSWERS

PROBLEMS AND APPLICATIONS

1. **a.** The restaurant's production possibility curve is shown below. (34-36)

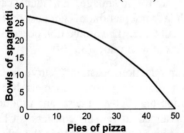

b. The number of pizza pies that must be given up to make an additional bowl of spaghetti increases as the number of bowls of spaghetti produced increases. (37)

c. If the restaurant found a way to toss and cook pizzas faster, the production possibility curve would rotate out along the pizza axis as shown below. (38)

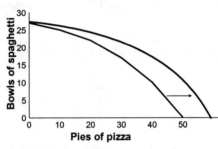

d. The production possibility curve would shift out to the right as shown in the figure below. (38)

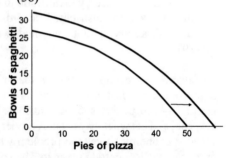

2. **a.** The production possibility curve is a straight line as shown below. (34-46)

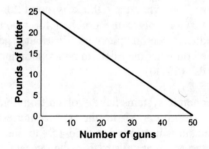

b. The opportunity cost of increasing the production of guns from 20 to 30 is 0.5 pounds of butter per gun. The opportunity cost of increasing the production of guns from 40 to 50 is also 0.5 pounds of butter per gun. (34-36)

c. The opportunity cost of producing guns stays the same as the production of guns increases. (34-36)

d. The opportunity cost of increasing the production of butter from 10 to 15 is 2 guns per pound of butter. The opportunity cost of increasing the production of butter from 20 to 25 is 2 guns per pound of butter. (34-36)

e. The opportunity cost of producing butter stays the same as the production of butter increases. (34-36)

f. Producing 26 guns and 13 pounds of butter is not attainable given this production possibility curve. We can produce 20 guns and 15 pounds of butter. To produce six more guns, Ecoland must give up 3 pounds of butter. Ecoland can produce only 26 guns and 12 pounds of butter. (34-36)

g. Ecoland can produce 34 guns and 7 pounds of butter. To see this, begin at 30 guns and 10 pounds of butter. To produce 4 more guns, 2 pounds of butter must be given up. Ecoland can produce 34 guns and 8 pounds of butter, which is more than 34 guns and 7 pounds of butter. This is an inefficient point of production. (34-36)

3. The production possibility of producing food and machinery for both Japan and the United States is shown in the graph below. The combined production possibility curve with trade is also shown. Clearly, trade shifts the production possibility curve out, showing that the two countries are better off with trade. The United States has a comparative advantage in the production of machinery. It must give up only 0.4 tons of food for each additional thousand units of machinery produced. Japan must give up 2.5 tons of food for each additional thousand units of machinery produced. A specific example is if Japan produced 12.5 tons of food and no machines while the United States produced 0 tons of food and 25 thousand units of machinery, Japan could offer the United States 2 tons of food for 3 thousand units of machinery. The United States would be at point A and Japan would be at point B. Each would be able to attain a level of production not attainable before. (34-36)

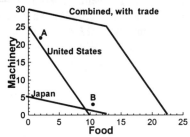

4. a. In France, the opportunity cost of producing wine is 5 pounds of butter. In Italy, the opportunity cost of producing wine is 1.6 pounds of butter. Calculate this by finding how much butter must be forgone for each bottle of wine in each

country. (34-36)

b. France has the comparative advantage in producing butter because it can produce butter for a lower opportunity cost. (34-36)

c. Italy should specialize in producing wine and France should specialize in producing butter assuming one can produce only wine and the other must produce only butter. This is concluded from the principle of comparative advantage. (34-36)

ANSWERS

A BRAIN TEASER

1. a. Production possibility B. Why? Because consumer products provide for *current* satisfaction, and at B we are getting a relatively larger amount of consumer products.

b. 3 units of consumer products.

c. Point A. Producing a relatively larger amount of capital products now means workers will have more plant and equipment to work with in the future. This will increase worker's productivity and the nation's production possibilities over time. Producing more capital is an ingredient for economic growth (greater production possibilities).

ANSWERS

MULTIPLE CHOICE

1. b   As discussed on page 28, markets require private property rights because these give people the framework within which they can trade and markets rely on trading. Markets also require government, but government and public property rights are not the same thing, which rules out a and c. And d is a throwaway answer.

2. c   As discussed on pages 28-29, c represents the concept of fairness in a pure capitalist economy. In a welfare capitalist economy d would be a possible answer. We should also point out that c leaves out issues of inheritance and luck, which complicate the ethics of capitalism, but c is nevertheless by far the best answer.

3.   a   As discussed on page 30, a is the correct answer. If the question had said "Soviet-style socialism," b would have been an acceptable answer, but Soviet-style socialism was a response to real-world implementation problems, not part of the theory of socialism.

4.   b   As discussed on page 30, b is the correct answer. If the question had said simply "socialism." An acceptable answer would have been a, but given that it said Soviet-style socialism, b is the preferable answer.

5.   b   Under capitalism, firms decide what to produce based on what they think will sell.

6.   d   As discussed on page 30, under Soviet-style socialism, central planners decide what to produce based upon what they believe society needs. We should point out that this is *ideally*; in practice, central planners may not be concerned with society. Thus c is a possible answer, but the term "profit" makes it unacceptable. Planners would not get profit—they might get rich, but it wouldn't be through profits.

7.   c   As discussed on page 33, since in the U.S. the market is allowed to operate, but the government intervenes in determining distribution, the U.S. is best described as welfare capitalist.

8.   a   As discussed on pages 34-36, the production possibility curve tells how much of one good you must give up to get more of the other good; here you must give up 2Y to get one X, making a the correct answer.

9.   c   As discussed on pages 34-36, the production possibility curve tells how much of one good you must give up to get more of another good. Opportunity cost is a ratio; it determines the slope, not the position, of the ppc curve. Thus, the correct answer is c because the 12 to 6 trade-off reduces to a 2 to 1 trade-off.

10. d   As discussed on pages 34-36, the production possibility curve tells how much of one good you must give up to get more of the other good. Opportunity cost is a ratio; it determines the slope, not the position, of the ppc curve. Since all have the same correct slope, all three are correct, so d is the right answer.

11. b   As discussed on pages 34 and 35 of the book, if the opportunity costs are constant, the ppc is a straight line, so b must be the answer.

12. c   As discussed on pages 35 and 36 of the book, with increasing marginal opportunity costs, as you produce more and more of a good, you will have to give up more and more of the other good to do so. This means that the slope of the ppc must be bowed outward, so c is the correct answer. (See Figure 2-2, page 40 for an in-depth discussion.)

13. d   As discussed on pages 34-36, the slope of the ppc measures the trade-off of one good for the other. Since moving from point c to b means giving up 3 guns for 2 pounds of butter, the correct answer is 3/2 or d.

14. b   As discussed on pages 35-37, the flatter the slope, the higher the opportunity cost of the good measured on the vertical axis; alternatively, the flatter the slope the lower the opportunity cost of that good measured on the horizontal axis. In the AB range the slope is flat so guns have a low opportunity cost in terms of butter; one need give up only one pound of butter to get four guns.

15. c   As discussed on page 38 (See Figure 2-3), point A is an inefficient point.

16. a   As discussed on page 38 (See Figure 2-3), technological change that improves the efficiency of producing a good shifts the ppc out in that good, but not in the other good. So a is the correct answer.

17. d   The answer is "You can't say," as discussed on pages 38-39. The term "efficiency" involves *achieving a goal as cheaply as possible*. Without specifying one's goal one cannot say what method is more efficient. The concept efficiency generally presumes that the goal includes preferring more to less, so if any method is more productive, it will be method A. But because there are distributional effects that involve making additional judgments, the correct answer is d. Some students may have been tempted to choose c because their goals involve more equity, but that is their particular judgment, and not all people may agree. Thus c would be incorrect, leaving d as the correct answer.

18. d As discussed in Figure 2-6 on page 38, with trade, both countries can attain a point outside each production possibility curve. The only point not already attainable is D.

A1. b As discussed on page 49, in feudalism tradition reigned.

A2. b As discussed on page 50, in mercantilism government directed the economy.

A3. b See page 51.

A4. c See page 52. To the degree that government was controlled by capitalists, d would be a correct answer, but it is not as good an answer as c, which represents the primary conflict. Remember, you are choosing the answer that best reflects the discussion in the text.

A5. d See page 53.

ANSWERS

POTENTIAL ESSAY QUESTIONS

The following are annotated answers. They indicate the general idea behind the answer.

1. a. Although there is no debate over the existence of market failures there is much debate over the extent to which they exist. Controversy often begins with equally reasonable and well intentioned people assessing the extent of the problem differently. (For example, consider the controversy surrounding the extent of ozone damage.) If a consensus is reached, then the same equally reasonable, equally well intentioned people will likely measure the benefits and costs associated with government involvement differently. This gives rise to debate concerning the appropriate extent of government involvement.

b. There will likely always be some degree of inefficiency in measuring the benefits and the costs associated with any problem and of any government involvement. However, greater reliance upon positive economic analysis, because it is "objective" and deals with "what is," should help everyone to avoid emotion and to see more clearly the extent of any problem. Moreover, it should help everyone to more clearly assess the benefits and costs associated with government action, or inaction, in a particular case. This is because positive economics helps us to predict or anticipate consequences. As was stated in the first chapter, "the art of economics is the application of the knowledge learned in positive economics to the achievement of the goals determined in normative economics. In the art of economics, it is difficult to be objective but it is important to try." People can argue until they are blue in the face about "what ought to be" the appropriate role for government. But that emotionally held belief, when enacted as policy, usually has little to do with the resulting real-world consequences. Too often, dismal consequences were predicted using positive economic analysis, but were ignored. This applies with equal weight to many "conservative" and "liberal" positions alike. We have experienced a rich history of real-world cases to show that sometimes government can help while at other times it only makes matters worse. That which is effective, however, may not be "politically correct" at the time.

2. Both economic systems have to answer the three central economic problems. (1) What to produce? In capitalism, firms produce what they believe people want and will make a profit. In socialism, in practice central planners decide what was produced. (2) How to produce? In capitalism firms decide how to produce efficiently, guided by their desire to make a profit. In socialism, central planners decide how to produce. (3) For whom to produce? In capitalism, distribution is decided according to ability and inherited wealth. In socialism, distribution is according to individuals' needs (as determined by central planners).

3. A decision tree is a visual description of sequential choices. It points out that decisions are made in context. See pages 45-46.

THE U.S. ECONOMY IN A GLOBAL SETTING

CHAPTER AT A GLANCE

This review is based upon the learning objectives that open the chapter.

1. Businesses, households and government interact in a market economy. (56)

    For a bird's-eye view of the U.S. economy see Figure 3-1 (sometimes called the "circular flow of income model"). Be able to draw and explain it.

    Note: there are 3 basic economic institutions:

    - *Businesses:*
      a. Supply goods in goods market
      b. Demand factors in factor market
      c. Pay taxes and receive benefits from government

    - *Households:*
      a. Supply factors
      b. Demand goods
      c. Pay taxes and receive benefits from government

    - *Government:*
      a. Demands goods
      b. Demands factors
      c. Collects taxes and provide services

2. The advantages and disadvantages of the three forms of business are shown in a table on page 59.

    Know the advantages and disadvantages of the three forms of business:
    - *Sole Proprietorship*
    - *Partnership*
    - *Corporation*

3. Although, in principle, ultimate power resides with the people and households (consumer sovereignty), in practice the representatives of the people–firms and government–are sometimes removed from the people and, in the short run, are only indirectly monitored by the people. (57)

    Note:
    - *Do we control business and government, or do they control us?*
    - *The distribution of income (rich vs. poor) determines the "for whom" question. If you're rich you get more.*
    - *Social forces affect what business and government do or don't do.*

4. Two general roles of government are: (63-64)

    - *As an actor:* Collects taxes and spends money.
    - *As referee:* Sets the rules governing relations between households and businesses. (68)

5. Canada and Mexico are our two largest trading partners. Other primary partners are countries in the European Union and the Pacific Rim.

    See Figure 3-6 on page 69 for U.S. exports and imports by region.

6. Two ways in which *inter*national trade differs from *intra*national (domestic) trade are: (69-71)

    - International trade involves potential barriers to trade; and

    Free and open international trade along the lines of comparative advantage is mutually beneficial to all economies involved.

- International trade involves multiple currencies.

  Foreign exchange markets exist to swap currencies.

7. Three global trade organizations include: (73)

- The World Trade Organization (WTO),
- The General Agreement on Tariffs and Trade (GATT); and
- The North American Free Trade Agreement (NAFTA).

  These are organizations that work toward lowering trade barriers among countries. Economists generally like markets and favor trade being as free as possible.

8. Four important international economic institutions are: (74)
- The UN
- The WTO
- The World Bank; and
- The IMF.

  They are designed to enhance trade negotiations (to avoid trade wars).

  Think internationally because we live in a global economy.

SHORT-ANSWER QUESTIONS

1. Draw a diagram of the U.S. economy showing the three groups that comprise the U.S. economy. What is the role of each group in the economy?

2. Although businesses decide what to produce, who ultimately makes the decision what to produce?

3. Your friend wants to buy a coin-operated Laundromat. Her brother has offered to be a partner in the operation and put up half the money to buy the business. They have come to you for advice about what form of business to create. Of course you oblige, letting them know the three possibilities and the advantages and disadvantages of each.

4. Why is much of the economic decision-making done by business and government even though households have the ultimate power?

5. What are two general roles of government?

6. What two countries are the largest trading partners of the U.S.? With what two other areas does the U.S. primarily trade?

7. State two ways international trade differs from domestic trade.

8. Name 3 important free trade organizations and 4 important international economic policy organizations.

MATCHING THE TERMS
Match the terms to their definitions

b 1.	consumer sovereignty	**a.** A free trade association of 15 western European countries.
i 2.	corporations	**b.** Principle that the consumer's wishes rule what's produced.
h 3.	entrepreneurship	**c.** Corporations with substantial operations on both production and sales in more than one country.
a 4.	European Union	
f 5.	foreign exchange market	**d.** Businesses that have only one owner.
c 6.	global corporation	**e.** The stockholder's liability is limited to the amount that stockholder has invested in the company.
k 7.	IMF	
e 8.	limited liability	**f.** Market in which one country's currency can be exchanged for another country's.
g 9.	NAFTA	
j 10.	quotas	**g.** A U.S.-Canada-Mexico free trade zone that is phasing in reductions in tariffs.
d 11.	sole proprietorship	
m 12.	tariffs	**h.** The ability to organize and get something done.
l 13.	trade deficit	**i.** Businesses that are treated as a person, and are legally owned by their shareholders who are not liable for the actions of the corporate "person."
		j. Limitations on how much of a good can be shipped into a country.
		k. A multinational, international financial institution concerned primarily with monetary issues.
		l. The result of a country's imports exceeding its exports.
		m. A tax on an imported good.

PROBLEMS AND APPLICATIONS

1. For each of the following, state for which form or forms of business it is an advantage: Sole proprietorships, partnerships, corporations.

a. Minimum bureaucratic hassle.
Sole proprietorship

b. Ability to share work and risks
Partnership

c. Direct control by owner.
sole pro

d. Relatively easy to form.
Partnership

e. No personal liability.
Corp.

f. Increasing ability to get funds.
Corp

2. For each of the following, state for which form or forms of business it is a disadvantage: Sole proprietorships, partnerships, corporations.

a. Unlimited personal liability.
sole proprietor

b. Possible double taxation of income.
Corp.

c. Limited ability to get funds
sole pro & partnership

d. Legal hassle to organize.
Corp

3. State whether the trade restriction is a quota, tariff, or nontariff barrier.

    a. The EU requires beef to be free of growth-inducing hormones in order to be traded in EU markets.

    Nontariff

    b. Hong Kong has maintained rice import controls on quantity since 1955 in order to keep local rice importers in business and to secure a steady wartime food supply.

    Quota

    c. To encourage domestic production of automobile parts, Japan limits the importation of automobile parts according to a rigid schedule of numbers.

    Quota

    d. The United States charges French wineries 10% of the value of each case of French wine imported into the United States.

    Tariff

4. Complete the blanks in the table below.

Currency	USD equivalent	Currency per USD
British pound	1.6393	0.61
German mark (DM)	0.5263	1.90
Sri Lankan rupee	0.0138	72.50
Japanese yen	0.0095	105.26
EU euro	1.03	.97

a. How many Sri Lankan rupees buys one Japanese yen?

b. How many USD (U.S. dollars) are needed to buy a German Porsche at a cost of 92,000 DM?

c. How many British pound(s) buys one euro?

A1. Choose which of the following offerings you would prefer having. (Refer to the present value table on page 78.)

    a. $1,500 today or $2,000 in 5 years. The interest rate is 5%.

    b. $1,500 today or $2,000 in 5 years. The interest rate is 10%.

    c. $2,000 today or $10,000 in 10 years. The interest rate is 15%

    d. $3,000 today or $10,000 in 15 years. The interest rate is 10%.

A2. A bond has a face value of $5,000 and a coupon rate of 10 percent. (A 10 percent coupon rate mans that it pays annual interest of 10 percent of its face value.) It is issued in 2001 and matures in 2006. Using this information, calculate the following:

    a. What is the annual payment for that bond?

b. If the bond is currently selling for $6,000, is its yield greater or less than 10 percent?

b. If the bond is currently selling for $4,000, is its yield greater or less than 10 percent?

d. What do your answers to (b) and (c) tell you about what the bond must sell for, relative to its face value, if the interest rate is 10%? Rises above 10%? Falls below 10%?

A BRAIN TEASER

1. **a.** What are the three general types of trade barriers which a nation's government might impose on foreign producers?

b. Assuming one of these trade barriers is going to be imposed, which one do you think might be most beneficial to the government imposing the trade barrier? Why?

MULTIPLE CHOICE

Circle the one best answer for each of the following questions:

1. In the factor market:
   a. businesses supply goods and services to households and government.
   b. government provides income support to households unable to supply factors of production to businesses.
   c. households supply labor and other factors of production to businesses.
   d. households purchase goods and services from businesses.

2. The ability to organize and get something done generally goes under the term
   a. the corporate approach.
   b. entrepreneurship.
   c. efficiency.
   d. consumer sovereignty.

3. By number, the largest percentage of businesses are
   a. partnerships
   b. sole proprietorships
   c. corporations
   d. nonprofit companies

4. By receipts, the largest percentage of business is undertaken by
   a. partnerships
   b. sole proprietorships
   c. corporations
   d. nonprofit companies

5. When a corporation's stock price goes up
   a. the corporation gets more revenue.
   b. the corporation gets less revenue.
   c. the corporation's revenue does not change.
   d. the yield on that company increases.

6. In reality, businesses are usually controlled by
   a. stockholders.
   b. managers.
   c. government.
   d. consumers.

7. Initial public offerings are a way for businesses to:
   a. finance expansion of an existing privately held business.
   b. finance expansion of an existing publicly-held business.
   c. increase sales by bringing in new customers.
   d. consolidate ownership of a company among a few stockholders.

8. The largest percentage of federal government expenditures is on
   a. education
   b. health and medical care
   c. infrastructure
   d. income security

9. The largest percentage of state and local expenditures is on:
   a. education.
   b. health and medical care.
   c. highways.
   d. income security.

10. All of the following are examples of government as referee *except*:
    a. setting limitations on when someone can be fired.
    b. collecting social security taxes from workers' paychecks.
    c. setting minimum safety regulations for the workplace.
    d. disallowing two competitors to meet to fix prices of their products.

11. Debtor nations will
    a. run trade deficits.
    b. run trade surpluses.
    c. not necessarily run a trade surplus or a trade deficit.
    d. run foreign exchange sales.

12. If a country has a trade deficit, it is:
    a. consuming more than it is producing.
    b. borrowing from foreigners.
    c. selling financial assets.
    d. selling real assets.

13. In the late-1990s the United States' trade balance has:
    a. had large surpluses.
    b. had large deficits.
    c. been in an approximate balance.
    d. fluctuated between deficits and surpluses.

14. An important way in which international trade differs from domestic trade is:
    a. international trade involves potential barriers to the flow of inputs and outputs.
    b. the use of different communication systems.
    c. the use of different transportation systems.
    d. that money is not used in international trade.

15. In a foreign exchange market:
    a. imports are exchanged for exports.
    b. exports are exchanged for imports.
    c. labor services, exports, imports and currencies are exchanged.
    d. one currency is exchanged for another.

16. The general plan of NAFTA is
    a. to adjust tariffs so that they are equal across products and countries.
    b. to replace tariffs with quotas.
    c. to move towards political integration among Canada, Mexico, and the United States.
    d. to remove tariffs on most goods traded in North America within 15 years of signing.

17. The EU is an economic free trade area
    a. but not a political organization.
    b. and a loose political organization.
    c. and a federation of individual countries.
    d. and a nation-state.

18. The Group of Five consists of
    a. Japan, Germany, Britain, France and the United States.
    b. Japan, Germany, Britain, France and Italy.
    c. Italy, Japan, Germany, Britain, and the United States
    d. Canada, Japan, Germany, the United States, and France.

19. The WTO is an organization mainly committed to
    a. increasing competitive quotas and tariffs among countries
    b. legalizing international trade by getting countries to refrain from imposing new tariffs or restrictions.
    c. creating independent trade zones throughout the world
    d. increasing security alliances around the world

20. If a country is found guilty in the World Court
    a. its leaders will be put in jail.
    b. it will be forced by the UN to pay a fine.
    c. it may or may not comply with the remedy decreed by the Court, depending on whether it chooses to comply or not.
    d. its dues to finance the World Court will be doubled.

A1. If the interest rate falls, the value of a fixed rate bond
    a. rises.
    b. falls.
    c. remains the same.
    d. cannot be determined as to whether it rises or falls.

A2. Two bonds, one a 30-year bond and the other a 1-year bond, have the same interest rate. If the interest rate in the economy falls, the value of the
    a. long-term bond rises by more than the value of the short-term bond rises.
    b. short-term bond rises by more than the value of the long-term bond rises.
    c. long-term bond falls by more than the value of the short-term bond falls.
    d. short-term bond falls by more than the value of the long-term bond falls.

POTENTIAL ESSAY QUESTIONS

You may also see essay questions similar to the "Problems & Applications" and "Brain Teasers" exercises.

1. Uglies is a brand of boxer shorts sold on the Internet. Their claim to fame is that each side of the shorts don't match. Their marketing ploy is boxer-short-of-the-month club. Suppose you were the one who came up with the idea for Uglies and wanted to start the business. What form of business would you select and why? (Thinking about where the funds to start the business will come from, who will make the shorts, and how the shorts will be sold will help you answer the question.)

2. Is it better to be a creditor nation or a debtor nation? Explain your answer.

3. Large trade deficits often inspire politicians to call for trade restrictions prohibiting imports. However, most economists oppose such restrictions because of the negative effects they may create. What are some of the problems associated with trade restrictions?

ANSWERS

SHORT-ANSWER QUESTIONS

1. As seen in the diagram below, the three groups that comprise the U.S. economy are households, business, and government. Households supply factors of production to businesses; businesses produce goods and services and sell them to households and government. The government taxes businesses and households, buys goods and services from businesses and labor services from households, and provides goods and services to each of them. (56-57)

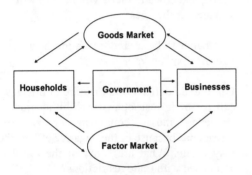

2. Although businesses decide what to produce, they are guided by consumer sovereignty. Businesses want to make a profit, so they will produce what they believe consumers will buy. That is not to say that businesses don't affect the desires of consumers through advertising. (57)

3. I would advise each of them to think hard about their situation. There are three possibilities: sole proprietorship, partnership and a corporation. Each form of business has its disadvantages and advantages. If your friend wants to minimize bureaucratic hassle and be her own boss, the best form of business would be a sole proprietorship. However, she would be personally liable for all losses and might have difficulty obtaining additional funds should that be necessary. If her brother has some skills to offer the new business and is willing to share in the cost of purchasing the company, she might want to form a partnership with him. Beware, though: Both partners are liable for any losses regardless of whose fault it is. I would ask her if she trusts her brother's decision-making abilities.

    As a partnership they still might have problems getting additional funds. What about becoming a corporation? Her liability would be limited to her initial investment, her ability to get funds is greater, and she can shed personal income and gain added expenses to limit taxation. However, a corporation is a legal hassle to organize, may involve possible double taxation of income, and if she plans to hire many employees it involves monitoring problems once she becomes less involved. I would tell her she needs to weigh the costs and benefits of each option and choose the one that is best for her. (57-60)

4. Business and government do much of the economic decision-making even though households retain the ultimate power. This is because in practice people have delegated much of that power to institutions and representatives – firms and the government–that are sometimes removed from the people. In the short run, households only indirectly control government and business. (61-62)

5. Two general roles of the government are as referee and actor. (63)

6. Canada and Mexico are the two countries with which the U.S. trades the most. The European Union and the Pacific Rim are the regions with which the U.S. trades the most. (69)

7. The two ways in which international trade differs from intranational trade are: (1) International trade involves potential barriers to trade; that is, producers' rights to sell can be limited by government-imposed quotas, tariffs, and nontariff barriers. (2) International trade involves multiple currencies that are traded in foreign exchange markets. (69-72)

8. Three important free trade organizations are the World Trade Organization (WTO), The North American Free Trade Association (NAFTA), and the General Agreement on Tariffs and Trade (GATT)—the predecessor to the WTO. Four important international economic policy organizations are the United Nations (U.N.), World Bank, World Court, and the International Monetary Fund (IMF). (73-74)

ANSWERS

MATCHING

1-b; 2-i; 3-h; 4-a; 5-f; 6-c; 7-k; 8-e; 9-g; 10-j; 11-d; 12-m; 13-l.

ANSWERS

PROBLEMS AND APPLICATIONS

1. a. Sole proprietorship. No special forms are required to begin one. (59)
    b. Partnership. The owners have another to work with and risks are shared. (59)
    c. Sole proprietorship. This is a firm of one person who controls the business. (59)
    d. Partnership. This is easy to form relative to the easiest (sole proprietorship) and the hardest (corporation). (59)
    e. Corporation. The individual liability is limited by the individual investment. (59)
    f. Corporation. They are more developed firms and have more access to capital. (59)

2. a. Sole proprietorship and partnership. (59)
    b. Corporation. (59)
    c. Sole proprietorship and partnership. (59)
    d. Corporation. (59)

3. a. Nontariff barrier because this a regulation that has the final effect of reducing imports without a tax or numerical limitation. (71)
    b. Quota. It is a numerical restriction on the amount of rice entering the country. (71)
    c. Quota because it is a numerical restriction on imports. (71)
    d. Tariff because it is a tax on imports. (00)

4. The table is filled in below. (71-72)

Currency	USD equivalent	Currency per USD
British pound	1.6393	0.61
German mark (DM)	0.5263	1.90
Sri Lankan rupee	0.0138	72.50
Japanese yen	0.0095	105.26
EU euro	1.03	0.97

    a. 0.6888 rupees buys one Japanese yen. Calculate this by first finding the yen per dollar (105.26) and Sri Lankan rupees per dollar (72.50). To find rupees per yen, divide rupees per dollar by Japanese yen per dollar. (71-72)
    b. $48,421.05 are needed to buy a German Porsche Carrera at a cost of 92,000 DM. To calculate this, find the German mark per U.S. dollar (1.90) and divide this into the cost of the Porsche in marks. (71-72)
    c. 0.6289 pounds are needed to buy one Euro.

Calculate this by finding the British pound per USD (0.61) and euro per dollar (0.97). To find British pounds per euro, divide British pounds per dollar euro per dollar. (71-72)

A1. Using the table to calculate the present value of $100 to be received in the future, we find that the better value is
    a. $2,000 in 5 years, valued today at $1,568. (78)
    b. $1,500 today. $2,000 in 5 years when the interest rate is 10% is worth only $1,242 today. (78)
    c. $10,000 in 10 years, valued at $2,470 when the interest rate is 15%. (78)
    d. $3,000 today. $10,000 in 15 years when interest rate is 10% is worth only $2390 today. (78)

A2. a. The annual payment for that bond is $500 annually. (80)
    b. If the bond is currently selling for $6000, its yield is less than 10 percent. (80)
    c. If the bond is currently selling for $4,000, its yield is greater than 10 percent. (80)
    d. My answer to (b) and (c) tell me that the bond must sell for its face value if the interest rate is 10%, less than face value if it rises above 10%, and more than face value if it falls below 10%. (80)

ANSWERS

A BRAIN TEASER

1. a. The three general types of trade barriers a nation's government might impose on foreign producers are tariffs, quotas, and nontariff barriers. (71)
    b. Although all barriers will be costly for the host government to "police," only tariffs (a tax on an imported product) will raise revenues for the government. (72)

ANSWERS

MULTIPLE CHOICE

1. c   See page 56.

2. b   See page 57.

3. b   See Figure 3-2 on page 58.

4. c   See Figure 3-2 on page 58.

5. c   A corporation's revenue is derived from the sale of its products, not its stock. See pages 60-61.

6. b   Although stockholders "own" businesses, they are run by managers. See page 60.

7. a   An initial public offering is when a company first offers some of its stock to the general public. See page 61.

8. d   See Figure 3-4 on page 64.

9. a   See Figure 3-3 on page 63.

10. b   Collecting social security taxes to fund the social security system is government as an actor. Government as referee refers to laws regulating interaction between households and businesses. See page 63.

11. c   A debtor nation may currently be running a surplus if it ran deficits in the past. See p. 68.

12. a   If a country has a trade deficit, it is importing (consuming) more than it is exporting (producing). See page 68.

13. b   See page 68.

14. a   International trade involves potential barriers to trade. See pages 69-71.

15. d   See page 71.

16. d   See page 73.

17. b   See page 73.

18. a   See page 74 for the list of the Group of Five.

19. b   See page 73.

20. c   The World Court has no enforcement mechanism. See page 74.

A1. a   The present value formula tells us that the value on any fixed interest rate bond varies inversely with the interest rate in the economy. See page 226.

A2. a   Since bond values vary inversely with interest rate changes, the answer must be a or b. Judging between a and b will be hard for you at this point unless you have studied present value in another course. However, based on the discussion in the text on pages 237 and 238, you can deduce that since a long-term bond is not paid back for a long time, it will be much more strongly affected be interest rate changes.

ANSWERS

POTENTIAL ESSAY QUESTIONS

The following are annotated answers. They indicate the general idea behind the answer.

1. The answer to this question will vary from person to person and will depend upon personal finances, how much risk one is able and willing to undertake, how much responsibility one wants to take on, and whether or not you want to share in any profits. Given limited financial resources, I'd find a partner I can trust who has the funds needed to launch a web site, hire a firm to carry out transactions and build inventory. With a partnership I can share the work and the risks of the venture. Since the liability associated with selling boxer shorts is not too great, unlimited liability with a partnership is not a problem. Not a corporation because establishing one is a legal hassle requiring even more money. Not a sole proprietorship because I don't have the funds to start the company on my own.

2. Whether it is better to be a creditor or debtor nation is debatable. A debtor nation is able to consume more that it produces. Countries can do this by living off foreign aid, past savings, or loans. The U.S. finances its deficits (as a debtor nation) by selling financial assets (such as stocks and bonds) and real assets (such as real estate and corporations) to foreigners. The problem with being a debtor nation is that country has to make interest payments on those bonds and has to pay profits to the foreigners who own the corporations. A creditor nation receives those interest payments and profits, but must consume less than it is producing.

3. Generally, there are two problems. First, trade restrictions reduce competition. Less competition means consumers have to pay higher prices than if the foreign competition were allowed. Second, trade restrictions often bring retaliation from other countries (they impose stricter trade restrictions as well). This reduces the amount domestic firms would otherwise be able to sell abroad.

SUPPLY AND DEMAND

CHAPTER AT A GLANCE

This review is based upon the learning objectives that open the chapter.

1. The <u>law of demand</u> states that the quantity of a good demanded is <u>inversely related</u> to a good's price. When price goes up, quantity demanded goes down. When price goes down, quantity demanded goes up. (83)

    Law of Demand (Inverse Relationship):
    arrows move in $\uparrow P \Rightarrow \downarrow Q_d$
    opposite directions $\downarrow P \Rightarrow \uparrow Q_d$

    Law of Demand expressed as a <u>downward-sloping curve</u>:

    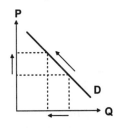

2a. The law of demand is based upon opportunity cost and individuals' ability to substitute. If the price of a good rises, the opportunity cost of purchasing that good will also rise and consumers will substitute for it a good with a lower opportunity cost. (83)

    As the P of beef ↑s, we buy more chicken.

2b. The law of supply, like the law of demand, is based on opportunity cost and the individual firm's ability to substitute. Suppliers will substitute toward goods for which they receive higher relative prices. (90)

    If the P of wheat ↑s, farmers grow more wheat and less corn.

3. Changes in quantity demanded are shown by movements along a demand curve. Shifts in demand are shown by a shift of the entire demand curve. (84-86) *(Note: "Δ"means "change.")*

    Don't get this confused on the exam!

ΔQ_d is caused <u>only</u> by a Δ in the P of the good itself.

$\Delta P \Rightarrow \Delta Q_d \Rightarrow$ movement along a given D curve.

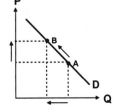

$\uparrow P \Rightarrow \downarrow Q_d$: movement along a curve (e.g. from point A to point B).

ΔD is caused only by Δs in the shift factors of D (<u>not</u> a Δ in the P of the good itself!)
<u>Δ in shift factors of D ⇒ ΔD ⇒ shift of a D curve</u>

Know what can cause an increase and decrease in demand:
↑D ⇒ <u>Rightward Shift</u> ↓D ⇒ <u>Leftward Shift</u>

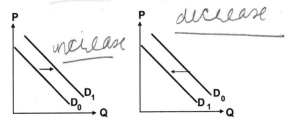

4. To derive a demand curve from a demand table you plot each point on the demand table on a graph and connect the points. (86-87)

    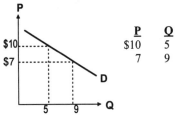

P	Q
$10	5
7	9

5. The <u>law of supply</u> states that the quantity supplied of a good is <u>directly related</u> to the good's price. When price goes up, quantity supplied goes up. When price goes down, quantity supplied goes down. (90-91)

Law of Supply (Direct Relationship):
arrows move in $\uparrow P \Rightarrow \uparrow Q_s$
same direction $\downarrow P \Rightarrow \downarrow Q_s$

Law of Supply expressed as an <u>upward-sloping curve</u>:

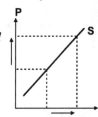

6. Just as with demand, it is important to distinguish between a shift in supply (a shift of the entire supply curve) and a movement along a supply curve (a change in the quantity supplied due to a change in price). (91-93)

    Don't get this confused on the exam!
    ΔQ_s is caused <u>only</u> by a Δ in the P of the good itself.

    $\Delta P \Rightarrow \Delta Q_s \Rightarrow$ movement along a given S curve.

    $\uparrow P \Rightarrow \uparrow Q_s$: movement along a curve (e.g. from point A to point B).

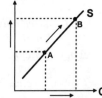

    ΔS is caused only by Δs in the shift factors of S (<u>not</u> a Δ in the P of the good itself!)
    Δ <u>in shift factors of S</u> $\Rightarrow \Delta S \Rightarrow$ <u>shift of a S curve</u>

    Know what can cause an increase and decrease in supply:
    $\uparrow S \Rightarrow$ <u>Rightward Shift</u> $\downarrow S \Rightarrow$ <u>Leftward Shift</u>

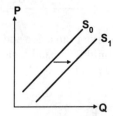 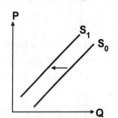

7. To derive a supply curve from a supply table, plot each point on the supply table on a graph and connect the points. (93-94)

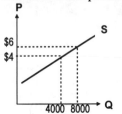

P	Q
$6	8000
$4	4000

8. Equilibrium is where quantity supplied equals quantity demanded: (95-97)
    - If quantity demanded is greater than quantity supplied, prices tend to rise;
    - If quantity supplied is greater than quantity demanded, prices tend to fall.
    - When quantity demanded equals quantity supplied, prices have no tendency to change.

    <u>*Know this!*</u>
    - If $Q_d > Q_s \Rightarrow$ Shortage $\Rightarrow$ P will $\uparrow$.
    - If $Q_s > Q_d \Rightarrow$ Surplus $\Rightarrow$ P will $\downarrow$.
    - If $Q_s = Q_d \Rightarrow$ Equilibrium $\Rightarrow$ no tendency for P to change (because there is neither a surplus nor a shortage).

Shortage	**Surplus**	**Equilibrium**
$(Q_d > Q_s)$	$(Q_s > Q_d)$	$(Q_s = Q_d)$
P is below equilibrium	P is above equilibrium	

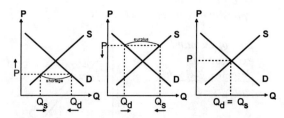

9. Equilibrium maximizes consumer and producer surplus. (97-99)
    <u>*Consumer surplus*</u> *is the difference between what buyers would have been willing to pay and what they actually had to pay. <u>Equal to Area A</u>.*

    <u>*Producer surplus*</u> *is the difference between what the seller would have been willing to accept as payment and what they actually received as payment. <u>Equal to Area B</u>.*

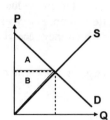

Hint for answering numerical problems about consumer and producer surplus: The area of a triangle = 1/2 base × height.

SHORT-ANSWER QUESTIONS

1. What is the law of demand?

   Quantity demanded inversely related to price

2. What does the law of supply say that most individuals would do if their wage increased? Explain the importance of substitution in this decision.

3. Demonstrate graphically a shift in demand.

4. Demonstrate graphically a movement along a demand curve.

5. Draw a demand curve from the following demand table.

   Demand Table

Q	P
50	1
40	2
30	3
20	4

6. State the law of supply.

7. Demonstrate graphically the effect on the supply of Red Hot Chili Pepper CDs of a new technology that reduces the cost of producing Red Hot Chili Pepper CDs.

8. Demonstrate graphically the effect of a rise in the price of Red Hot Chili Pepper CDs on the quantity supplied.

9. Draw a supply curve from the following supply table.

   SupplyTable

Q	P
20	1
30	2
40	3
50	4

10. What are three things to note about supply and demand which help to explain how they interact to bring about equilibrium in a market?

11. Given the graph below, at what price is there no pressure on price to change? Why?

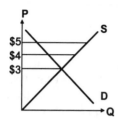

12. What are consumer surplus and producer surplus?

MATCHING THE TERMS
Match the terms to their definitions

_m_ **1.** demand
_b_ **2.** demand curve
_j_ **3.** equilibrium
_l_ **4.** equilibrium price
_n_ **5.** equilibrium quantity
_o_ **6.** excess demand
_i_ **7.** excess supply
_f_ **8.** law of demand
_g_ **9.** law of supply
_m_ **10.** market demand curve
_p_ **11.** movement along a demand curve
_e_ **12.** movement along a supply curve
_a_ **13.** quantity demanded
_q_ **14.** quantity supplied
_k_ **15.** shift in demand
_c_ **16.** shift in supply
_r_ **17.** supply
_d_ **18.** supply curve

a. A specific amount that will be demanded per unit of time at a specific price, other things constant.

b. Curve that tells how much of a good will be bought at various prices.

c. The effect of a change in a nonprice factor on the supply curve.

d. Curve that tells how much of a good will be offered for sale at various prices.

e. The graphic representation of the effect of a change in price on the quantity supplied.

f. Quantity demanded rises as price falls, other things constant.

g. Quantity supplied rises as price rises, other things constant.

h. A schedule of quantities of a good that will be bought per unit of time at various prices, other things constant.

i. Quantity supplied is greater than quantity demanded.

j. A concept in which opposing dynamic forces cancel each other out.

k. The effect of a change in a nonprice factor on the demand curve.

l. The price toward which the invisible hand (economic forces) drives the market.

m. The horizontal sum of all individual demand curves.

n. Amount bought and sold at the equilibrium price.

o. Quantity demanded is greater than quantity supplied.

p. The graphic representation of the effect of a change in price on the quantity demanded.

q. A specific amount that will be offered for sale per unit of time at a specific price.

r. A schedule of quantities a seller is willing to sell per unit of time at various prices, other things constant.

● PROBLEMS AND APPLICATIONS

1. Draw two linear curves on the same graph from the following table, one relating P with Q_1 and the other relating P with Q_2.

P	Q_1	Q_2
$30	60	100
35	70	90
40	80	80
45	90	70

   a. Label the curve that is most likely a demand curve. Explain your choice.

   b. Label the curve that is most likely a supply curve. Explain your choice.

   c. What is equilibrium price and quantity? Choose points above and below that price and explain why each is not the equilibrium price.

2. Correct the following statements, if needed, so that the terms "demand," "quantity demanded," "supply," and "quantity supplied" are used correctly.

   a. As the price of pizza increases, consumers demand less pizza.

   b. Whenever the price of bicycles increases, the supply of bicycles increases.

   c. The price of electricity is cheaper in the northwestern part of the United States and therefore the demand for electricity is greater in the northwest.

   d. An increase in incomes of car buyers will increase the quantity demanded for cars.

   e. An increase in the quantity demanded of lobsters means consumers are willing and able to buy more lobsters at any original price.

   f. A decrease in the supply of frog legs means suppliers will provide fewer frog legs at any original price.

3. You are given the following individual demand tables for compact discs.

Price	Juan	Philippe	Ramone
$7	3	20	50
$10	2	10	40
$13	1	7	32
$16	0	5	26
$19	0	3	20
$22	0	0	14

   a. Determine the market demand table.

   b. Graph the individual and market demand curves.

   c. If the current market price is $13, what is the total market quantity demanded? What happens to total market quantity demanded if the price rises to $19 a disc?

   d. Say that a new popular 'N Sync compact disc hits the market which increases demand for compact discs by 25%. Show with a demand table what happens to the individual and market demand curves.

Demonstrate graphically what happens to market demand.

4. The following table depicts the market supply and demand for oranges in the United States (in thousands of bushels).

Price	Quantity supplied	Quantity demanded
$15	7000	2000
$14	5500	3000
$13	4000	4000
$12	2500	5000
$11	1000	6000

a. Graph the market supply and demand for oranges.

b. What is the equilibrium price and quantity of oranges in the market? Why?

c. Suppose the price is $14. Would we observe a surplus (excess supply) or a shortage (excess demand)? If so, by how much? What could be expected to happen to the price over time? Why?

d. Suppose the price is $12. Would we observe a surplus or a shortage? If so, by how much? What could be expected to happen to the price over time? Why?

5. Draw a hypothetical demand and supply curve for cyber cafes — coffee houses with computers hooked up to the Internet with access to daily newspapers (among other things) at each table. Show how demand or supply is affected by the following:

a. A technological breakthrough lowers the cost of computers.

b. Consumers' income rises.

c. A per-hour fee is charged to coffee houses to use the Internet.

d. The price of newspapers in print rises.

e. Possible suppliers expect Cyber cafes to become more popular.

6. Draw demand and supply curves. Illustrate market equilibrium. Also illustrate the areas representing consumer and producer surplus at market equilibrium. Can consumer and producer surplus be increased any more than when we are at market equilibrium?

● A BRAIN TEASER

1. The invention of a self-milking cow machine allows cows to milk themselves. Not only does this reduce the need for higher-cost human assistance in milking, but it also allows the cow to milk herself three times a day instead of two, leading to both a healthier cow and increased milk production.

    a. Show the effect of this innovation on the equilibrium quantity and price of milk.

    b. Show the likely effect on equilibrium price and quantity of apple juice (a substitute for milk).

● MULTIPLE CHOICE

Circle the one best answer for each of the following questions:

1. The law of demand states
   a. quantity demanded increases as price falls, other things constant.
   b. more of a good will be demanded the higher its price, other things constant.
   c. people always want more.
   d. you can't always get what you want at the price you want.

2. There are many more substitutes for good A than for good B.
   a. The demand curve for good B will likely shift out further.
   b. The demand curve for good B will likely be flatter.
   c. You can't say anything about the likely relative flatness of the demand curves.
   d. The demand curve for good A will likely be flatter.

3. If the weather gets very hot, what will most likely happen?
   a. The supply of air conditioners will increase.
   b. Quantity demanded of air conditioners will increase.
   c. Demand for air conditioners will increase.
   d. The quality demanded of air conditioners will increase.

4. If the price of air conditioners falls, there will be
   a. an increase in demand for air conditioners.
   b. an increase in the quantity demanded of air conditioners.
   c. an increase in the quantity supplied of air conditioners.
   d. a shift in the demand for air conditioners.

5. An increase in demand
   a. is reflected as a rightward (outward) shift of the demand curve.
   b. is caused by a decrease in price.
   c. means demanders are buying less at any price
   d. shifts the demand curve to the left (inward).

6. The demand curve will likely shift outward to the right if
   a. society's income falls.
   b. the price of a substitute good falls.
   c. the price of the good is expected to rise in the near future.
   d. the good goes out of style.

7. The difference between the quantity demanded and demand is
   a. the quantity demanded is associated with a whole set of prices, whereas demand is associated with a particular price.
   b. the quantity demanded is associated with a particular price, whereas demand is associated with a whole set of prices.
   c. the quantity demanded is the whole demand curve, whereas demand is a particular point along a demand curve.
   d. a change in the quantity demanded is reflected graphically as a shift of the demand curve, whereas a change in demand is reflected as movement along a given demand curve.

8. If there is a flood, what will most likely happen in the market for bottled water?
   a. Demand will increase.
   b. Demand will fall.
   c. Supply will increase.
   d. Supply will decrease.

9. The movement in the graph below from point A to point B represents

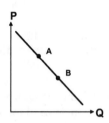

    a. an increase in demand.
    b. an increase in the quantity demanded.
    c. an increase in the quantity supplied.
    d. an increase in supply.

10. Using the standard axes, the demand curve associated with the following demand table is

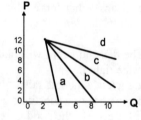

    a. a
    b. b
    c. c
    d. d

11. To derive a market demand curve from two individual demand curves
    a. one adds the two demand curves horizontally.
    b. one adds the two demand curves vertically.
    c. one subtracts one demand curve from the other demand curve.
    d. one adds the demand curves both horizontally and vertically.

12. The market demand curve will always
    a. be unrelated to the individual demand curves and slope.
    b. be steeper than the individual demand curves that make it up.
    c. have the same slope as the individual demand curves that make it up.

    d. be flatter than the individual demand curves that make it up.

13. The law of supply states that
    a. quantity supplied increases as price increases, other things constant.
    b. quantity supplied decreases as price increases, other things constant.
    c. more of a good will be supplied the higher its price, other things changing proportionately.
    d. less of a good will be supplied the higher its price, other things changing proportionately.

14. In the graph below, the arrow refers to

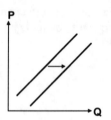

    a. a shift in demand.
    b. a shift in supply.
    c. a change in the quantity demanded.
    d. a change in the quantity supplied.

15. If there is an improvement in technology one would expect
    a. a movement along the supply curve.
    b. a shift upward (or to the left) of the supply curve.
    c. a shift downward (or to the right) of the supply curve.
    d. a movement down along the supply curve.

16. The market supply curve for the two individual supply curves S_1 and S_2 below would be

    a. S_3.
    b. S_4.
    c. S_5.
    d. S_6.

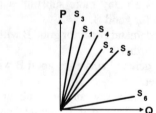

17. You're the supplier of a good and suddenly a number of your long-lost friends call you to buy your product. Your good is most likely
  a. in excess supply.
  b. in excess demand.
  c. in equilibrium.
  d. in both excess supply and demand.

18. At which point on the graph below will you expect the strongest downward pressure on prices?

  a. a.
  b. b.
  c. c.
  d. d.

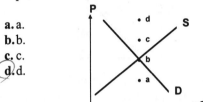

19. If at some price the quantity supplied exceeds the quantity demanded then:
  a. a surplus (excess supply) exists and the price will fall over time as sellers competitively bid down the price.
  b. a shortage (excess demand) exists and the price will rise over time as buyers competitively bid up the price.
  c. the price is below equilibrium.
  d. equilibrium will be reestablished as the demand curve shifts to the left.

20. If the price of a good
  a. rises it is a response to a surplus (excess supply).
  b. falls it is a response to a shortage (excess demand).
  c. is below equilibrium then a shortage will be observed.
  d. is below equilibrium then a surplus will be observed.

21. Consumer surplus
  a. is minimized in equilibrium.
  b. is the price the producer sells a product for minus the cost of producing it.
  c. is represented by the area above the supply curve but below the price.
  d. is the value the consumer gets from buying a good less its price.

22. In the graph below, producer surplus is greatest when the price is
  a. P_1
  b. P_2
  c. P_3
  d. P_4

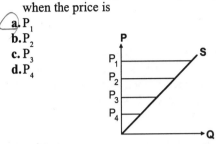

● POTENTIAL ESSAY QUESTIONS

You may also see essay questions similar to the "Problems & Applications" and "Brain Teaser" exercises.

1. Many university campuses sell parking permits to their students allowing them to park on campus in designated areas. Although most students complain about the relatively high cost of these parking permits, what annoys many students even more is that after having paid for their permits, vacant parking spaces in the designated lots are very difficult to find during much of the day. Many end up having to park off campus anyway, where permits are not required. Assuming the University is unable to build new parking facilities on campus due to insufficient funds, what recommendation might you make to remedy the problem of students with permits being unable to find places to park on campus?

2. Some products are considered to be "inferior" by most consumers. The key characteristic of inferior products is that the demand for these goods decreases as consumer incomes rise. List a few "inferior" goods.

ANSWERS

SHORT-ANSWER QUESTIONS

1. The law of demand states that the quantity of a good demanded is inversely related to the good's price. When price goes up, quantity demanded goes down, other things constant. (83)

2. The law of supply states that quantity supplied rises as price rises; the quantity supplied falls as price falls. According to this law, most individuals would choose to supply a greater quantity of labor hours if their wage increased. That is, they will substitute work for leisure. (90)

3. A shift in demand is shown by a shift of the entire demand curve resulting from a change in a shift factor of demand as shown in the graph below. (86)

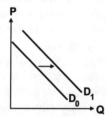

4. A movement along a demand curve is a change in quantity demanded resulting from a change in price as is shown in the graph below as a movement from *A* to *B*. (86)

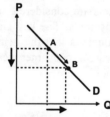

5. To derive a demand curve from a demand table, you plot each point on the demand table on a graph and connect the points. This is shown on the graph below. (86-87)

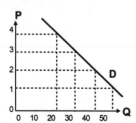

6. The law of supply states that the quantity supplied rises as price rises. Or alternatively: Quantity supplied falls as price falls. (90)

7. A new technology that reduces the cost of producing Red Hot Chili Pepper CDs will shift the entire supply curve to the right from S_0 to S_1, as shown in the graph below. (92)

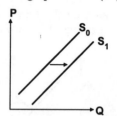

8. A rise in the price of Red Hot Chili Pepper CDs from P_0 to P_1 results in a movement up along a supply curve; quantity of Red Hot Chili Pepper CDs supplied will rise from Q_0 to Q_1 as shown in the graph below. (91-92)

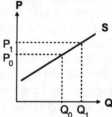

9. To derive a supply curve from a supply table, you plot each point on the supply table on a graph and connect the points. This is shown on the graph below. (94)

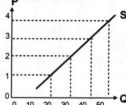

10. The first things to note is that when quantity demanded is greater than quantity supplied, prices tend to rise and when quantity supplied is greater than quantity demanded, prices tend to fall. Each case is demonstrated in the graph below. Price tends away from P_1 and P_2 and toward P_0.

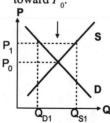 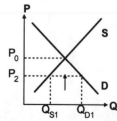

The second thing to note is that the larger the difference between quantity supplied and quantity demanded, the greater the pressure on prices to rise (if there is excess demand) or fall (if there is excess supply). This is demonstrated in the graph below. At P_2, the pressure for prices to fall toward P_0 is greater than the pressure at P_1 because excess supply is greater at P_2 compared to excess supply at P_1.

The third thing to note is that when quantity demanded equals quantity supplied, the market is in equilibrium. (95-97)

11. Because we are in equilibrium at $3 there is no pressure to change at this price. At the other prices, surpluses exist putting downward pressure on price. (96-97)

12. Consumer surplus is the difference between what buyers would have been willing to pay and what they actually had to pay. Producers surplus is the difference between what the sellers would have been willing to accept as payment and what they actually received as payment. (98)

━━━━ ANSWERS ━━━━

MATCHING

1-h; 2-b; 3-j; 4-l; 5-n; 6-o; 7-i; 8-f; 9-g; 10-m; 11-p; 12-e; 13-a; 14-q; 15-k; 16-c; 17-r; 18-d.

━━━━ ANSWERS ━━━━

PROBLEMS AND APPLICATIONS

1. The linear curves are shown on the right. (87, 94)

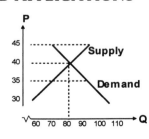

a. As shown in the graph, the downward sloping curve is a demand curve. We deduce this from the law of demand: quantity demanded rises (falls) as the price decreases (increases). (84)

b. As shown in the graph, the upward sloping curve is a supply curve. We deduce this from the law of supply: quantity supplied rises (falls) as the price rises (falls). (90-91)

c. The equilibrium price and quantity are where the demand and supply curves intersect. This is at $P = \$40$, $Q = 80$. At a price above $40, such as $45, quantity supplied exceeds quantity demanded and there is pressure for price to fall. At a price below $40, such as $35, quantity demanded exceeds quantity supplied and there is pressure for price to rise. (95-97)

2. a. As the price of pizza increases, the *quantity demanded* of pizza decreases. (84-86)

    Note that a change in the price of an item will cause a change in the quantity demanded; not demand! A change in something else other than the price may cause a change in demand–such as a change in one of the shift factors of demand discussed in the textbook.

    b. Whenever the price of bicycles increases, the *quantity supplied* also increases. (91-93)

    Note that a change in the price will cause a change in the quantity supplied; not supply! A change in something else other than the price may cause a change in supply–such as a change in one of the shift factors of supply discussed in the textbook.

    c. The price of electricity is cheaper in the northwestern part of the United States and therefore the *quantity demanded* of electricity is greater in the northwest. (84-86)

    d. An increase in incomes of car buyers will increase the *demand* for cars. (84-86)

    Notice that a change in a shift factor of demand, such as income, will change demand; not the quantity demanded!

    e. An increase in the *demand* for lobsters means consumers are willing and able to buy more lobsters at any given price (whatever the current price is). (84-86)

    In order for there to be an increase in the quantity demanded there would have to be a decrease in the price. Moreover, recall that an increase in demand is reflected as a rightward shift of the demand curve. Upon viewing a graph where the demand curve has shifted to the right you will see that more will be purchased at any given price.

f. This is a correct usage of the term "supply." Also note that a decrease in supply is reflected graphically as a leftward shift of the curve. Upon viewing a graph where the supply curve has shifted to the left you will see that less will be provided in the market at any given price. (91-93)

3. a. The market demand table is the summation of individual quantities demanded at each price as follows (88-89):

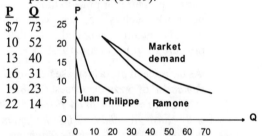

P	Q
$7	73
10	52
13	40
16	31
19	23
22	14

b. The individual and market demand curves are shown to the right of the demand table. (88-89)

c. At $13 a disc, total market quantity demanded is 40 discs. Total market quantity demanded falls to 23 when the price of discs rises to $19 per disc. (88-89)

d. Quantity demanded at each price rises by 25% for each individual and for the market as a whole. The new demand table is shown below. Graphically, both the individual and market demand curves shift to the right. The graph below shows the rightward shift in market demand. (88-89)

Price	Juan	Philippe	Ramone	Market
$7	3.75	25	62.50	91.25
$10	2.50	12.5	50	65
$13	1.25	8.75	40	50
$16	0	6.25	32.5	38.75
$19	0	3.75	25	28.75
$21	0	0	17.5	17.5

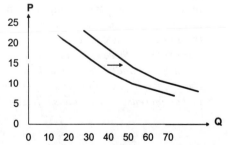

4. a. See the graph below. (87, 94)

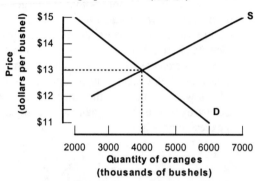

b. The equilibrium price is $13, the equilibrium quantity is 4000. This is an equilibrium because the quantity supplied equals the quantity demanded at this price. That is, there is neither a surplus (excess supply) nor a shortage (excess demand) and hence no tendency for the price to change. (95-97)

c. Because the quantity supplied exceeds the quantity demanded when the price is $14 per bushel, we would observe a surplus of 2,500 bushels (in thousands of bushels). We can expect the price of oranges per bushel to fall as sellers scramble to rid themselves of their excess supplies.

d. Because the quantity demanded exceeds the quantity supplied at $12 per bushel, we would observe a shortage of 2,500 bushels (in thousands of bushels). We can expect the price of oranges per bushel to rise as some buyers competitively bid up the price just to get some oranges. (95-97)

5. A hypothetical market for cyber cafes shows an upward sloping supply curve, a downward sloping demand curve and an equilibrium price and quantity where the two curves intersect.

a. A technological breakthrough that lowers the cost of computers will shift the supply of cyber cafes to the right as shown in the graph below. (91-92)

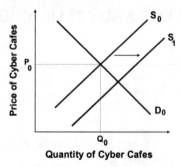

b. A rise in consumers' income will shift the demand for cyber cafes to the right as shown in the graph below. (85)

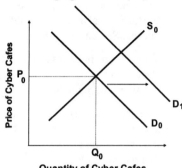

Quantity of Cyber Cafes

c. If a fee is charged to coffee houses to use the Internet, the supply of cyber cafes will shift to the left as shown below. (85)

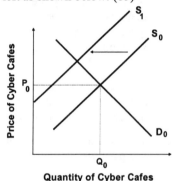

Quantity of Cyber Cafes

d. If the price of newspapers in print rises, the demand for cyber cafes will shift to the right as shown in the graph for answer (b). (85)

e. If possible suppliers expect cyber cafes to become more popular, the supply of cyber cafes will shift to the right as shown for answer (a). (91-92)

6. Equilibrium is found at the point of intersection between the demand and supply curves because there is neither a surplus nor a shortage at this price. Consumer surplus is shown as triangular area A. Producer surplus is shown as triangular area B. Both consumer and producer surpluses are at a maximum in equilibrium. (98)

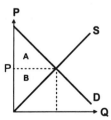

━━━━━ ANSWERS ━━━━━

A BRAIN TEASER

1. **a.** This innovation will shift the supply curve to the right as shown in the graph on the left below. As a result, this creates excess supply and the equilibrium price falls while the equilibrium quantity rises. (91-92)

    b. The market demand and supply for apple juice is shown below on the right. As a result of the fall in milk prices, the demand for apple juice shifts to the left. This creates excess supply of apple juice. The equilibrium price will fall. The equilibrium quantity will also fall. (91-93)

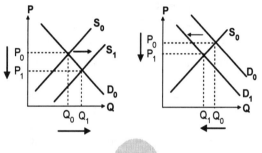

━━━━━ ANSWERS ━━━━━

MULTIPLE CHOICE

1. a   As discussed on page 83, the correct answer is a. A possible answer is d, which is a restatement of the law of demand, but since the actual law was among the choices, and is more precise, a is the correct answer.

2. d   An equal rise in price will cause individuals to switch to other goods more, the more substitutes there are. See page 83.

3. c   As discussed on pages 84-86, it is important to distinguish between a change in the quantity demanded and a change in demand. Weather is a shift factor of demand, so demand, not quantity demanded, will increase. Supply will not increase; the quantity supplied will, however. Who knows what will happen to the quality demanded? We don't.

4. b   As discussed on pages 84-86, when the price falls there is a movement along the demand curve which is expressed by saying the quantity demanded increased.

5. a   As discussed on pages 85-86, an increase in

5. a   As discussed on pages 85-86, an increase in demand is expressed as an outward (or rightward) shift of the demand curve. It is caused by something else other than the price. It means people will buy more at any price or pay a higher price for a given quantity demanded.

6. c   All of these are shift factors of demand. However, only c will increase demand and shift the demand curve to the right. See pages 85-86.

7. b   As is discussed on pages 84-86, especially page 85, b is the only correct response.

8. a   A flood will likely bring about a significant increase in the demand for bottled water since a flood makes most other water undrinkable. A flood would be a shift factor of demand for bottled water. See pages 85-86.

9. b   The curve slopes downward, so we can surmise that it is a demand curve; and the two points are on the demand curve, so the movement represents an increase in the quantity demanded, not an increase in demand. A shift in demand would be a shift of the entire curve. (See the figures on page 86 of the text.)

10. b   This demand curve is the only demand curve that goes through all the points in the table. See page 87.

11. a   As discussed in the text on pages 88-89 (Figure 4-4), market demand curves are determined by adding individuals' demand curves horizontally.

12. d   Since the market demand curve is arrived at by adding the individual demand curves horizontally, it will always be flatter. See pages 88-89.

13. a   As discussed on page 90, the law of supply is stated in a. The others either have the movement in the wrong direction or are not holding all other things constant.

14. b   It is a shift in supply because the curve is upward sloping; and it's a shift of the entire curve, so it is not a movement along. See page 92 and Figure 4-6.

15. c   As discussed on page 91, technology is a shift factor of supply so it must be a shift of the supply curve. Since it is an improve-

ment, it must be a shift rightward (or downward). (See also page 92, Figure 4-6)

16. c   The market supply curve is determined by the horizontal addition of individual supply curves. See page 93, Figure 4-7.

17. b   When there is excess demand, demanders start searching for new suppliers, as discussed on page 95.

18. d   The greater the extent to which the quantity supplied exceeds the quantity demanded, the greater the pressure for the price to fall. See pages 95-96.

19. a   As discussed on pages 95-96, this is a surplus (excess supply) when the price is above equilibrium. A surplus will motivate sellers to reduce price to rid themselves of their excess supplies. As the price falls, the quantity demand rises and the quantity supplied rises; demand and supply curves do *not* shift.

20. c   As discussed on pages 95-97 whenever the price is below equilibrium, a shortage is observed, and the price rises.

21. d   This is a definition of consumer surplus. See page 98.

22. a   Producer surplus is the price received minus the cost of producing the product, or the area between the price and the supple curve. That area is greatest at the highest price, P_1. See page 98 and Figure 4-9.

ANSWERS

POTENTIAL ESSAY QUESTIONS

The following are annotated answers. They indicate the general idea behind the answer.

1.   The shortage of parking spaces implies that permit prices are below equilibrium. The price of a permit should be increased. At least with the purchase of a permit you could be reasonably certain that a space would be available.

2.   Examples include lower grade liquor, wine, beer, "cheaper" grades of meat, and used clothes.

USING SUPPLY AND DEMAND

● CHAPTER AT A GLANCE

This review is based upon the learning objectives that open the chapter.

1. Demand and supply curves enable us to determine the equilibrium price and quantity. In addition, changes (shifts) in demand and supply curves enable us to predict the effect on the equilibrium price and quantity in a market. (104)
   Anything other than price that affects demand or supply will shift the curves.
   Know how a change in demand or supply affects the equilibrium price and quantity! Note:

$\uparrow D \Rightarrow \uparrow P; \uparrow Q$ $\downarrow D \Rightarrow \downarrow P; \downarrow Q$

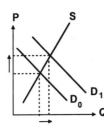 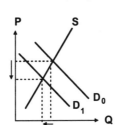

$\uparrow S \Rightarrow \downarrow P; \uparrow Q$ $\downarrow S \Rightarrow \uparrow P; \downarrow Q$

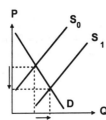 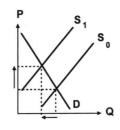

2. Changes (shifts) in demand and supply are what cause changes in the price and the quantity traded in real-world markets. (105-109)
   Shifts in both demand and supply can be tricky. But remember, simply locate the new point of intersection. When both curves shift, the effect on either price or quantity depends on the relative size of the shifts. Moreover, the effect on either price or quantity (one of them) will be certain, while the effect on the other will be uncertain. Note:

$\uparrow D$ and $\uparrow S \Rightarrow$?P; $\uparrow Q$ $\uparrow D$ and $\downarrow S \Rightarrow \uparrow P;$?Q

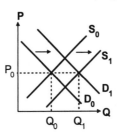 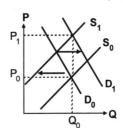

$\downarrow D$ and $\uparrow S \Rightarrow \downarrow P;$?Q $\downarrow D$ and $\downarrow S \Rightarrow$?P; $\downarrow Q$

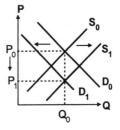 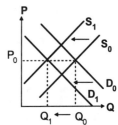

3. Price ceilings cause shortages; price floors cause surpluses. (110-112)
   A price ceiling is a legal price set by government below equilibrium. An example is rent controls. A price floor is a legal price set by government above equilibrium. An example is the minimum wage.

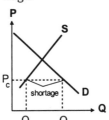 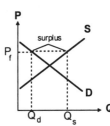

Price Ceiling   **Price Floor**

4. Taxes and tariffs raise price and reduce quantity. Quotas are a numerical limit on the number imported. (113-115)

A tariff is an excise tax on an imported good. Any excise tax imposed on suppliers shifts the supply curve up by the amount of the tax. Rarely is the tax <u>entirely</u> passed on to consumers in the form of a higher price. Although a quota can have the same effect as a tariff, suppliers prefer quotas because the suppliers get the revenues.

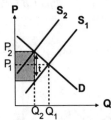

With tax t, price rises to P_2 and the government collects revenue shown by the shaded region. A quota Q_2 has the same effect on price and quantity. The difference is in who gets the additional revenue.

5. Simple supply and demand analysis holds other things constant. Sometimes supply and demand are interconnected, making it impossible to hold other things constant. When there is interdependence between supply and demand, a movement along one curve can cause a shift of the other curve. Thus, supply and demand analysis used alone is not enough to determine where the equilibrium will be. (115-116)

When the "other things are constant" assumption is not realistic, then feedback or ripple effects can become relevant. The degree of interdependence differs among various sets of issues. That is why there is a separate micro and macro analysis–microeconomics and macroeconomics.

The fallacy of composition is the false assumption that what is true for a part will also be true for the whole. This means that what is true in microeconomics, may not be true in macroeconomics.

6. There are six roles of government in a market economy: (116-119)

- Provide a stable set of institutions and rules.
  The government specifies "the rules of the game."

- Promote effective and workable competition.
  Know the different consequences associated with competition vs. monopoly power.

- Correct for externalities.
  Government attempts to restrict the production and consumption of negative externalities; while promoting the production and consumption of positive externalities.

- Ensure economic stability and growth.
  Government tries to ensure:
  Full employment
  Low inflation
  Economic growth (which increases the standard of living)

- Provide for public goods.
  Government provides public goods by collecting taxes from everyone to try to eliminate the free-rider problem.

- Adjust for undesired market results.
  Governments often attempt to redistribute income in a more "fair" manner through the use of taxes (and other methods). Know the difference between progressive, regressive, and proportional taxes. Government sometimes encourages merit (socially desirable) goods by subsidizing them, and discourages demerit (socially undesirable) goods or activities by taxing them. But, should government decide what is "good" or "bad" for us?

Government intervenes in the economy in an attempt to correct for "market failures." But just as the market can sometimes provide undesirable results, there is also government failure– government intervention that makes things worse.

See also, "Appendix A: Algebraic Representation of Supply, Demand, and Equilibrium."

SHORT-ANSWER QUESTIONS

1. Demonstrate graphically what happens to the equilibrium price and quantity of M&Ms if they suddenly become more popular.

2. Demonstrate graphically what happens to the equilibrium price and quantity of oranges if a frost destroys 50 percent of the orange crop.

3. Demonstrate graphically what happens in the following situation: Income in the U.S. rose in the 1990s and more and more people began to buy luxury items such as caviar. However, about that same time, the dissolution of the Soviet Union threw suppliers of caviar from the Caspian Sea into a mire of bureaucracy, reducing their ability to export caviar. Market: Caviar sold in the United States.

4. What is a price ceiling? Demonstrate graphically the effect of a price ceiling on a market.

5. What is a price floor? Demonstrate graphically the effect of a price floor on a market.

6. Why are rent controls likely to worsen an existing shortage of housing?

7. Demonstrate graphically what happens to equilibrium price and quantity when a tariff is imposed on imports.

8. What is the fallacy of composition and how is it related to why economists separate micro from macro economics?

9. What are six roles of government?

MATCHING THE TERMS
Match the terms to their definitions

_e_ 1. price ceiling
_h_ 2. price floor
_g_ 3. demerit goods
___ 4. externality
___ 5. market failure
___ 6. rent control
___ 7. excise tax
___ 8. tariff
___ 9. quota
___ 10. merit goods
___ 11. fallacy of composition
___ 12. government failure
___ 13. macroeconomic externality
___ 14. minimum wage laws
___ 15. progressive tax
___ 16. regressive tax
___ 17. public good
___ 18. proportional tax
___ 19. monopoly power
___ 20. free rider

a. The lowest wage a firm can legally pay an employee.

b. The ability of individuals or firms currently in business to prevent other individuals or firms from entering the same kind of business.

c. Tax that is levied on a specific good.

d. The false assumption that what is true for a part will also be true for the whole.

e. A government-imposed limit on how high a price can be charged.

f. A quantitative restriction on the amount that one country can export to another.

g. Price ceiling on rents set by government.

h. A government-imposed limit on how low a price can be charged.

i. The effect of a decision on a third party not taken into account by the decision maker.

j. A good which if supplied to one person must be supplied to all and whose consumption by one individual does not prevent its consumption by another individual.

k. Excise tax on an imported good.

l. A person who participates in something for free because others have paid for it.

m. An externality that effects the levels of unemployment, inflation, or growth in the economy as a whole.

n. A tax whose rates increase as a person's income increases.

o. A tax whose rates decrease as a person's income increases.

p. A tax whose rates are constant at all income levels, no matter what a taxpayer's total annual income is.

q. Goods or activities that society believes are bad for people even though they choose to use the goods or engage in the activities.

r. Situation where the market does not lead to a desired result.

s. Situation where the government intervenes and makes things worse.

t. Goods or activities that government believes are good for you even though you may not choose to engage in the activities or consume the goods.

PROBLEMS AND APPLICATIONS

1. Use supply and demand curves to help you determine the impact that each of the following events has on the market for surfboards in Southern California.

   a. Southern California experiences unusually high temperatures, sending an unusually large number of people to its beaches.

   b. Large sharks are reported feeding near the beaches of Southern California.

c.   Due to the large profits earned by surfboard producers there is a significant increase in the number of producers of surfboards.

d.   There is a significant increase in the price of epoxy paint used to coat surfboards.

2.   Use supply and demand curves to help you determine the impact that each of the following events has on the market for beef.

a.   New genetic engineering technology enables ranchers to raise healthier, heavier cattle significantly reducing costs.

b.   The CBS program "60 Minutes" reports on the unsanitary conditions in poultry processing plants that may increase the chances of consumers getting sick by eating chicken.

c.   In addition to developing new genetic engineering technology, we have been mistaken in the past. Highly credible new research results report that abundant consumption of fatty red meats actually prolongs average life expectancy.

d.   Consumers expect the price of beef to fall in the near future.

3.   Suppose you are told that the price of Cadillacs has increased from last year as well as the number bought and sold. Is this an exception to the law of demand, or has there been a change in demand or supply that could account for this?

4.   The following table depicts the market supply and demand for milk in the United States.

Price in dollars per gal	Quantity of gals supplied in 1,000	Quantity of gals demanded in 1,000
$1.50	600	800
$1.75	620	720
$2.00	640	640
$2.25	660	560
$2.50	680	480

a.   Graph the market supply and demand for milk.

b.   What is the equilibrium market price and quantity in the market?

c.   Show the effect of a government imposed price floor of $2.25 on the market price, quantity supplied, and quantity demanded.

d. Show the effect of a government imposed price ceiling of $1.75 on the quantity supplied and quantity demanded.

e. What would happen to equilibrium price and quantity if the government imposes a $1 per gallon tax on the sellers and as a result supply decreases by 100 thousand gallons? What price would the sellers receive?

5. Suppose the United States government imposes stricter entry barriers on Japanese cars imported into the United States. This could be accomplished by the U.S. government either raising tariffs or by imposing a stricter quota.

a. What impact would this have on the market for Japanese cars in the United States?

b. What impact would this likely have on the market for American-made cars in the United States?

c. What do you think could motivate the U.S. government to pursue these stricter entry barriers on Japanese cars coming into the U.S.?

d. Would Japanese car manufacturers prefer a tariff or a quota? Why?

6. Describe what likely happens to market price and quantity for the particular goods in each of the following cases:

a. A technological breakthrough lowers the costs of producing tractors in India while there is an increase in incomes of all citizens in India. Market: tractors.

b. The United States imposes a ban on the sale of oil by companies that do business with Libya and Iran. At the same time, very surprisingly, a large reserve of drillable oil is discovered in Barrington, Rhode Island. Market: Oil.

c. In the summer of 1996, many people watched the Atlanta Summer Olympics on NBC instead of going to the movies. At the same time, thinking that summer time is the peak season for movies, Hollywood released a record number of movies. Market: movie tickets.

d. After a promotional visit by Michael Jordan to France, a craze for Nike Air shoes develops, while workers in Nike's manufacturing plants in China go on strike decreasing the production of these shoes. Market: Nike shoes.

7. For each of the following determine which role government is exercising.

    a. Government enforces legal and binding contracts.

    b. Government bans the use of a particular pesticide that has been determined to significantly increase the chances of those exposed to it getting cancer.

    c. Government deregulates an industry making it easier for entrepreneurs to enter into that business activity.

    d. Government raises tax rates on upper-income individuals because it has been politically determined that they are not paying their "fair" share.

    e. Government builds a new interstate highway system.

    f. Government increases the federal budget deficit because it is argued this will help to reduce unemployment and provide for greater rates of economic growth.

    g. Government subsidizes the "arts" (e.g. symphony orchestras).

A1. The supply and demand equations for strawberries are given by $Q_s = -10 + 5P$ and $Q_d = 20 - 5P$ respectively, where P is price in dollars per quart, Q_s is millions of quarts of strawberries supplied, and Q_d is millions of quarts of strawberries demanded.

    a. What is the equilibrium market price and quantity for strawberries in the market?

    b. Suppose a new preservative is introduced that prevents more strawberries from rotting on their way from the farm to the store. As a result supply of strawberries increases by 20 million quarts at every price. What effect does this have on market price and quantity sold?

    c. Suppose it has been found that the spray used on cherry trees has ill effects on those who eat the cherries. As a result, the demand for strawberries increases by 10 million quarts at every price. What effect does this have on market price for strawberries and quantity of strawberries sold?

A2. The supply and demand equations for roses are given by $Q_s = -10 + 3P$ and $Q_d = 20 - 2P$ respectively, where P is dollars per dozen roses and Q is dozens of roses in hundred thousands.

    a. What is the equilibrium market price and quantity of roses sold?

b. Suppose the government decides to make it more affordable for individuals to be able to give roses to their significant others, and sets a price ceiling for roses at $4 a dozen. What is the likely result?

c. Suppose the government decides to tax the suppliers of roses $1 per dozen roses sold. What is the equilibrium price and quantity in the market? How much do buyers pay for each dozen they buy for their significant others? How much do suppliers receive for each dozen they sell?

d. Suppose the government decides instead to impose a $1 tax on buyers for each dozen roses purchased. (Government has determined buying roses for love to be a demerit good.) What is the equilibrium price and quantity in the market? How much do the buyers pay, and the sellers receive?

● A BRAIN TEASER

1. Buchananland wants to restrict its number of auto imports from Zachstan. It is trying to decide whether it should impose a tariff or set quotas on Zachstani cars. With the help of a diagram, explain why auto makers in Zachstan have hired a lobbyist to persuade the government of Buchananland to set quotas instead of imposing tariffs.

● MULTIPLE CHOICE

Circle the one best answer for each of the following questions:

1. If the demand for a good increases you will expect
   a. price to fall and quantity to rise.
   b. price to rise and quantity to rise.
   c. price to fall and quantity to fall.
   d. price to rise and quantity to fall.

2. Compared to last year, fewer oranges are being purchased and the selling price has decreased. This could have been caused by
   a. an increase in demand.
   b. an increase in supply.
   c. a decrease in demand.
   d. a decrease in supply.

3. If demand and supply both increase, this will cause
   a. an increase in the equilibrium quantity, but an uncertain effect on the equilibrium price.
   b. an increase in the equilibrium price, but an uncertain effect on the equilibrium quantity.
   c. an increase in the equilibrium price and quantity.
   d. an decrease in the equilibrium price and quantity.

4. An increase in demand for a good will cause
    a. excess demand (a shortage) before price changes.
    b. movement down along the demand curve as price changes.
    c. movement down along the supply curve as price changes.
    d. a higher price and a smaller quantity traded in the market.

5. If a frost in Florida damages oranges, what will likely happen to the market for Florida oranges?
    a. Demand will increase.
    b. Demand will fall.
    c. Supply will increase.
    d. Supply will decrease.

6. Assume that the cost of shipping automobiles from the U.S. to Japan decreases. What will likely happen to the equilibrium price and quantity of cars made in the U.S. and sold in Japan?
    a. The price will rise, and quantity will fall.
    b. Both price and quantity will rise.
    c. The price will fall, and quantity will rise.
    d. The price will fall, what happens to quantity is not clear.

7. What will likely happen to the price and quantity of cricket bats in Trinidad as interest in cricket dwindles following the dismal performance of the national cricket team, while at the same time taxes are repealed on producing cricket bats?
    a. The price will decrease, but what happens to quantity is not clear.
    b. The price will decrease, and quantity will increase.
    c. The price will increase, but what happens to quantity is not clear.
    d. It is not clear what happens to either price or quantity.

8. If there is an effective price ceiling
    a. the quantity demanded exceeds the quantity supplied.
    b. the price is above equilibrium.
    c. then a surplus is created.
    d. the supply exceeds demand.

9. Effective rent controls
    a. are examples of price floors.
    b. cause the quantity demanded to exceed the quantity supplied of rental occupied housing.
    c. create a greater amount of higher quality housing to be made available to renters.
    d. create a surplus of rental occupied housing

10. An increase in the minimum wage can be expected to
    a. cause unemployment for some workers.
    b. cause a shortage of workers.
    c. increase employment.
    d. help businesses by reducing their costs of production.

11. A quota
    a. is a tax imposed on an imported good.
    b. is a quantitative restriction on the amount that one country can export to another.
    c. imposed on a good will shift the supply of that good outward to the right.
    d. imposed on a good , like a tariff, will reduce the price of the good to consumers.

12. For governments
    a. tariffs are preferred over quotas because tariffs can help them collect revenues.
    b. quotas are preferred over tariffs because quotas can help them collect revenues.
    c. neither quotas nor tariffs can help collect revenues.
    d. both quotas and tariffs are sources of revenues.

13. The fallacy of composition is
    a. the false assumption that what is false for a part will also be false for the whole.
    b. the false assumption that what is true for a part will also be true for the whole.
    c. the false assumption that what is false for a whole will also be false for the part.
    d. the false assumption that what is true for a whole will also be true for the part.

14. When government attempts to adjust for the effect of decisions on third parties not taken into account by the decision makers, the government is attempting to
    a. provide for a stable set of institutions and rules.
    b. promote effective and workable competition.
    c. provide for public goods and services.
    d. correct for externalities.

15. A progressive income tax
    a. is a tax whose rates increase as a person's income increases.
    b. is a tax whose rates decrease as a person's income increases.
    c. is a tax whose rates are constant at all income levels, no mater what a taxpayer's total annual income
    d. is not used in the United States.

16. If the consumption of a good by one individual does not prevent its consumption by another individual, that good is called
    a. a public good.
    b. a private good.
    c. a macroeconomic good.
    d. a demerit good.

17. Economic theory says government should
    a. follow a policy of laissez-faire.
    b. get intricately involved in the economy.
    c. not get involved in the economy.
    d. base government intervention upon costs and benefits.

A1. The supply and demand equations for Nantucket Nectar's Kiwi-berry juice are given by $Q_s = -4 + 5P$ and $Q_d = 18 - 6P$ respectively, where price is dollars per quart and quantity is thousands of quarts. The equilibrium market price and quantity is
    a. P = $2, Q = 6 thousand quarts.
    b. P = $3, Q = 6 thousand quarts.
    c. P = $14, Q = 66 thousand quarts.
    d. P = $22, Q = 106 thousand quarts.

A2. The supply and demand equations for sidewalk snow removal in a small town in Montana are given by $Q_s = -50 + 5P$ and $Q_d = 100 - 5P$ respectively, where price is in dollars per removal.and quantity is numbers of removals per week. It snows so much that demand for sidewalk snow removals increases by 30 per week. The new equilibrium market price and quantity is
    a. P = $15, Q = 6 sidewalk snow removals.
    b. P = $15, Q = 6 sidewalk snow removals.
    c. P = $18, Q = 66 sidewalk snow removals.
    d. P = $18, Q = 40 sidewalk snow removals.

A3. The supply and demand equations for Arizona Ice Tea in Arizona is given by $Q_s = -10 + 6P$ and $Q_d = 40 - 8P$; P is price of each bottle in dollars; and quantity is in hundreds of thousands of bottles per month. Suppose the state government imposes a $1 per bottle tax on the suppliers. The market price the suppliers receive and the equilibrium quantity in the market are
    a. $3 per bottle and 8 hundred thousand bottles per month.
    b. $3 per bottle and 16 hundred thousand bottles per month.
    c. $4 per bottle and 8 hundred thousand bottles per month.
    d. $4 per bottle and 16 hundred thousand bottles per month.

● POTENTIAL ESSAY QUESTIONS

You may also see essay questions similar to the "Problems & Applications" and "Brain Teaser" exercises.

1. Discuss how a change in demand or supply impacts a market equilibrium price and quantity.

2. Discuss the six roles of government in a market economy. According to economic theory, to what extent should government intervene in our economy?

ANSWERS

SHORT-ANSWER QUESTIONS

1. Increasing popularity of M&Ms means that at every price, more M&Ms are demanded. The demand curve shifts out to D_1, and both equilibrium price and quantity rise to P_1 and Q_1 respectively. (104)

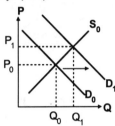

2. A frost damaging oranges means that at every price, suppliers are willing to supply fewer oranges. The supply curve shifts to the left to S_1, and equilibrium price rises to P_1, and quantity falls to Q_1 . (106-107)

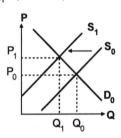

3. The demand curve for Russian caviar shifts out; the supply shifts in; the price rises substantially. What happens to quantity depends upon the relative sizes of the shifts. (105, 109)

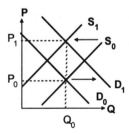

4. A price ceiling is a government imposed limit on how high a price can be charged. An effective price ceiling below market equilibrium price will cause $Q_D > Q_S$ (a shortage) as shown in the graph below. (110-111)

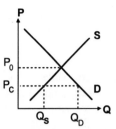

5. A price floor is a government imposed limit on how low a price can be charged. An effective price floor above market equilibrium price will cause $Q_S > Q_D$ (a surplus) as shown in the graph below. (111-112)

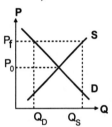

6. Rent controls are price ceilings and result in shortages in rental housing. As time passes and as the population rises, the demand for rental housing rises. On the supply side, other ventures become more lucrative relative to renting out housing. Owners have less incentive to repair existing buildings, let alone build new ones, reducing the supply of rental housing over time. The housing shortage increases. The shortage becomes more acute over time (110-111)

7. As a tariff of t is imposed, the supply curve shifts leftward to S_1 by the amount of the tariff. The equilibrium price goes up and quantity goes down. (113-114)

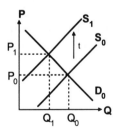

8. Fallacy of composition is the false assumption that what is true for a part will also be true for the whole. In micro, economists isolate an individual person's or firm's behavior and consider its effects, while the many side effects are kept in the background. In macro, those side effects become too large and can no longer be held constant. These side effects are what account for the interdependence of supply and demand. Macro, thus, is not simply a summation of all micro results; it would be a fallacy of composition to take the sum of each individual's (micro) actions and say that it is the aggregate (macro) result. (116)

9. Six roles of government are (1) provide a stable set of institutions and rules, (2) promote effective and workable competition, (3) correct for externalities, (4) provide public goods, (5) ensure economic stability and growth, and (6) adjust for undesired market results. (116-120)

━━━━━━ ANSWERS ━━━━━━

MATCHING

1-e; 2-h; 3-q; 4-i; 5-r; 6-g; 7-c; 8-k; 9-f; 10-t; 11-d; 12-s; 13-m; 14-a; 15-n; 16-o; 17-j; 18-p; 19-b; 20-l.

━━━━━━ ANSWERS ━━━━━━

PROBLEMS AND APPLICATIONS

1. **a.** This will increase the demand for surfboards shifting the demand curve to the right. At the original price a temporary shortage would be observed putting upward pressure on price. We end up with a higher equilibrium price and a greater equilibrium quantity as illustrated in the graph below. (*When dealing with a change in D or S curves, just remember to go from the initial point of intersection between the curves to the new point of intersection. The initial point of intersection will give you the initial equilibrium P and Q and the new point of intersection the new equilibrium P and Q. Then recall that if the price went up in the*

market, it was a response to a temporary shortage (excess demand). If the equilibrium price went down, then it was a response to a temporary surplus (excess supply). (104-109)

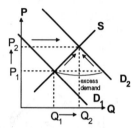

b. This would cause a decrease in the demand for surfboards shifting the demand curve to the left. At the original price a temporary surplus would be observed putting downward pressure on price. We end up with a lower equilibrium price and a lower equilibrium quantity as illustrated in the graph below. (104-109)

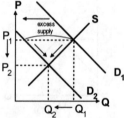

c. This would cause an increase in the supply of surfboards shifting the supply curve to the right. At the original price a temporary surplus would be observed putting downward pressure on price. We end up with a lower equilibrium price and a higher equilibrium quantity as illustrated in the graph below. (104-109)

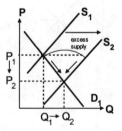

d. This would cause a decrease in the supply of surfboards shifting the supply curve to the left. At the original price a temporary shortage would be observed putting upward pressure on price. We end up with a higher equilibrium price and a lower equilibrium quantity as illustrated in the graph below. (104-109)

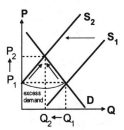

2. **a.** An increase in production technology will increase the supply of beef. The temporary surplus (excess supply) of beef at the original price will cause the market price to fall. Eventually we get a lower equilibrium price of beef and a greater amount bought and sold in the market. (104-109)

    b. Chicken and beef are substitute goods–they can be used instead of each other. Therefore, this "60 Minutes" report will likely increase the demand for beef. The temporary shortage (excess demand) at the original price will cause the price to be competitively bid up. Eventually we observe a higher equilibrium price and a greater equilibrium quantity. (104-109)

    c. The new development would increase the supply of beef while the reports of the health benefits of beef would increase the demand for beef. Quantity of beef sold would rise. The impact on equilibrium price depends upon the relative sizes of the shifts. (104-109)

    d. Because people will postpone their purchases of beef until the price decreases this will reduce the demand for beef today. A decrease in demand is reflected as a leftward shift of the demand curve. The temporary excess supply (surplus) that is created at the original price puts downward pressure on the market price of beef. Eventually we get a lower equilibrium price and quantity. (104-109)

3. This is not an exception to the law of demand (there are very few exceptions). Instead, an increase in demand could account for a higher price and a greater amount bought and sold as is illustrated in the figure below. (104-109)

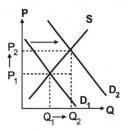

4. **a.** The market supply and demand for milk is graphed below.

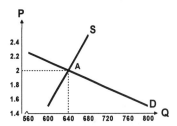

    b. The equilibrium market price is $2 and equilibrium quantity in the market is 640 thousand gallons of milk. This is point *A* on the graph above. (104-109)

    c. A government imposed price floor of $2.25 is shown in the figure below. Since it is a price above market price, quantity supplied (660) exceeds quantity demanded (560) by 100 thousand gallons. (111-112)

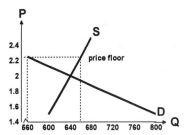

    d. A government-imposed price ceiling of $1.75 is below market price. Quantity supplied (620 thousand gallons) will be less than quantity demanded (720 thousand gallons) by 100 thousand gallons as shown below. (110-111)

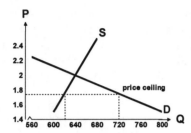

e.   Because of the tax, the quantity supplied for every price level will decline by 100 thousand gallons. The supply and demand table will change as follows:

Price in dollars per gal	Quantity of gals supplied 1,000	Quantity of gals demanded 1,000
$1.50	500	800
$1.75	520	720
$2.00	540	640
$2.25	560	560
$2.50	580	480

The market equilibrium price would be $2.25 and quantity would be 560 thousand gallons. Since the sellers will have to pay $1 tax on every gallon they sell, they will receive $1.25 per gallon milk. (113-114)

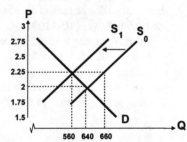

5.   a.   A higher tariff or more strict quota imposed on Japanese cars would decrease the supply of Japanese cars in the United States. The leftward shift of the supply curve, such as from S_1 to S_2 shown in the figure below, creates a temporary shortage (excess demand) at the original price that puts upward pressure on the prices of Japanese cars. The result will be higher prices for Japanese cars as well as a decrease in the amount bought and sold in the U.S. market. (113-114)

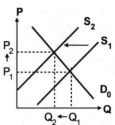

b.   Because Japanese and American-made cars are substitutes for each other, some people will switch from buying the now relatively more expensive Japanese cars (law of demand in action) to buying more American-made cars. (Notice that "relative" prices are what are relevant.) This increases the demand for American-made cars, increasing their prices as well as the amount bought and sold. This is illustrated in the figure below. (104)

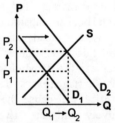

c.   These trade barriers may be advocated by American car manufacturers. They could obviously benefit from the higher prices and greater sales. American automotive workers could also benefit from the greater job security that comes with more cars being produced and sold. These "special interest groups" may put political pressure on government, and the government may succumb to that pressure. (113-114)

d.   The Japanese would prefer a quota over a tariff. This is because a tariff would require them to pay taxes to the U.S. government; a quota would not. Moreover, a quota would increase revenues and therefore profits to the Japanese. (114-115)

6.   a.   The supply curve will shift out from S_0 to S_1 as the new technology makes it cheaper to produce tractors. Increased incomes will shift the demand for tractors out from D_0 to D_1. Equilibrium price may

go up, remain the same, or go down, depending on the relative shifts in the two curves. Equilibrium quantity, however, will definitely increase. (104-109)

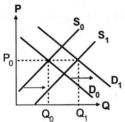

b. The ban on the companies doing business with Libya and Iran will shift the supply curve in from S_0 to S_1. The discovery of oil will, however, shift it back out to S_2. Depending on the relative shifts, equilibrium price and quantity will change. In the case shown in the diagram, the shift resulting from the discovery of the new oil source dominates the shift resulting from the ban, and the equilibrium price falls and quantity goes up. (104-109)

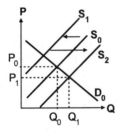

c. With more people watching the Olympics, the demand for movies shifts in from D_0 to D_1. At the same time the increased supply of movies will shift the supply curve out from S_0 to S_1. Equilibrium price will fall, and the change in equilibrium quantity will depend on the relative shifts in the curves. (104-109)

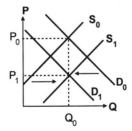

d. With more people demanding Nike Air shoes, the demand curve will shift out from D_0 to D_1. The worker strike will, however, reduce supply and shift it in from S_0 to S_1. The resulting equilibrium price will be higher, and the change in quantity depends on the relative shifts in the curves. (104-109)

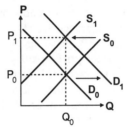

7. a. Providing a stable set of institutions and rules. (117)

b. Correcting for an externality (a negative externality in this case). (117-118)

c. Promoting effective and workable competition. (117)

d. Adjusting for undesired market results (an "unfair" distribution of income in this case). (119)

e. Providing for public goods. (118-119)

f. Ensuring economic stability and growth. (118)

g. Adjusting for undesired market results (subsidizing a merit activity in this case). (119)

A1. a. Equating Q_s to Q_d and then solving for equilibrium price gives us $3 per quart. Substituting $3 into the demand and supply equations, we find that equilibrium quantity is 5 million quarts. (123-125)

b. Since supply increases by 20 million quarts, the new supply equation is $Q_s = 10 + 5P$. Equating this with the demand equation, we find the new equilibrium price to be $1 per quart. Substituting into either the new supply equation or the demand equation we find that equilibrium quantity is 15 million quarts. (123-125)

c. With demand increasing, the new demand equation is $Q_d = 30 - 5P$. Setting Q_s equal to Q_d and solving for price we find equilibrium price to be $4 per quart. Substituting this into either the new demand or the supply equation we find equilibrium quantity to be 10 million quarts. (123-125)

A2. a. Equating Q_s and Q_d, then solving gives equilibrium price $6 and quantity 8 hundred thousand dozen. (125-126)

b. If price ceiling is set at $4, $Q_s = 2$, and $Q_d = 12$; the resulting shortage is 10 hundred thousand dozen. (125-126)

c. If a $1 tax is imposed on suppliers, the new supply equation will be $Q_s = -10 + 3(P-1) = -13 + 3P$. Equating this with Q_d gives equilibrium price $6.60 and quantity 6.8 hundred thousand. Buyers pay $6.60 for each dozen they buy, and the sellers receive $1 less than that, or $5.60, for each dozen they sell. (126)

d. As a result of the tax, the new demand equation will be $Q_d = 20 - 2(P+1) = 18 - 2P$. Equating this with Q_s gives equilibrium price $5.60 and quantity 6.8 hundred thousand. Buyers pay $6.60 ($P + 1$) for each dozen they buy, and the sellers receive $5.60 for each dozen they sell. (126)

ANSWERS

A BRAIN TEASER

1. The supply and demand equilibrium are at price P_e and quality Q_e. If quotas for Zachstani cars are set at Q_2, the price received for each car sold is P_2, which is well above P_t, the price they would normally sell for at that quantity. A tariff of $t (P_2 - P_t)$ would have to be imposed to reduce imports to Q_2 reflected by the supply curve shifting in to S_1. In both cases, consumers pay Zachstan producers P_2 for each car. In the case of the quota, Zachstan producers keep P_2 for each car. In the case of the tariff, Zachstan producers must give up t for each car sold. Profits are higher with the quota. For this reason they have the lobbyist lobbying for quotas. (113-115)

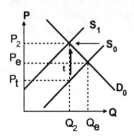

ANSWERS

MULTIPLE CHOICE

1. **b** Since this statement says demand increases, it is the demand curve shifting. There is no change in the supply curve. Assuming an upward sloping supply curve, that means that price will rise and quantity will rise. See page 104.

2. **c** Only a decrease in demand will result in a decrease in quantity and a decrease in price. See page 104.

3. **a** An increase in demand has a tendency to increase price and increase the quantity. An increase in supply has a tendency to *decrease* the price and increase the quantity. So, on balance, we are certain of an increase in the equilibrium quantity, but we are uncertain about the impact on the price in the market. See page 108.

4. **a** An increase in demand causes the quantity demanded to exceed the quantity supplied creating excess demand (a shortage). This increases the price causing movement *up* along the demand and supply curves resulting in a *greater* quantity traded in the market. See page 104.

5. **d** A frost will reduce the quantity of oranges available for sale at every price. Supply will decrease. See page 104.

6. **c** The supply curve will shift out, market price will fall and the quantity will rise. See page 104.

7. **a** Demand for cricket bats will fall, shifting the demand curve in, while the tax repeal will shift the supply curve out. Price will fall, and quantity may change depending on the relative shifts of the supply and demand curves. Related issues are discussed in pages 105-107 of the textbook.

8. **a** As discussed on pages 110-111, the quantity demanded exceeds the quantity supplied. The price is *below* equilibrium, and a *shortage* is created. You don't use the

terms supply and demand because that usage refers to the entire schedule (curve).

9. b   Rent controls are price ceilings and therefore cause the quantity demanded to exceed the quantity supplied. Indeed, the quantity demanded rises while the quantity supplied falls creating a shortage. See pages 110-111 in the text.

10. a   Because the minimum wage is a price floor it increases the quantity supplied and decreases the quantity demanded (*decreasing* employment) and creating a *surplus* of workers (causing some unemployment). The higher minimum wage would *increase* costs of production to businesses. See pages 111-112 in the textbook.

11. b   The correct answer is b by definition. Also, a quota will decrease supply, shifting the supply curve inward to the left. This causes the price consumers must pay to rise. See pages 114-115 in the text.

12. a   See the discussion on page 115 of the textbook.

13. b   See definition of fallacy of composition on page 116 of the textbook.

14. d   See pages 117-118 of the textbook.

15. a   See definition of progressive income tax on page 119 of the textbook.

16. a   See definition of public good on page 118 of the textbook.

17. d   Government should get involved in our economy only if the benefits outweigh the costs. See page 120.

A1. a   Equating the supply and demand equations gives equilibrium P = $2. Substituting this into either the supply or demand equation tells us that Q = 6 thousand quarts. See page 124.

A2. d   The new demand becomes $Q_d = 130 - 5P$. Equating the supply and demand equations gives equilibrium P = $18. Substituting this

into either the supply or demand equation tells us that Q = 40 sidewalk snow removals. See pages 123-125.

A3. c   A $1 per bottle tax on suppliers makes the supply equation $Q_s = -10 + 6(P - 1) = -16 + 6P$. Equating this with the demand equation gives equilibrium P = $4 and Q = 8 hundred thousand. The supplier receives $3 ($4 - $1). See page 126 of the textbook.

ANSWERS

POTENTIAL ESSAY QUESTIONS

The following are annotated answers. They indicate the general idea behind the answer.

1. Suppose there is an increase in demand. The demand curve shifts out to the right, creating a temporary shortage (excess demand) at the original price. As a result, buyers competitively bid up the price. The quantity demanded falls (movement up along the demand curve toward the new point of intersection) and the quantity supplied rises (movement up along the supply curve toward the new point of intersection). Eventually, the price rises enough until the quantity demanded is once again equal to the quantity supplied. Because there is neither a shortage nor a surplus at this new point of intersection, the new market equilibrium price and quantity is obtained. The market equilibrium price and quantity will both increase as a result of an increase in demand. *You should be able to illustrate this graphically as well.*

2. Six roles of government are (1) provide a stable set of institutions and rules, (2) promote effective and workable competition, (3) correct for externalities, (4) provide public goods, (5) ensure economic stability and growth, and (6) adjust for undesired market results. Economic theory tells us that the government should intervene in our economy only if the benefits outweigh the costs. However, equally reasonable people are likely to weigh the benefits and costs of government involvement differently.

Pretest
Chapters 1 - 5

I

Take this test in test conditions, giving yourself a limited amount of time to complete the questions. Ideally, check with your professor to see how much time he or she allows for an average multiple choice question and multiply this by 25. This is the time limit you should set for yourself for this pretest. If you do not know how much time your teacher would allow, we suggest 1 minute per question, or 25 minutes.

1. Scarcity could be reduced if
   a. individuals work less and want fewer consumption goods.
   b. individuals work more and want fewer consumption goods.
   c. world population grows and world production remains the same.
   d. innovation comes to a halt.

2. In arriving at a decision, a good economist would say that
   a. one should consider only total costs and total benefits.
   b. one should consider only marginal costs and marginal benefits.
   c. after one has considered marginal costs and benefits, one should integrate the social and moral implications and reconsider those costs and benefits.
   d. after considering the marginal costs and benefits, one should make the decision on social and moral grounds.

3. If at Female College there are significantly more females than males (and there are not a significant number of gays) economic forces
   a. will be pushing for females to pay on dates.
   b. will be pushing for males to pay on dates.
   c. will be pushing for neither to pay on dates.
   d. are irrelevant to this issue. Everyone knows that the males always should pay.

4. Which of the following is an example of a macroeconomic topic?
   a. The effect of a frost on the Florida orange crop.
   b. Wages of cross-country truckers.
   c. How the unemployment and inflation rates are related.
   d. How income is distributed in the United States.

5. "Given certain conditions, the market achieves efficient results" is an example of a
   a. positive statement.
   b. normative statement.
   c. art-of-economics statement.
   d. subjective statement.

6. For a market to exist, you have to have
   a. public property rights.
   b. private property rights.
   c. a combination of public and private property rights.
   d. coordination rights.

7. In capitalism, the "what to produce" decision is made by
   a. consumers.
   b. the market.
   c. government.
   d. firms.

8. If the opportunity cost of good X in terms of good Y is 2Y, so you'll have to give up 2Y to get one X, the production possibility curve would look like
   a. a.
   b. b.
   c. c.
   d. d.

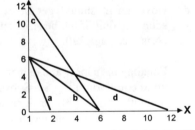

9. In the accompanying production possibility diagram, point A would be

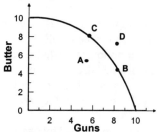

   a. an efficient point.
   b. a super-efficient point.
   c. an inefficient point.
   d. a non-attainable point.

10. If the United States and Japan have production possibility curves as shown in the diagram below, at what point would they most likely be after trade?
    a. A
    b. B
    c. C
    d. D

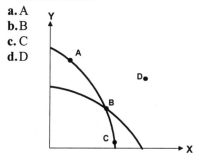

11. By receipts, the largest percentage of business is undertaken by
    a. partnerships
    b. sole proprietorships
    c. corporations
    d. nonprofit companies

12. The largest percentage of federal government expenditures is on
    a. education
    b. health and medical care
    c. infrastructure
    d. income security

13. If a country has a trade deficit, it is:
    a. consuming more than it is producing.
    b. borrowing from foreigners.
    c. selling financial assets.
    d. selling real assets.

14. In a foreign exchange market:
    a. imports are exchanged for exports.
    b. exports are exchanged for imports.
    c. labor services, exports, imports and currencies are exchanged.
    d. one currency is exchanged for another.

15. The WTO is an organization mainly committed to
    a. increasing competitive quotas and tariffs among countries
    b. legalizing international trade by getting countries to refrain from imposing new tariffs or restrictions.
    c. creating independent trade zones throughout the world
    d. increasing security alliances around the world

16. If the weather gets very hot, what will most likely happen?
    a. The supply of air conditioners will increase.
    b. Quantity demanded of air conditioners will increase.
    c. Demand for air conditioners will increase.
    d. The quality demanded of air conditioners will increase.

17. The difference between the quantity demanded and demand is
    a. the quantity demanded is associated with a whole set of prices, whereas demand is associated with a particular price.
    b. the quantity demanded is associated with a particular price, whereas demand is associated with a whole set of prices.
    c. the quantity demanded is the whole demand curve, whereas demand is a particular point along a demand curve.
    d. a change in the quantity demanded is reflected graphically as a shift of the demand curve, whereas a change in demand is reflected as movement along a given demand curve.

18. To derive a market demand curve from two individual demand curves
    a. one adds the two demand curves horizontally.
    b. one adds the two demand curves vertically.
    c. one subtracts one demand curve from the other demand curve.
    d. one adds the demand curves both horizontally and vertically.

19. In the graph below, the arrow refers to

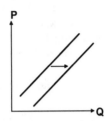

a. a shift in demand.
b. a shift in supply.
c. a change in the quantity demanded.
d. a change in the quantity supplied.

20. If at some price the quantity supplied exceeds the quantity demanded then:
a. a surplus (excess supply) exists and the price will fall over time as sellers competitively bid down the price.
b. a shortage (excess demand) exists and the price will rise over time as buyers competitively bid up the price.
c. the price is below equilibrium.
d. equilibrium will be reestablished as the demand curve shifts to the left.

21. If the demand for a good increases you will expect
a. price to fall and quantity to rise.
b. price to rise and quantity to rise.
c. price to fall and quantity to fall.
d. price to rise and quantity to fall.

22. An increase in demand for a good will cause
a. excess demand (a shortage) before price changes.
b. movement down along the demand curve as price changes.
c. movement down along the supply curve as price changes.
d. a higher price and a smaller quantity traded in the market.

23. If there is an effective price ceiling
a. the quantity demanded exceeds the quantity supplied.
b. the price is above equilibrium.
c. then a surplus is created.
d. the supply exceeds demand.

24. The fallacy of composition is
a. the false assumption that what is false for a part will also be false for the whole.
b. the false assumption that what is true for a part will also be true for the whole.
c. the false assumption that what is false for a whole will also be false for the part.
d. the false assumption that what is true for a whole will also be true for the part.

25. If the consumption of a good by one individual does not prevent its consumption by another individual, that good is called
a. a public good.
b. a private good.
c. a macroeconomic good.
d. a demerit good.

ANSWERS

1.	b	(1:2)	14.	d	(3:15)
2.	c	(1:8)	15.	b	(3:19)
3.	a	(1:12)	16.	c	(4:3)
4.	c	(1:15)	17.	b	(4:7)
5.	a	(1:17)	18.	a	(4:11)
6.	b	(2:1)	19.	b	(4:14)
7.	b	(2:5)	20.	a	(4:19)
8.	c	(2:9)	21.	b	(5:1)
9.	c	(2:15)	22.	a	(5:4)
10.	d	(2:18)	23.	a	(5:8)
11.	c	(3:4)	24.	b	(5:13)
12.	d	(3:8)	25.	a	(5:16)
13.	a	(3:12)			

Key: The figures in parentheses refer to multiple choice question and chapter numbers. For example (1:2) is multiple choice question 2 from chapter 1.

ECONOMIC GROWTH, BUSINESS CYCLES, UNEMPLOYMENT, AND INFLATION

CHAPTER AT A GLANCE

This review is based upon the learning objectives that open the chapter.

1. The long-run framework focuses on supply. The short-run framework focuses on demand. (133)

    Issues of growth are considered in a long-run framework. Business cycles are generally considered in a short-run framework. Unemployment and inflation fall within both frameworks.

2a. Growth is usually measured by changes in real GDP. U.S. economic output has grown at an annual 2.5 to 3.5 percent rate. (133-134)

    Today's growth rates are high by historical standards.

2b. The range in growth rates among countries is wide. (134-135)

    African economies have consistently grown at below average rates. Japan and Western Europe grew quickly in the last half of the 20th century.

2c. Since 1945 the United States has had 9 recessions. (136-138)

2d. In the 1980s and 1990s the target rate of unemployment has been between 5 percent and 6 percent. (141)

    The target rate of unemployment has been called the "natural" rate of unemployment.

2e. Since World War II, the U.S. inflation rate has remained positive and relatively stable. (148-149)

3. The four phases of the business cycle are: the peak, the downturn, the trough, and the upturn. (137-138)

    Note!
    - *There is an overall upward secular growth trend of 2.5-3.5% shown by the dotted line.*
    - *We want to smooth out fluctuations because of the problems associated with them.*
    - *Two problems with a downturn (recession) are (a) cyclical unemployment and (b) low growth rate.*
    - *One problem with upturn (expansion) is demand-pull inflation.*

    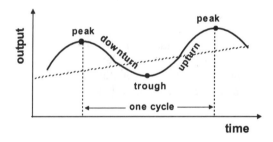

4a. The unemployment rate is measured by dividing the number of unemployed individuals by the number of people in the civilian labor force and multiplying by 100. (144-145)

    Unemployment measures are imperfect but are still a good gauge of the economy's performance.

4b. Some microeconomic categories of unemployment are: reason for unemployment, demographic unemployment, duration of unemployment, and unemployment by industry. (147-148)

    Know the different types of unemployment.

5. Potential output is defined as the output that will be achieved at the target rate of unemployment and the target level of capacity utilization. It is difficult to know precisely where potential output is. (146-147)

    Recession: Actual output (income) < Potential output.

    Expansion: Actual output (income) > Potential output.

    Target rate of unemployment (about 5%) is the lowest rate of unemployment that policymakers believe is achievable under existing conditions (where inflation is not accelerating). It is the rate of unemployment that exists when the economy is operating at potential.

6a. Inflation is a continual rise in the price level. (148)

    Price indexes are used to measure inflation; The most often used are the Producer Price Index (PPI), GDP deflator, and the Consumer Price Index (CPI).

6b. The "real" amount is the nominal amount divided by the price index. It is the nominal amount adjusted for inflation. (152)
    Real means "inflation-adjusted."

$$\text{Real output} = \frac{\text{nominal output}}{\text{price index}} \times 100.$$

7. While inflation may not make the nation poorer, it does cause income to be redistributed and it can reduce the amount of information that prices are supposed to convey. (153-154)

    Inflation hurts those who cannot or do not raise their prices, but benefits those who can and do raise their prices.

    See also Appendix A, "Nonmainstream Approaches to Macro"

● SHORT-ANSWER QUESTIONS

1. What are the two frameworks economists use to analyze unemployment, inflation, growth, and business cycles? What distinguishes the two frameworks from one another?

long run → supply
short run → demand

2. What is the average rate of real growth in output in the United States since 1890 to the present? What are the costs and the benefits of growth?

3. How long has the average expansion since mid-1945 lasted?

56 months

4. In the 1980s and 1990s, what has been the target rate of unemployment?

5 & 6%

5. How did the inflation rate in the U.S. change in this century from pre-World War II to the post-World War II period (1950 to the present)?

↑

6. Label the four phases of the business cycle in the graph below.

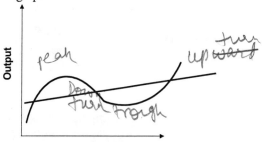

peak   *up trough*   *Down*   *full trough*

7. How is the unemployment rate calculated?

$$\frac{\text{\# of unemployed individual}}{\text{\# of people in civilian labor}} \times 100$$

8. Who in the United States does not work and is nevertheless not counted as unemployed?

students, retirees, homemaker etc

9. State two categories of unemployment for which microeconomic policies are appropriate. Why are such categories important to follow?

10. How is the target rate of unemployment related to potential output? *→ achieved at target rate of unemployment*

11. Define inflation. If there were no inflation what would happen to the distinction between a real concept and a nominal concept?

inflation - continues ↑ in price

12. Suppose the price of a Maserati in 1975 was $75,000 and the price of a Maserati in 1995 was $200,000. Your parents exclaim that the prices of Maseratis have risen by 166%! Wow! You tell them that the price of a Maserati really hasn't risen that much. They are confusing real and nominal concepts. Explain what you mean.

13. What is the difference between expected and unexpected inflation?

surprise

14. What are two important costs of inflation?

MATCHING THE TERMS
Match the terms to their definitions

K **1.** business cycle
e **2.** consumer price index
o **3.** cyclical unemployment
m **4.** frictional unemployment
f **5.** GDP deflator
h **6.** hyperinflation
b **7.** inflation
g **8.** labor force participation rate
c **9.** Okun's rule of thumb
i **10.** potential output
j **11.** real output
a **12.** recession
n **13.** structural unemployment
d **14.** target rate of unemployment
l **15.** unemployment rate

a. A downturn that persists for more than two consecutive quarters.

b. A continual rise in the price level.

c. A one percentage point change in the unemployment rate will cause income to change in the opposite direction by 2 percent.

d. Lowest sustainable rate of unemployment policymakers believe is achievable under existing conditions.

e. Index of inflation measuring prices of a fixed "basket" of consumer goods, weighted according to each component's share of an average consumer's expenditures.

f. Index of the price level of aggregate output of the average price of the components in GDP relative to a base year.

g. Labor force as a percentage of the total population at least 16 years old.

h. Inflation that hits triple digits (100 percent) or more per year.

i. Output that would materialize at the target rate of unemployment and the target rate of capacity utilization.

j. The total amount of goods and services produced, adjusted for price level changes.

k. The upward or downward movement of economic activity that occurs around the growth trend.

l. The percentage of people in the labor force who can't find a job.

m. Unemployment caused by new entrants to the job market and people who have left their jobs to look for and find other jobs.

n. Unemployment resulting from changes in the economy itself.

o. Unemployment resulting from fluctuations in economic activity.

● PROBLEMS AND APPLICATIONS

1. State Okun's law. For each of the following increases in the unemployment rate, state what will likely happen to income in the United States:

    a. Unemployment rate falls 2 percentage points.

    1% change cause effect 2%
    income ↑ 4%.

    b. Unemployment rate falls 1 percentage point.

    income ↑ 2%.

    c. Unemployment rate increases 3 percentage points.

    Income ↓ 6%.

2. For each, state whether the unemployment is structural or cyclical.

    a. As the United States becomes a more high-tech producer, labor-intensive factories relocate to low-wage countries. Factory workers lose their jobs and the unemployment rate rises.

    Structural because it is a structural change in economy

    b. As it becomes more acceptable for mothers to work, more women enter the labor market looking for work. The unemployment rate rises.

    Structural .

    c. Foreign economies slow and demand fewer U.S. exports. Unemployment rate rises.

    Cyclical

3. Calculate the following given the information about the economy in the table:

Total population	260 million
Noninstitutional population	200 million
Incapable of working	60 million
Not in the labor force	66 million
Employed	134 million
Unemployed	10 million

    a. Labor force.

    employed + unemployed =
    134 + 10 = 144 m.
    Labor force = 144-145.

    b. Unemployment rate.

    unemployed = 10m X 100
    Labor force

4. Create a price index for Green Bay Packer fans using the following basket of goods with 2000 prices as the base year.

    base year – index must be 100

Quantities in 2000	Prices 2000	2001
90 lbs of cheese	$2.50/lb	$2.00/lb
12 flannel shirts	$15/shirt	$20/shirt
16 football tickets	$25/ticket	$30/ticket

    a. What is the price of the basket of goods in each year? Show how the price index is 100 in the base year 2000.

    b. Using 2000 as the base year, what is the Price index in 2001? By how much have prices risen?

    c. What are some potential flaws of this price index?

5. Calculate the following given the following information about the economy in 1985, 1995, and 1999:

	1985	**1995**	**1999**
Nominal GDP (in billions of dollars)	4,213	____	9,256.1
GDP deflator (index,1996=100)	73.7	98.1	____
Real GDP (in billions of 1996 dollars)	____	7,543.8	8,848.2
Population (in millions)	238	265	275

a. Nominal GDP in 1995.

b. Real GDP in 1985.

c. Rise in the price level from 1985 to 1999.

d. Growth in real output from 1985 to 1999.

e. Per capita real GDP in 1985, 1995, 1999. What was the growth in real output from 1985 to 1999?

6. Answer each of the following questions about nominal output, real output, and inflation:
   a. Nominal output increased from $8.8 trillion to $9.3 trillion from 1998 to 1999. The GDP deflator rose over that same year by 1.5%. By how much did real output increase?

b. Real output increased from $7.5 trillion to $7.8 trillion from 1995 to 1996. The GDP deflator rose over that same year by 2.0%. By how much did nominal output increase?

c. Real output decreased from $6.70 billion in 1990 to $6.67 billion in 1991. Nominal output rose by 3.2%. By how much did the price level rise from 1990 to 1991?

A BRAIN TEASER

1. How could output and unemployment rise in an economy at the same time?

MULTIPLE CHOICE

Circle the one best answer for each of the following questions:

1. Inflation and unemployment are
   a. best studied in the long-run framework.
   b. best studied in the short-run framework.
   c. fall within both the short-and long-run frameworks.
   d. are not problems of today and therefore are not studied.

2. All of the following are long-run growth policies *except*:
   a. increasing government spending to spur consumer spending.
   b. reducing tax rates to increase incentives to work.
   c. providing funding for research.
   d. following policies to reduce interest rates and increase business investment.

3. If a country of 270 million people has a total income of $8 trillion, its per capita income is
   a. $29.63.
   b. $29,630.
   c. $33.75.
   d. $33,750.

4. The secular trend growth rate in the United States is approximately
   a. 1 to 1.5 percent per year.
   b. 2.5 to 3.5 percent per year.
   c. 5 to 5.5 percent per year.
   d. 7 to 7.5 percent per year.

5. Some people have argued that the two goals of (1) environmental protection and (2) economic growth that involves increased material consumption by individuals do not necessarily contradict each other because spending on the environment can create growth and jobs. This argument
   a. offers great hope for the future.
   b. is incorrect because environmental issues are not as important as material consumption.
   c. is correct because material consumption is not as important as the environment.
   d. is incorrect because the environmental projects will use the resources generated from growth, leaving little or nothing for increased personal consumption.

6. From 1950 to 2000, which geographic area or country had the highest per capita growth rate?
   a. China.
   b. Japan.
   c. North America.
   d. Latin America.

7. The business cycle characterized by the Great Depression occurred in the early
   a. 1900s.
   b. 1930s.
   c. 1950s.
   d. 1960s.

8. Leading indicators include
   a. manufacturing and trade sales volume.
   b. number of employees on non-agricultural payrolls.
   c. industrial production.
   d. new orders for goods and materials.

9. At what stage of the business cycle would a Classical economist be most likely to support government intervention?
   a. Peak.
   b. Trough.
   c. Depression.
   d. Upturn.

10. Under pure capitalism, the main deterrent of unemployment was
    a. pure government intervention.
    b. pure market intervention.
    c. the fear of hunger.
    d. immigration.

11. In the 1980s and 1990s the target rate of unemployment generally has been
    a. between 2 and 4 percent.
    b. between 3 and 5 percent.
    c. between 4 and 6 percent.
    d. between 7 and 9 percent.

12. Keynesians
    a. generally favor activist government policies.
    b. generally favor laissez-faire policies.
    c. believe that frictional unemployment does not exist.
    d. believe that all unemployment is cyclical unemployment.

13. Classicals
    a. generally favor activist government policies.
    b. generally favor laissez-faire policies.
    c. believe that frictional unemployment does not exist.
    d. believe that all unemployment is cyclical unemployment.

14. The level of output that would materialize at the target rate of unemployment and the target rate of capital utilization is called
    a. nominal output.
    b. actual output.
    c. potential output.
    d. utilized output.

15. Okun's rule of thumb states that
    a. a 1 percentage-point change in the unemployment rate will cause income to change in the same direction by 2 percent.
    b. a 1 percentage-point change in the unemployment rate will cause income to change in the opposite direction by 2 percent.
    c. a 2 percentage-point change in the unemployment rate will cause income to change in the same direction by 1 percent.
    d. a 2 percentage-point change in the unemployment rate will cause income to change in the opposite direction by 1 percent.

16. Using Okun's rule of thumb, if unemployment rises from 5 to 6 percent, one would expect total output of $5 trillion to
    a. rise by $5 billion.
    b. rise by $100 billion.
    c. fall by $100 billion.
    d. fall by $5 billion.

17. A one-time rise in the price level is
    a. inflation if that rise is above 5 percent.
    b. inflation if that rise is above 10 percent.
    c. inflation if that rise is above 15 percent.
    d. not inflation.

18. Food and beverages make up about 20 percent of total expenditure. If food and beverage prices rise by 10 percent while the other components of the price index remain constant, approximately how much will the price index rise?
    a. 1 percent.
    b. 2 percent.
    c. 20 percent.
    d. 25 percent.

19. Real output is
    a. total amount of goods and services produced.
    b. total amount of goods and services produced adjusted for price level changes.
    c. total amount of goods produced, adjusted for services that aren't real.
    d. total amount of goods and services that are really produced as opposed to ones that are resold.

20. If the price level rises by 20 percent and real output remains constant, by how much will nominal output rise?
    a. 1 percent.
    b. 5 percent.
    c. 20 percent.
    d. 40 percent.

21. A cost of inflation is that
    a. it makes everyone poorer.
    b. it makes the poor poorer but the rich richer.
    c. There are no costs of inflation because inflation does not make the society as a whole poorer.
    d. it reduces the informational content of prices.

22. Unexpected inflation
    a. makes everyone poorer.
    b. redistributes income from those who raised their prices to those who didn't.
    c. transfers income from those who didn't raise their prices to those who did.
    d. is impossible since firms always plan price increases.

A1. Economists who believe in the liberty of all individuals first and social goals second are:
    a. Austrian economists.
    b. Post Keynesian economists.
    c. radical economists.
    d. Classical economists.

● POTENTIAL ESSAY QUESTIONS

You may also see essay questions similar to the "Problems & Applications" and "Brain Teasers" exercises.

1. Full employment, keeping inflation under control, and economic growth are among the major macroeconomic goals of all societies. Why is economic growth a major macroeconomic goal?

2. What is potential output and how is it related to the target rate of unemployment and the target level of capacity utilization? Which is greater: potential or actual output during a recession? During an economic boom?

3. What are some of the problems with the interpretation of unemployment statistics that can cause unemployment statistics to underestimate and to overestimate the true rate of unemployment? How do Classical and Keynesian economists differ in this regard?

ANSWERS

SHORT-ANSWER QUESTIONS

1. Economists use the long-run framework and the short-run framework to analyze macroeconomic problems. The long-run framework focuses on supply while the short-run framework focuses on demand. (133)

2. The average rate of real growth in output in the United States from 1890 to the present is 2.5 - 3.5% per year. The benefits of growth are improvements in the standard of living, on average. The costs are pollution, resource exhaustion and destruction of natural habitat. (134-135)

3. The average expansion since mid-1945 has lasted more than 56 months. (137)

4. In the 1980s and 1990s, the target rate of unemployment has been between 5 and 6 percent. (141-142)

5. The inflation rate in the U.S. before World War II fluctuated and was sometimes positive and sometimes negative. Since World War II the price level has continually risen. (148-149)

6. The four phases of the business cycle are: the peak, the downturn, the trough, and the upturn. They are labeled in the graph below. (137)

7. Unemployment is calculated by dividing the number of unemployed individuals by the number of people in the civilian labor force, and multiplying the result by 100. (144-145)

8. Those who are not in the labor force and those incapable of working are not employed and are not counted as unemployed. They include students, retirees, homemakers, those incapable of working, and those who choose not to participate in the labor force. (145-146)

9. Two microeconomic subcategories of unemployment include how people become unemployed and demographic unemployment. Others are duration of unemployment and unemployment by industry. These categories are important to follow because policies affect different types of unemployment differently and sometimes macro policies should be supplemented by micro policies. (147-148)

10. Potential output is that level of output that will be achieved at the target rate of unemployment. (147)

11. Inflation is a continual rise in the price level. If there were no inflation there would be no difference between real and nominal concepts. A real concept is the nominal concept adjusted for inflation. (148-152)

12. Nominally Maseratis have risen by 166% from 1975 to 1995, but all other prices have risen during that time period too, including wages. You must adjust the rise in the aggregate price level to find out how much Maseratis have risen in real terms. From 1975 to 1995, the price level rose by 156%. (We used the *Economic Report of the President* to find this information.) So, the real price of the Maserati rose by only approximately 10% from 1975 to 1995. (152)

13. Expected inflation is the amount of inflation that people expect. Unexpected inflation is inflation that is a surprise. (152-153)

14. Two important costs of inflation are that it redistributes income from people who do not raise their price to people who do raise their price; and it can reduce the amount of information that prices are supposed to convey. (153-154)

━━━━━━━━ ANSWERS ━━━━━━━━

MATCHING

1-k; 2-e; 3-o; 4-m; 5-f; 6-h; 7-b; 8-g; 9-c; 10-i; 11-j; 12-a; 13-n; 14-d; 15-l.

━━━━━━━━ ANSWERS ━━━━━━━━

PROBLEMS AND APPLICATIONS

1. Okun's rule of thumb states that a 1-percentage point change in the unemployment rate will cause income in the economy to change in the opposite direction by 2 percent.
    a.   Income rises 4 percent. (147)
    b.   Income rises 2 percent. (147)
    c.   Income falls 6 percent. (147)

2. a.   Structural because this is a structural change in the economy. (140)
    b.   Structural because this is a change in social structure. (140)
    c.   Cyclical because this is unemployment due to a change in economic activity. (140)

3. a.   Labor force = employed + unemployed = 144 million. (144-145)
    b.   Unemployment rate = (unemployed/labor force)×100 = 6.9%. (144-145)

4. a.   The price of the basket in 2000 is $805 and in 2001 is $900. Since 2000 is the base year, the index must be 100. This is calculated as (price of the basket in 2000)/(price of the basket in 2000) = $805/$805 × 100=100. (149-150)
    b.   The price index in 2001 is (price of the basket in 2001)/(price of the basket in 2000) = $900/$805 × 100= 112. Prices rose by 12%. (149-150)
    c.   Some potential flaws are that (1) the basket of goods is small and might not reflect the true basket of goods purchased by Green Bay Packer fans, (2) the basket of goods is fixed (since the price of cheese fell, fans might be buying more cheese and fewer football tickets), (3) the basket does not reflect quality improvements (since the Green Bay Packers won the Super Bowl in 1997, the quality of subsequent games in 1998 might improve, but the tickets are counted as if they were the same as in 1997). (149-150)

5. a.   Nominal GDP in 1995 is $7,400 billion dollars. Calculate this by multiplying real GDP in 1995 by the GDP deflator and dividing by 100. (152)
    b.   Real GDP in 1996 dollars in 1985 is $5,763 billion. Calculate this by dividing nominal GDP by the GDP deflator and multiplying by 100. (152)
    c.   The price level rose by 42% from 1985 to 1999. Calculate this by dividing the change in the GDP price deflator by the base year deflator and multiplying by 100: (104.6 − 73.7)/73.7 × 100. (152)
    d.   Real output grew by 54% from 1985 to 1999. Calculate this by dividing the change in nominal GDP from 1985 to 1999 by the base year nominal GDP and multiplying by 100: (8848.2 − 5763)/5763 × 100. (152)
    e.   Per capita real GDP in 1985 was $24,214; in 1995 it was $28,467; in 1990 it was $2,175. Calculate this by dividing real GDP by the population. Per capita real GDP rose by 15% from 1985 to 1999. (152)

6. a.   Nominal output increased by 5.7% from 1998 to 1999. Since the GDP deflator rose over that same year, we know that real output increased by less—specifically by 4.2% from 1998 to 1999. Subtract inflation from the change in nominal output to get the change in real output: 5.7% − 1.5%=4.2%. (152)
    b.   Real output increased 4.0% from 1995 to 1996. Since the GDP deflator rose 2% over that same year, we know that nominal output increased 6.0% from 1995 to 1996. Add inflation to the change in real output to find the change in nominal output: 2%+4% = 6%. (152)
    c.   Real output fell 0.45% from 1990 to 1991. Since nominal output rose by 3.2%, we know the price level rose 3.65% from 1990 to 1991. Subtract the change in real output from the change in nominal output to find the inflation rate: 3.2% − (−0.45%) = 3.65%. (152)

ANSWERS

A BRAIN TEASER

1. Usually one would expect unemployment to fall as output rises because it takes more workers to produce more output. However, an increase in productivity of workers can cause an increase in output without any reduction in unemployment. Another possibility is that the labor force participation rate could be rising so that the labor force is rising at a faster pace than the rise in employment. This would cause unemployment to rise even though output is expanding and the economy is growing. (144-146)

ANSWERS

MULTIPLE CHOICE

1. c   As the text states on page 133, inflation and unemployment are both short- and long-run problems.

2. a   As stated on page 146, the long run focuses on supply issues that increase the incentive to work, create new technologies, and invest in capital.

3. b   Per capita income is calculated by dividing total income by total population as stated on page 134.

4. b   See page 134.

5. d   As more material goods made available by growth are used for antipollution equipment, less is available for personal consumption. The added material goods have already been used. See pages 135-136.

6. b   As seen in the table on page 134, Japan's per capita growth rate averaged 4.8 percent from 1950 to 2000. China's per capita growth rate was 3.4 percent.

7. b   See page 138.

8. d   The others are coincidental indicators.

Even if you didn't remember this, you should be able to figure out that the change in inventory predicts what firms think will be happening in the future, whereas the others tell what is happening now. See page 139.

9. c   Almost all economists believe government should intervene during a depression. See page 138.

10. c   As discussed on page 140, the fear of hunger was the main deterrent to unemployment. A second deterrent would have been emigration, but that would not be as good an answer. Since d says immigration (the flowing in of people), not emigration, d is definitely wrong.

11. c   See page 141.

12. a   See pages 142-143.

13. b   See pages 142-143.

14. c   As discussed on page 147, the statement that begins the question is the definition of potential output.

15. b   See page 147.

16. c   Total output moves in the opposite direction by 2% times $5 trillion, which equals a fall of $100 billion. See page 147.

17. d   As the text points out on page 148, inflation is a continiual rise in the price level, so the use of the term "one-time" should have clued you that d is the answer.

18. b   To determine the price level rise you multiply each component by its price rise. Since only 20% of the total rose, you get 10% times 20% = 2% . See pages 149-150.

19. b   See page 152. A reminder: A service is considered just as much a good and a component of real output as is a physical good.

20. c   If real output remains constant, then the nominal output must also rise by 20%, as discussed on page 152.

21. d Inflation does not make society richer or poorer, and the distributional consequences of inflations differ, eliminating answers a and b. While the second part of c is true, that doesn't mean that there are no costs of inflation and, as discussed on pages 153-154, one of those costs is the reduction in the informational content of prices.

22. c As discussed on pages 153-154, unexpected inflation is inflation that surprises people. Those people who didn't raise their prices are surprised. Income is redistributed from those people who didn't raise their prices to those who did.

A1. a Austrian economists are defined on page 157.

ANSWERS

POTENTIAL ESSAY QUESTIONS

The following are annotated answers. They indicate the general idea behind the answer.

1. Economic growth is a major macroeconomic goal because it provides for more jobs for a growing population. If output increases more than population increases then per capita growth occurs. Assuming there is no change in the distribution of the nation's income then everybody gets a "bigger piece of the pie." In this way economic growth increases the average absolute standard of living for people. *Remember, economic growth is valued by all nations because it raises the standard of living.*

2. Potential output is the output that would materialize at the target rate of unemployment and the target level of capacity utilization. Potential output grows at the secular (long-term) trend rate of 2.5 to 3.5 percent per year. When the economy is in a recession, actual output is below potential output. When the economy is in a boom, actual output is above potential output.

3. The Bureau of Labor Statistics (BLS) estimates the rate of unemployment. Underestimation can occur because of discouraged workers who are not counted as unemployed as well as others who may not be counted. Also, many people may be working part-time but would like to work full-time. This "underemployment" is not reflected in unemployment statistics and suggests that it underestimates the true problem. On the other hand, some people may be counted as being unemployed when they are working in the underground economy–working for "cash under the table." The Classicals and Keynesians differ most when it comes to the number of discouraged workers. Some Keynesians argue that the BLS underestimates unemployment significantly because a great number of discouraged workers are not counted as being unemployed.

NATIONAL INCOME ACCOUNTING

CHAPTER AT A GLANCE

This review is based upon the learning objectives that open the chapter.

1. National income accounting enables us to measure and analyze how much a nation is producing and consuming. (161)

    GDP:

    - *Most common measure of a nation's output (income)*

    - *Calculated by either:*
      a) expenditures approach, or
      b) income approach

2a. Gross domestic product (GDP): Aggregate final output of residents and businesses in an economy in a one-year period. (161)

    GDP is total market ($) value of all final goods and services produced in a one-year period.

    GDP is output produced within a country's borders; GNP is output produced by a country's citizens wherever they may be in the world.

    GNP = GDP + Net foreign factor income where:

    Net foreign factor income Add the foreign income of one's citizens and subtract the income of residents who are not citizens.

2b. To avoid double counting, you must eliminate intermediate goods, either by calculating only final output (expenditures approach), or by calculating only final income (income approach) by using the value added approach. (163-164)

Know what is and is not included in calculating GDP.

GDP does not include:
- *intermediate goods (sold for resale or further processing);*
- *second-hand sales;*
- *government transfers, housespouse production or any other non-market activity;*
- *underground economic activity.*

3. GDP can be calculated using either the income or expenditures approach because of the national income identity. (166-170)

    The definition of profit is key to the equality of income and expenditures. Profit is total output less payments to the factors of production.

    Hint: In most "non-technical" discussions, "output" (GDP) and "income" (NI) are used interchangeably—that is, GDP is assumed to be equal to NI for purposes of simplification.

4. GDP = C + I + G + (X − M) is an accounting identity because it is defined as true. (166-167)

    The above identity is really the expenditures approach, which states:

    > *Total output = Total expenditures*
    > *Total output = GDP;*
    > *Total expenditures=C+I+G+(X−M)*

    By substitution: GDP = C + I + G + (X−M)

    Know what C, I, G, X − M stand for!

    Also note:
    $X_n = (X − M) =$ *Net exports.*
    If X_n is positive, then X>M ⇒ Trade surplus.
    If X_n is negative, then X<M ⇒ Trade deficit.
    If X_n is zero, then X=M ⇒ Trade balance.

5. A real concept is a nominal concept adjusted for inflation. (173-174)

    GDP is a price times quantity (P×Q) phenomenon. GDP can rise due to an increase in P (price level) and/or an increase in Q (real quantity of output).

    Real GDP, in essence, holds prices (P) constant. Hence, real GDP is inflation (or deflation) adjusted.

6. Limitations of national income accounting include: (174-177)

    - Measurement problems.
    - GDP measures national activity, not welfare; and
    - Subcategories are often interdependent.

    GDP is not and was never intended to be a measure of social well-being.

7. Using GDP to compare standards of living among countries has problems. (172-173)

    GDP only measures market activity. In developing countries individuals often produce and trade outside the market.

    Market prices often vary considerably among countries making the value of the same income in terms of purchasing power different.

● SHORT-ANSWER QUESTIONS

1. What is the purpose of national income accounting?

2. What is GDP?

final output of Residents

3. What is GNP? How does it differ from GDP?

final output of Citizens

4. Calculate the contribution of Chex cereal (from seeds to consumer) to GDP, using the following information:

Participants	Cost of materials	Value of Sales
Farmer	0	200
Chex factory	200	500
Distributor	500	800
Grocery store	800	1000

5. What are the four components of gross domestic product? What are the four components of national income?

6. Say the price level rises 10% from an index of 1 to an index of 1.1 and nominal GDP rises from $4 trillion to $4.6 trillion. What is nominal GDP in the second period? What is real GDP in the second period?

7. As pointed out by the quotation that begins the chapter on national income accounting, statistics can be misleading. In what way can national income statistics be misleading? Given your answer, why use them at all?

MATCHING THE TERMS
Match the terms to their definitions

a 1.	disposable personal income	a. National income minus personal taxes plus transfer payments made to individuals.
c 2.	gross domestic product	b. GDP calculated at existing prices.
f 3.	gross national product	c. Aggregate final output of residents and businesses in an economy in a one-year period.
i 4.	intermediate products	d. Total income earned by citizens and businesses of a country.
d 5.	national income (NI)	e. GDP adjusted to take account of depreciation.
l 6.	national income accounting	f. Aggregate final output of citizens and businesses of an economy in a one-year period.
e 7.	net domestic product	g. Income from foreign domestic factor sources minus foreign factor incomes earned domestically.
g 8.	net foreign factor income	
b 9.	nominal GDP	h. Nominal GDP adjusted for inflation.
h 10.	real GDP	i. Products of one firm used in some other firm's production of another firm's product.
k 11.	value added	j. A balance sheet of an economy's stock of assets and liabilities.
j 12.	Wealth Accounts	k. The increase in value that a firm contributes to a product or service.
		l. A set of rules and definitions for measuring economic activity in the aggregate economy.

PROBLEMS AND APPLICATIONS

1. For each of the following, calculate how much the action described has added to GDP:

   a. A used car dealer buys a car for $3,000 and resells it for $3,300.

   $ 300

   b. A company sells 1,000 disks for $500 each. Of these, it sells 600 to other companies and 400 to individuals.

   500,000
   200,000
   600 X 500 = 300,000
   500 - 300,000

   PS 163-164

   c. A company sells 50 computers at a retail price of $1,000 apiece and 100 software packages at a retail price of $50 apiece to consumers. The same company sells 25 computers at $800 and 50 software packages at $30 apiece to wholesalers. The wholesalers then sell the 25 computers at $1,250 apiece and the 50 software packages at $75 apiece.

   GDP
   50 X 1000 + 100 X 50
   55,000
   + sales of wholesal
   25 X 1250
   + 50 X 75 = 35,000 total to GDP
   = 90,000

   d. Fred purchases 100 stock certificates valued at $5 apiece and pays a 10% commission. When the price declines to $4.50 apiece, Fred decides to sell all 100 certificates, again at a 10% commission.

   Only Commis — GDP
   $95

   e. Your uncle George receives $600 in social security each month for one year.

2. Use the following table showing the production of 500 boxes of Wheaties cereal to calculate the contribution to GDP using the value-added approach.

Participants	Cost of materials	Value of sales
Farmer	$ 0	$ 150
Mill	$ 150	$ 250
Cereal maker	$ 250	$ 600
Wholesaler	$ 600	$ 800
Grocery store	$ 800	$ 1,000

a. Calculate the value added at each stage of production.

b. What is the total value of sales?

c. What is the total value added?

d. What is the contribution to GDP for the production of those Wheaties?

3. There are three firms in an economy: X, Y, and Z. Firm X buys $200 worth of goods from firm Y and $300 worth of goods from firm Z, and produces 250 units of output at $4 per unit. Firm Y buys $150 worth of goods from firm X, and $250 worth of goods from firm Z, and produces 300 units of output at $6 per unit. Firm Z buys $75 worth of goods from X, and $50 worth goods from firm Y, and produces 300 units at $2 per unit. All other products are sold to consumers. Answer the following:

a. What is GDP?

b. How much government revenue would a value added tax of 10% generate?

c. How much government revenue would an income tax of 10% generate?

d. How much government revenue would a 10% sales tax on final output generate?

4. You have been hired as a research assistant and are given the following data about the economy: All figures are in billions of dollars.

Transfer payments	$70
Interest paid by consumers	5
Net exports	10
Indirect business taxes	44
Net foreign factor income	3
Corporate income tax	69
Contribution for social insurance	37
Personal tax and non-tax payments	92
Undistributed corporate profits	49
Gross private investment	200
Government purchases	190
Personal consumption	550
Depreciation	65

You are asked to calculate the following:

a. GDP.

b. GNP.

c. NDP.

d. NI.

e. Personal income.

f. Disposable personal income.

5. You have been hired as a research assistant and are given the following data about another economy (profits, wages, rents, and interest are measured nationally):

Corporate income tax	$200
Profits	475
Wages	800
Rents	30
Depreciation	20
Indirect business taxes	110
Undistributed corporate profits	50
Net foreign factor income	-5
Interest	175
Social security contribution	0
Transfer payments	0
Personal taxes	150

Calculate the following:

a. GDP.

b. GNP.

c. NDP.

d. National income.

e. Personal income.

f. Disposable personal income.

6. Use the following table to answer the questions:

Real output in year	Nominal output billions of 1996 $	GDP deflator billions of $ (1996=100)
1995	7,543.8	7,400.5	_____
1996	7,813.2	7,813.2	100.0
1997	8,144.8	_____	101.9
1998	_____	_____	103.1
1999	_____	9,256.1	104.6

a. What is output for 1999 in 1996 dollars?

b. What is the output in nominal terms in 1997?

c. What is the GDP deflator (1996=100) in 1995?

d. Real output grew by 4.3% from 1997 to 1998. By how much did nominal output grow in 1998?

● A BRAIN TEASER

1. Why must imports be subtracted in calculating GDP?

● MULTIPLE CHOICE

Circle the one best answer for each of the following questions:

1. GDP is:
   a. the total market value of all final goods and services produced in an economy in a one-year period.
   b. the total market value of all goods and services produced in an economy in a one-year period.
   c. the total market value of all final goods and services produced by a country's citizens in a one-year period.
   d. the sum of all final goods and services produced in an economy in a one-year period.

2. To move from GDP to GNP, one must:
   a. add net foreign factor income.
   b. subtract inflation.
   c. add depreciation.
   d. subtract depreciation.

3. If a firm's cost of materials is $100 and its sales are $500, its value added is:
   a. $100.
   b. $400.
   c. $500.
   d. $600.

4. If you, the owner, sell your old car for $600, how much does GDP increase?
   a. By $600.
   b. By the amount you bought it for, minus the $600.
   c. By zero.
   d. By the $600 you received and the $600 the person you sold it to paid, or $1,200.

5. There are two firms in an economy, Firm A and Firm B. Firm A produces 100 widgets and sells them for $2 apiece. Firm B produces 200 gadgets and sells them for $3 apiece. Firm A sells 30 of its widgets to Firm B and the remainder to consumers. Firm B sells 50 of its gadgets to Firm A and the remainder to consumers. What is GDP in this economy?
   a. $210.
   b. $590.
   c. $600.
   d. $800.

6. If a woman divorces her husband (who has been cleaning the house) and hires him to continue cleaning her house for $20,000 per year, GDP will:
   a. remain constant.
   b. increase by $20,000 per year.
   c. decrease by $20,000 per year.
   d. remain unchanged.

7. The national income identity shows that:
   a. the value of factor services is equal to the value of final goods plus investment.
   b. the value of factor services is equal to the value of final goods plus savings.
   c. the value of factor services is equal to the value of final goods sold.
   d. the value of consumption goods is equal to the value of factor services.

8. Which of the following correctly lists the components of total expenditures?
   a. consumption, investment, deprecation, exports minus imports.
   b. consumption, investment, government expenditures, exports minus imports.
   c. rent, profit, interest, wages.
   d. consumption, net foreign factor income, investment, government expenditures.

9. The largest component of expenditures in GDP is
   a. consumption.
   b. investment.
   c. net exports.
   d. government purchases of goods and services.

10. The largest component of national income is
    a. rents.
    b. net interest.
    c. profits.
    d. compensation to employees.

11. Gross investment differs from net investment
    by:
    a. net exports.
    b. net imports.
    c. depreciation.
    d. transfer payments.

12. While the size of the U.S. federal government
    budget is approximately $2 trillion, the
    federal government's contribution in the GDP
    accounts is approximately:
    a. $0.5 trillion.
    b. $1.5 trillion.
    c. $2.0 trillion.
    d. $5.0 trillion.

13. Which of the following factors serves to equate
    income and expenditure?
    a. profit.
    b. depreciation.
    c. net foreign factor income.
    d. value added.

14. Switching from the exchange rate approach to
    the purchasing power parity approach for
    calculating GDP generally:
    a. does not make a significant difference for a
       developing country's GDP relative to a
       developed country's GDP.
    b. generally increases a developing country's
       GDP relative to a developed country's GDP.
    c. generally decreases a developing country's
       GDP relative to a developed country's GDP.
    d. changes the relative GDP of developing
       country's GDP, but not in a predictable
       fashion.

15. If inflation is 10 percent and nominal GDP goes
    up 20 percent, real GDP goes up approxi-
    mately
    a. 1 percent.
    b. 10 percent.
    c. 20 percent.
    d. 30 percent.

16. Which of the following is the *best* measure
    available to compare changes in standards of
    living among countries over time?
    a. changes in nominal income.
    b. changes in nominal per capita income.
    c. changes in real income.
    d. changes in real per capita income.

17. If nominal GDP rises:
    a. welfare has definitely increased.
    b. welfare has definitely decreased.
    c. welfare may have increased or decreased.
    d. welfare most likely has increased.

18. Estimates of the importance of the underground
    economy in the United States indicate that it
    is:
    a. very small—under 1 percent of the total
       economy.
    b. somewhere between 1.5 percent all the way to
       20 percent of the total economy.
    c. somewhere between 1.5 percent all the way to
       60 percent of the total economy.
    d. as large as the non-underground economy.

● POTENTIAL ESSAY QUESTIONS

*You may also see essay questions similar to the
"Problems & Applications" and "Brain Teasers"
exercises.*

1. Using the circular flow model explain why any
   dollar value of output must give rise to an
   identical amount of income (at least for all
   practical concerns)?

2. How might an economy experience an increase
   in nominal GDP but experience negative growth
   at the same time?

ANSWERS

SHORT-ANSWER QUESTIONS

1. The purpose of national income accounting is to measure and analyze how much the nation is producing and consuming. National income accounting defines the relationship among the sub-aggregates of aggregate production. (161)

2. GDP is the aggregate final output of *residents* and businesses *in* an economy in a one-year period. (161)

3. GNP is aggregate final output of *citizens* and businesses *of* an economy in a one-year period. GDP is output produced within a country's borders while GNP is output produced by a country's citizens. Add net foreign factor income to GDP to get GNP. (161-162)

4. $1,000. We could use either the value added approach or the final output approach. Summing the value added at each stage of production — the difference between cost of materials and value of sales —we get $1,000. (163-164)

Participants	Cost of materials	Value of Sales	Value Added
Farmer	$0	$200	$200
Chex factory	200	500	300
Distributor	500	800	300
Grocery store	800	1000	200
Sum (total output)			1000

5. The four components of gross domestic product are consumption, investment, government expenditures, and net exports (X − M). The four components that comprise NI are compensation to employees, rents, interest, and profits. (166-169)

6. A real value is a nominal value adjusted for inflation. So, nominal GDP in the second period is $4.6 trillion, but real GDP is $4.6 trillion divided by the price index, 1.1, or $4.18 trillion. (173-174)

7. National income accounting statistics can be misleading. They are subject to measurement error; they are based on samples of data and assumptions about behavior. For example, the measurement of inflation is widely believed to overestimate true inflation. Also, GDP does not include non-market activities such as housework. It measures national activity, not welfare; output could rise but welfare fall. Its subcategories are often interdependent; that is, arbitrary decisions were made when determining what goes in which subcategory. Nevertheless, national income accounting makes it possible to discuss the aggregate economy. It is important to be aware of the limitations of the data in those discussions. (174-177)

ANSWERS

MATCHING

1-a; 2-c; 3-f; 4-i; 5-d; 6-l; 7-e; 8-g; 9-b; 10-h; 11-k; 12-j.

ANSWERS

PROBLEMS AND APPLICATIONS

1. a. $300. Only the value added by the sale would be added to GDP, which in this case is the difference between the purchase price and the sale price. (163-164)

   b. $200,000. Total output produced is 1,000 × $500 = $500,000. Of this intermediate goods valued at 600 × $500 = $300,000. So, the company's contribution to GDP is ($500,000 − $300,000) = $200,000. (163-164)

   c. Only that amount that is sold to the consumer is counted in GDP. This is 50×1,000 + 100×50 = $55,000 sold by the first company plus the sales of the wholesaler, which is 25×$1250 + 50×$75 = $35,000. Total contribution to GDP is $90,000. (163-164)

   d. Only the commissions of $50 and $45 are counted in GDP. Together they contribute $95. (163-164)

   e. Nothing has been added to GDP. Government transfers are not included in GDP. (163-164)

2.

Participants	Cost of materials	Value of sales	Value added
Farmer	$ 0	$ 150	150
Mill	$ 150	$ 250	100
Cereal maker	$ 250	$ 600	350
Wholesaler	$ 600	$ 800	200
Grocery store	$ 800	$ 1,000	200

a. The value added at each stage of production is shown in the table above. (163-164)

b. The total value of sales is $2,800. Find this by adding the rows of the value of sales column. (163-164)

c. The total value added is $1,000. Find this by adding the value added at each stage of production. (163-164)

d. The contribution to GDP for the production of those Wheaties is $1,000. Value added at each stage of production is the contribution to GDP. This avoids double-counting. (163-164)

3. a. $2375: GDP is the sum of the value added by the three firms = 500 + 1,400 + 475. (163-164)

b. $237.50: A 10% value added tax would generate = (.10)($2,375) = $237.50 of revenue. (163-164)

c. $237.50: A 10% income tax would generate the same revenue as a 10% value added tax. (163-164)

d. $340: A 10% sales tax on final output would generate = $340 of revenue: (.10)(1,000 + 1,800 + 600). (163-164)

4. a. $950: GDP = $C + I + G + (X - M)$ = 550 + 200 + 190 + 10 = 950. (166-167)

b. $953: GNP = GDP + net foreign factor income = 953. (161-162)

c. $885: NDP = GDP − depreciation = 950 − 65 = 885. (166-167)

d. $844 : NI = NNP − indirect business taxes = 888 − 44 = 844. (171-172)

e. $759: PI = NI + transfers from government − corporate retained earnings − corporate income taxes − social security taxes = 844 + 70 − 49 − 69 − 37 = 759. (171)

f. $667: DPI = PI − personal income tax = 759 − 92 = 667. (171)

5. a. $1,615: GDP = NDP + Depreciation = NNP − net foreign factor income + depreciation = NI + indirect business tax − net foreign

factor income + depreciation = wages + rents + interest + profits + proprietors' income + indirect business taxes − net foreign factor income + depreciation = 800 + 30 + 175 + 475 + 110 − (−5) + 20 = 1615. (167-172)

b. $1,610: GNP = GDP + net foreign factor income = 1615 + (−5). (161, 162, 167-172)

c. $1,595: NDP = GDP − depreciation = 1615 − 20. (167-172)

d. $1,480: NI = NNP − indirect business taxes = 1590 − 110. (167-172)

e. $1,230: PI = NI + transfers − corporate income taxes − undistributed corporate profits − social security contributions = 1480 + 0 − 200 − 50 − 0. (167-172)

f. $1,080: DPI = PI − personal taxes = 1230 − 150. (167-172)

6. a. $8849.0 billion 1996 dollars: Real output = (Nominal output/deflator) × 100 = 9256.1/104.6 × 100. (173-174)

b. $8299.6 billion: Nominal output = (real output × deflator) / 100 = (8144.8 × 101.9)/100.(173-174)

c. 98.1: Deflator = (Nominal output/real output) × 100 = (7400.5/7543.8) × 100.1. (173-174)

d. Real output grew by 4.3% and inflation rose by 1.2%, so nominal output grew by 5.5%.(173-174)

━━━━━ ANSWERS ━━━━━

A BRAIN TEASER

1. Government expenditures, consumption, investment include all expenditures in those categories regardless of where the products were produced. That is, they include products produced in foreign countries. Since GDP measures domestic production, the total value of imports must be subtracted from total expenditures. (168)

━━━━━ ANSWERS ━━━━━

MULTIPLE CHOICE

1. a   As the text emphasizes on page 161, GDP is the market value of all final goods and services produced in an economy in a one-year period.

2. a   Since GNP is total market value of production of citizens in a country, and GDP is total market value of production within a country, one must add net foreign factor income to GDP to get GNP. See pages 161-162.

3. b   Value added equals value of sales minus cost of materials. See page 164.

4. c   As discussed on page 165, sales of used goods do not contribute to GDP except to the degree that they are sold by a second hand dealer. Then the dealer's profit would be the value added.

5. b   GDP doesn't include purchases made between businesses, only final sales to consumers. To calculate the answer, calculate total sales for Firms A and B ($600 + $200 = $800) and subtract those goods sold between the firms ($60 + $150 = $210) to get final sales ($800 − $210 = $590). See pages 163-164.

6. b   As discussed on page 165, GDP measures market transactions. The divorce-and-hire changes the housecleaning activities from nonmarket to market and hence increases GDP.

7. c   The national income identity shows that all income (value of factor services) equals all expenditures (value of goods sold to individuals). See pages 166-167.

8. b   GDP = C + I + G + (X − M). See pages 166-167.

9. a   Consumption makes up the majority of expenditures. See Table 7-3, page 169.

10. d   As you can see in Table 7-4 on page 170, compensation to employees is the largest percent of national income.

11. c   Net investment equals gross investment less depreciation. See pages 167-168.

12. a   As discussed on page 168 only government expenditures on goods and services are included as part of GDP. The government's entire budget also includes transfer payments.

13. a   Profit is what remains after all firm's other income is paid out. Thus, profit is the key to the income/expenditures equality. See pages 169-171.

14. b   In developing countries, living expenses are generally lower than in developed countries. Thus moving towards a purchasing power parity approach generally increases GDP in a developing country. In the example of China given on page 173, the switch increased China's GDP by more than 400 percent.

15. b   Subtract inflation from nominal GDP growth to find real GDP growth as a first approximation. See pages 173-174.

16. d   As discussed on pages 173-174 nominal GDP must be adjusted for price level increases before comparisons over time can be made. Dividing total real income by the population is a good indication of relative standards of living.

17. c   Nominal GDP must be adjusted by inflation to arrive at real GDP before one can even start to make welfare comparisons. And even if real GDP increases, it is not clear that welfare has increased, as discussed on pages 174-175.

18. b   On page 175 the text states that the underground economy in the United States is between 1.5 and 20 percent of the total economy.

━━━ **ANSWERS** ━━━

POTENTIAL ESSAY QUESTIONS

The following are annotated answers. They indicate the general idea behind the answer.

1.   Whenever the business community produces some $X value of output, that dollar value reflects costs of production which were incurred in producing that output level. Those costs of production are all paid out to the resource (input) owners as their income. Hence, any dollar output level (GDP) gives rise to an identical amount of national income (NI), at least for all practical purposes.

2.   The price level could have increased by a greater percentage than the decrease in the real quantity of goods and services produced. This would result in an increase in nominal GDP but a decrease in real GDP (negative growth).

GROWTH, PRODUCTIVITY AND THE WEALTH OF NATIONS

CHAPTER AT A GLANCE

This review is based upon the learning objectives that open the chapter.

1a. Growth is an increase in the amount of goods and services an economy produces. (182)

Growth can be measured either by increases in real GDP or increases in real GDP per person (per capita growth).

1b. Because growth, on average, makes more goods available for consumption, it improves physical standards of living. (182-183)

Because of compounding, small differences in growth rates can result in enormous differences in income per person.

Remember the Rule of 72: the number of years it takes for income to double equals 72 divided by the annual growth rate of income.

2. Markets create specialization and division of labor and have been empirically highly correlated with growth. The growth rate has increased as the importance of markets has increased. Five important sources of growth are: (184-189) *Pg 186*

- Capital accumulation–investment in productive capacity;

  Can be: (1) Privately owned by business, (2) publicly owned and provided by government– our infrastructure, (3) human capital–invest- ment in people, (4) social capital–institutions and conventions.

- Available resources;

  Technological advances can help overcome any lack of resources.

- Institutions with incentives compatible with growth;

  Government policy can help or hinder growth. Regulations have both costs and benefits, but too much regulation definitely hinders growth.

- Technological development;

  Technology not only causes growth, it changes the entire social and political dimensions of society.

- Entrepreneurship.

  This is the ability to get things done. It involves creativity, vision, and an ability to translate that vision into reality.

3. Most growth theories center around the production function: Output = A·f(labor, capital, land). (189-190)

Returns to scale describes what happens to output when all inputs are increased.

- *Constant returns to scale: output rises by same proportion as the increase in all inputs. (An example: ↑all inputs 10% ⇒ ↑output by 10%)*

- *Increasing returns to scale: output rises by a greater proportion than the increase in all inputs. (An example: ↑ all inputs 10% ⇒ ↑output by 15%)*

- *Decreasing returns to scale: output rises by a smaller proportion than the increase in all inputs. (An example: ↑all inputs 10% ⇒ ↑ output by 5%)*

Diminishing marginal productivity involves increasing one, not all, inputs. In general, economists assume diminishing marginal pro-ductivity—the increase in output falls as more of one input is added.

4a. The Classical growth model focuses on the role of capital accumulation in the growth process. Increases in capital lead to growth. (190-193)

The Classical growth model predicts that the rise in output per worker will eventually slow as additional amounts of capital are less productive. It also predicts that as economies add capital, capital-poor countries will grow faster than capital-rich countries.

The graph below depicts early economists' view of the effects of diminishing marginal productivity of labor. Increases in the population beyond N* leads to starvation. Below N*, the population grows because of the surplus output.

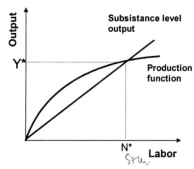

4b. The new growth theory emphasizes the role of technology in the growth process. Positive externalities and learning by doing mean that increasing returns may predominate and that growth rates can accelerate over time. (193-195)

According to some estimates, technology accounts for 35% of economic growth in the United States.

Technological advance is not necessarily the result of investment.

Technology often has positive externalities that can result in an acceleration in growth.

5. Six government policies to promote growth are: (195-200)

● Policies to encourage saving and investment;

Even though new growth theorists downplay the role of capital, they agree that capital and investment is still important.

Tax laws impact saving and consequently investment.

● Policies to control population growth;

Providing enough capital and education for a large population that is growing is difficult.

Perhaps a country needs to grow first. Then the residents will choose to have fewer children and the population growth will slow.

● Policies to increase the level of education;

Education increases the productivity of work-ers. Basic education is important to economic growth.

● Policies to create institutions that encourage technological innovation;

This means having institutions that provide incentives to innovate such as patents. Patents, however, also reduce the positive externalities associated with innovation.

Corporations and financial institutions reduce the risk of innovating.

● Provide funding for basic research;

The U.S. government funds 60 percent of all basic research in the United States.

● Policies to increase the economy's openness to trade.

Trade allows specialization, which leads to increases in productivity and innovation.

● SHORT-ANSWER QUESTIONS

1. What assumption do economists make that allows them to focus only on supply in the long run?

    Say's Law
    Supply creates its own demand

2. What are the two ways to measure growth?

    Real GDP
    mean per capita real GDP

3. You've been called in by a political think tank to develop a strategy to improve growth in the U.S. What are five things that would you recommend they concentrate on that would contribute positively to economic growth?

4. Write a production function. Use the production function to explain the difference between diminishing marginal returns from decreasing returns to scale.

5. Why did the early Classical model predict that output would gravitate toward a subsistence level?

6. What is the focus of new growth theory?

7. How do the prediction of the Classical growth theory differ from the predictions of the new growth theory?

8. What are six policies to promote growth?

MATCHING THE TERMS
Match the terms to their definitions

_h_ 1. Classical growth model	a. Output rises by a greater proportionate increase as all inputs.
_g_ 2. constant returns to scale	b. Producing more goods and services per person.
_k_ 3. decreasing returns to scale	c. Legal ownership of a technological innovation that gives the owner of the patent sole rights to its use and distribution for a limited time.
_d_ 4. growth	
_m_ 5. human capital	d. An increase in the amount of goods and services an economy produces.
_a_ 6. increasing returns to scale	
_o_ 7. law of diminishing marginal productivity	e. The habitual way of doing things that guides people in how they approach production.
_r_ 8. learning by doing	f. The way we make goods.
_n_ 9. new growth theories	g. Output will rise by the same proportionate increase as all inputs.
_c_ 10. patents	h. Model of growth that focuses on the role of capital accumulation in the growth process.
_b_ 11. per capita growth	
_l_ 12. positive externalities	i. Output per unit of input.
_i_ 13. productivity	j. Rule in which you divide 72 by the growth rate of income (or any variable) to get the number of years over which income (or any variable) will double.
_j_ 14. Rule of 72	
_q_ 15. Say's Law	
_e_ 16. social capital	k. Output rises by a smaller proportionate increase as all inputs.
_p_ 17. specialization	l. Positive effects on others not taken into account by the decision-maker.
_f_ 18. technology	
	m. The skills that are embodied in workers through experience, education and on-the-job training
	n. Theories that emphasize the role of technology rather than capital in the growth process.
	o. Increasing one input, keeping all others constant, will lead to smaller and smaller gains in output.
	p. The concentration of individuals on certain aspects of production
	q. Supply creates its own demand.
	r. Improving the methods of production through experience.

● PROBLEMS AND APPLICATIONS

1. According to the Classical growth model how will each of the following events affect a country's growth rate?

   a. An increase in the percent change in population.

   ↑ population ↓ growth rate

   b. An increase in the saving rate. *↑ growth rate*

   ↑

   c. An improvement in technology. *↑ growth rate*

d. The government passes a law extending the time frame in which the holder of a patent has sole ownership of a technological innovation.

2. State the Rule of 72. Answer each of the following questions:

a. How many years will it take for income to double if a country's total income grows at 2 percent? 4 percent? 6 percent?

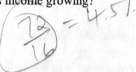

36 years – 2%
& year 4%
12 year – 6%

b. If a country's income doubles in 16 years, at what rate is its income growing?

$\frac{72}{16} = 4.5\%$

c. In 2000 per capita output in the United States was about $35,000. If real income per capita is growing at a 2% annual rate, what will per capita output be in 36 years? In 72 years?

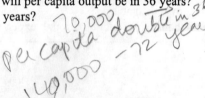

70,000 double in 36 year
140,000 – 72 year

d. If real income is rising at an annual rate of 4% per year and the population is growing at a rate of 1% per year, how many years will it take for per capita income to double?

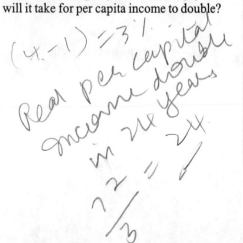

$(4 - 1) = 3\%$
Real per capital income double in 24 years
$\frac{72}{3} = 24$

3. Calculate per capita income for each of the following countries:

GDP (in millions of dollars)		Population (in millions)
Brazil	773,400	164
Ghana	6,600	18
Croatia	20,700	4
France	1,526,000	59

4. The inputs to an economy are labor and capital only. In each of the following state whether the production function exhibits (a) increasing returns to scale, (b) decreasing returns to scale, (c) constant returns to scale, or (d) diminishing marginal productivity.

a. Output rises by 16% when both labor and capital rise by 16%.

b. Output rises by 10% when both labor and capital rise by 16%.

c. Output rises by 10% when labor rises by 16%.

5. What prediction did Thomas Malthus make about growth?

a. Draw a graph that demonstrates his predictions and explain the predictions using the graph.

b.   What law are those predictions based upon?

c.   According to Classical economists, why didn't his predictions come true?

6.   Country A has per capita income of $10,000 while Country B has per capita income of $20,000.

a.   According to the Classical growth theory, which country is predicted to grow more quickly? Why?

b.   According to the new growth theory, which country is predicted to grow more quickly? Why?

⬤ A BRAIN TEASER

1.   How can two countries with equal population sizes have different levels of output?

⬤ MULTIPLE CHOICE

Circle the one best answer for each of the following questions:

1.   Long-run growth analysis focuses:
   a. on demand.
   b. on supply.
   c. on both supply and demand.
   d. on the distribution of output.

2.   According to Say's Law:
   a. aggregate supply will exceed aggregate demand.
   b. aggregate demand will exceed aggregate supply.
   c. there will be no relation between aggregate supply and demand.
   d. aggregate demand will equal aggregate supply.

3.   If the growth rate is 6%, how many years will it take for output to double?
   a. 4.
   b. 8.
   c. 12.
   d. 16.

4.   The average worker today:
   a. earns about the same as a worker in 1919 when earnings are adjusted for inflation
   b. earns less than a worker in 1919 when earnings are adjusted for inflation.
   c. earns more than a worker in 1919 when earnings are adjusted for inflation.
   d. is better off than a worker in 1919.

5.   Suppose output grew at 4% in China and 2% in the United States.
   a. Per capita income grew faster in China
   b. Per capita income grew faster in the U.S.
   c. We cannot say in which country per capita income grew faster.
   d. Per capita output grew faster in China.

6.   Investment is:
   a. the same thing as capital.
   b. the decrease in capital over time.
   c. the increase in capital over time.
   d. unrelated to capital.

7. Types of capital discussed in the book do *not* include:
    a. human capital.
    b. social capital.
    c. physical capital.
    d. investment capital.

8. Available resources:
    a. must always decrease.
    b. are always constant because of the entropy law.
    c. must always increase.
    d. may increase or decrease.

9. A production function:
    a. shows the relationship between inputs and outputs.
    b. is a type of technological manufacturing.
    c. is a type of manufacturing technology.
    d. is an important source of growth.

10. If there are increasing returns to scale:
    a. as inputs rise, outputs fall.
    b. as inputs rise, output rises by a smaller percentage.
    c. as inputs rise, output rises by a larger percentage.
    d. as one input rises, output rises by a larger percentage.

11. The law of diminishing marginal productivity states that:
    a. as inputs increase by equal percentages, output will increase by less than that percentage.
    b. as inputs increase by equal percentages output will eventually increase by less than that percentage.
    c. as one input increases by a certain percentage output will increase by less than that percentage
    d. as one input increases output will increase by decreasing percentages.

12. The Classical growth model focuses on:
    a. technology.
    b. saving and investment.
    c. entrepreneurship.
    d. available resources.

13. Early predictions of the Classical model of growth were that:
    a. the economy would grow without limit.
    b. the economy will end because of pollution.
    c. wages would be driven to subsistence because of diminishing marginal productivity.
    d. wages would be driven to subsistence because of decreasing returns to scale.

14. Which of the following is *not* an explanation for why the growth rates of rich and poor countries have not converged?
    a. Human capital has increased.
    b. Technology has increased.
    c. The law of diminishing marginal productivity is wrong.
    d. Both human capital and technology have increased.

15. In empirically explaining per capita growth an increase in:
    a. physical capital is the most important element.
    b. human capital is the most important element.
    c. technology is the most important element.
    d. the quantity of labor is the most important element.

16. New growth theories are theories that emphasize:
    a. technology.
    b. human capital.
    c. physical capital.
    d. entrepreneurship.

17. In the new growth theory which of the following may be true?
    a. The law of increasing marginal productivity overwhelms the law of diminishing marginal productivity.
    b. Learning by doing overwhelms the law of diminishing marginal productivity.
    c. The law of technology overwhelms the law of diminishing marginal productivity.
    d. The law of QWERTY overwhelms the law of diminishing marginal productivity.

18. QWERTY is a metaphor for:
    a. the invisible hand.
    b. technological lock-in.
    c. the law of diminishing marginal productivity.
    d. the pollution caused by positive spillovers.

19. In the borrowing circle case study:
    a. loans were made to large firms.
    b. loans were made to an entire circle of firms.
    c. guarantees of friends replaced traditional collateral.
    d. individuals were given collateral so they could get loans.

20. Growth usually leads to decreased birth rates because when there is growth because:
    a. men and women are too tired to have kids.
    b. the opportunity cost of having children rises.
    c. pollution reduces the fertility of the population.
    d. immigration crowds out endogenous population growth.

21. Patents create:
    a. incentives to innovate and hence are a good thing.
    b. barriers to entry and hence are a bad thing.
    c. both barriers to entry and incentives to innovate and hence are both a bad and good thing.
    d. common knowledge and hence are a good thing.

22. Which of the following policies will likely *slow* an economy's growth rate?
    a. Increased trade restrictions.
    b. Increase the level of education.
    c. Increasing saving.
    d. Protecting property rights.

● POTENTIAL ESSAY QUESTIONS

You may also see essay questions similar to the "Problems & Applications" and "Brain Teasers" exercises.

1. What does the Classical model predict about the growth rates of poor countries relative to rich countries? What accounts for that prediction?

2. How does human capital differ from physical capital?

3. How can patents be both a deterrent and a reason for growth?

ANSWERS

SHORT-ANSWER QUESTIONS

1. Economists assume that demand is sufficient to buy whatever is supplied. This assumption is called Say's law—supply creates its own demand. According to Say's law aggregate demand will always equal aggregate supply. This way, one can focus only on aggregate supply. (182)

2. Growth can be measured either as increases in the amount of goods and services an economy produces (real GDP), or as increases in the amount of goods and services an economy produces per person (per capita real GDP). Increases in per capita output is a better measure of improvements in the standard of living because it tells you how much income the average person has. (182-186)

3. I would tell them: (1) To promote institutions with incentives compatible with growth. Institutions that encourage hard work will lead to growth. (2) To promote institutions that foster creative thinking and lead to technological development; (3) To be creative in recognizing available resources. Growth requires resources and although it may seem that the resources are limited, available resources depend upon existing technology. New technology is a way of overcoming lack of resources. (4) To invest in capital. This would include not only buildings and machines, but also human and social capital. (5) To encourage entrepreneurship. An economy deficient in the other four areas can still grow if its population can translate vision into reality. Each of these will contribute to growth. (186-189)

4. A typical production function is: Output = A · f(labor, capital, land), where labor, capital and land are the only inputs. A is a factor that is used to capture changes in technology. Decreasing returns to scale describes the situation where output rises by a smaller percentage than the increase in all inputs. For example, if labor, capital and land all increase by 20%, but output increases by only 10%, the production function exhibits decreasing returns to scale. Diminishing marginal productivity describes what happens to output when only one input is changed—output rises by a percentage that is smaller than the percentage increase in one input (while all other inputs remain the same). (189)

5. The early Classical model predicted that output would gravitate toward a subsistence level because they focused on the law of diminishing marginal productivity of labor. As long as an additional worker could produce more than enough for him or herself, the population would grow. But land was relatively fixed. As more and more workers were added to a fixed amount of land, eventually, additional workers would not be able to produce enough additional output to survive. Workers would starve to death and the population would shrink. The equilibrium number of workers was where output was just enough to survive—no more and no less. (190-191)

6. New growth theory focuses on the role of technology rather than capital in the growth process. New growth theory considers the possibility that there are positive externalities associated with technological advance so that growth rates can accelerate. It also focuses on learning by doing. Just the process of producing results in lower costs and technological innovation. (193-194)

7. Classical growth theory predicts that the growth rates of poor countries will be higher than the growth rates of rich countries because the law of diminishing marginal productivity of capital is stronger in rich countries. Eventually the incomes of rich and poor countries will converge. New growth theory, because of the positive externalities associated with technological advance, is consistent with the possibility that rich countries may grow faster than poor countries because they have more technology. Classical growth theory also predicts that growth rates will slow over time whereas the new growth theory is consistent with an acceleration in growth rates. (190-195)

8. Six policies to promote growth are (1) policies to encourage saving and investment; (2) policies to control population growth; (3) policies to increase the level of education; (4) policies to create institutions that encourage technological innovation; (5) provide funding for basic research; and (6) policies to increase the economy's openness to trade. (195-200)

ANSWERS

MATCHING

1-h; 2-g; 3-k; 4-d; 5-m; 6-a; 7-o; 8-r; 9-n; 10-c; 11-b; 12-l; 13-i; 14-j; 15-q; 16-e; 17-p; 18-f.

ANSWERS

PROBLEMS AND APPLICATIONS

1. **a.** An increase in the percent change in population will lead to a reduction in the growth rate per capita because each worker will have less capital to produce with. (190-191)
    b. An increase in the saving rate will lead to an increase in the growth rate per capita because saving results in increased investment and more capital for each worker. Eventually, however, the law of diminishing marginal productivity of capital would set in and per capita income would cease to grow. (190-191)
    c. An improvement in technology will increase the growth rate per capita because each worker will be more productive. This will increase per capita output at the time of the technological improvement, but would not result in a lasting increase in the growth rate per capita. (190-191)
    d. Technological innovation is outside the model. Thus government policies to affect technological innovation would not affect the growth rate of an economy. (190-191)

2. The Rule of 72 is that the number of years that it takes income (or any variable) to double equals 72 divided by the annual growth rate of income (or that variable).
    a. 36 years if income grows at 2 percent per year; 18 years if income grows at 4 percent per year; 12 years if income grows at 6 percent per year. (183)
    b. Its income is growing at 4.5 percent per year. Divide 72 by 16 to find the answer. (183)
    c. If real income per capita is growing at 2 percent per year, per capita output will double in 36 years. So, real per capita output will be $70,000 in 36 years and $140,000 in 72 years. (183)
    d. Per capita real income is rising at an annual rate of 3% per year (4% - 1%). At 3% per year, real per capital income will double in 24 years (72/3 = 24). (183)

3. Divide GDP by the population to find per capita income:
    a. Brazil $4,716
    b. Ghana $367
    c. Croatia $5,175
    d. France $25,864 (See page 185.)

4. **a.** Since output is rising by the same percentage as the increase in all inputs, the production function exhibits constant returns to scale. (189)
    b. Since output is rising by a smaller percentage as the increase in all inputs, the production function exhibits decreasing returns to scale. (189)
    c. Since capital is fixed, the correct description involves marginal productivity. Since output rises by less than the percentage increase in labor only, the production function exhibits diminishing marginal productivity. (189)

5. Thomas Malthus predicted that since land was relatively fixed, as the population grew, diminishing marginal productivity would set in. The growth in output would not keep pace with the growth in the population and eventually people would starve.
    a. The graph below demonstrates Malthus' predictions. The production function is downward bowed because of diminishing marginal productivity. Each additional worker adds less output than the individual before. At population levels below N*, there is surplus output (because output per worker exceeds the subsistence level of output). Because there is surplus output, people have more children and the population grows. Once the population grows beyond N*, per capita output is not sufficient to feed the population (output per worker is less than the subsistence level of output) and people starve to death. The population declines to N*. (190-191)

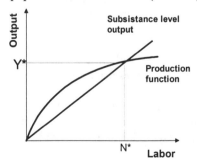

b. The predictions of Thomas Malthus are based upon the law of diminishing marginal productivity. (190-191)

c. According to Classical economists, his predictions didn't come true because some output produced is used to increase the amount of capital that workers have to work with. As capital increases, even if land is fixed, output can also increase. The economy could still grow if capital increased at the same rate that labor increased. (191)

6. a. According to the Classical growth theory, Country A is expected to grow more quickly because increases in capital per worker in country A are more productive than in country B due to the law of diminishing marginal productivity. (191)

b. According to the new growth theory, income doesn't need to converge. In fact, new growth theory stresses the possibility that countries with higher output will grow faster than poor countries because of positive externalities associated with technology and learning by doing. Increases in technology have significant positive externalities that can accelerate the growth rate. Further, as output increases, the benefits from learning by doing also increase. Therefore, greater output can lead to faster growth rates. (193-195)

ANSWERS

A BRAIN TEASER

1. Total output in the long run depends upon capital, labor, and land. It could be that the two countries have different levels of capital or natural resources (captured in land). For instance, the United States have many natural resources, but Japan does not. Japan overcomes its lack of natural resources by investing heavily in capital and importing natural resources. If two countries had equal amounts of capital, land and labor, however, their outputs could still differ if they had different amounts of human capital (the skills that are embodied in workers through experience, education, and on-the-job training) and social capital (the habitual way of doing things that guides people in how they approach production). (186-189)

ANSWERS

MULTIPLE CHOICE

1. **b** In the short run economists analysis focuses on demand; in the long run it focuses on supply. See page 182.

2. **d** Say's law states that supply creates its own demand. See page 182.

3. **c** According to the rule of 72 on page 183, divide 72 by the growth rate to determine the number of years in which output will double.

4. **c** As discussed in the text the average worker's wages buy many more goods now than in 1919. Whether that makes them better off is debatable, but they definitely earn more. See page 184.

5. **c** Per capita income (output) growth equals output growth less population growth. Without knowing population growth, we do not know for which country per capita income (output) growth is greater. See page 185.

6. **c** As defined in the text investment is the increase in capital over time. See page 186.

7. **d** Investment is the change in capital; it is not a description of capital. See page 186.

8. **d** Available resources depend on technology. That is why they can increase or decrease. See page 187.

9. **a** The definition given in the text on page 189 is the relationship between inputs and outputs.

10. **c** As discussed in the text on page 189 increasing returns to scale refers to the relation between all inputs and outputs. Increasing returns to scale exist when output increases by a greater percentage than the increase in all inputs.

11. **d** The law of diminishing marginal productivity refers to one input, not all, and to what will happen to output as that input is continually increases, keeping other inputs constant. See page 189.

12. b   The Classical growth focuses on increases in capital and hence on saving and investment. See page 190.

13. c   In the early Classical model, fixed land and diminishing marginal productivity meant that wages would be driven to subsistence. See page 190.

14. c   Economists continue to believe in the law of diminishing marginal productivity because there are many other explanations for the lack of convergence. See page 191.

15. c   Although increases in technology and increases in the quantity of labor are of almost equal importance in explaining total growth, per capita growth decreases the importance of the quantity of labor. See page 193.

16. a   New growth theories center their explanation of growth on technology. See page 193.

17. b   The only law mentioned in the book is the law of diminishing marginal productivity. The others are not laws and can't overwhelm anything. See page 194.

18. b   Qwerty stands for the upper left keys on a keyboard. Placing them there is not especially efficient, but once they were placed there, they were locked in. See page 195.

19. c   The essence of the borrowing circle was guarantees of friends. The loans were small loans to individuals, not to firms. See page 196.

20. b   In industrialized countries, people have chosen to have fewer children because the benefits of having children (such as being supported by them in your old age) is reduced. See page 197.

21. c   Patents have both good and bad aspects; the policy debate is about what the optimal length of the patent should be. See pages 198-199.

22. a   Economists generally believe that trade increases growth, so increasing trade restrictions would decrease growth. See page 200.

■ ■ ■   ANSWERS   ■ ■ ■

POTENTIAL ESSAY QUESTIONS

The following are annotated answers. They indicate the general idea behind the answer.

1. The Classical model predicts that poor countries with little capital will grow at faster rates than rich countries with a lot of capital. The reason for this prediction is the law of diminishing marginal productivity. Capital that is added in poor countries will be much more productive because the law of diminishing marginal productivity is weaker compared to that in rich countries.

2. Physical capital are the buildings and machines available for production while human capital are the skills that are embodied in workers through experience, education, and on-the-job training. Both are considered important to growth, but the connection between investment and each type of capital differs. Expenditures on plant and equipment (investment) clearly increase physical capital. Human capital can increase without direct investment—one example is just experience. Investment in human capital can also be unproductive and not lead to increases in human capital—an example would be providing education in areas that do not increase the productivity of its workers.

3. Patents provide an incentive for people to innovate because the holder of a patent has the right to be the sole provider of the innovation. As a sole provider, the holder can charge more for its use by others. Based upon the law of supply a greater incentive will result in a greater quantity of innovations supplied. On the other hand, patents, because they are privately held will be lower than if they could be used by all. Since the innovation is priced high, less of the innovation will be demanded and the innovation will have less of an impact on growth. Further, it is the common knowledge aspect of a technology that leads to positive externalities. Patents limit the common knowledge aspect of a technology and thus limit its impact on growth. Policymakers face a dilemma. Before the innovation is developed, the best strategy is to offer patents. Once the innovation is developed, the best strategy is to make it free to everyone.

AGGREGATE DEMAND, AGGREGATE SUPPLY, AND MODERN MACRO

CHAPTER AT A GLANCE

This review is based upon the learning objectives that open the chapter.

1. Keynesian economics developed as economists debated the cause of the Great Depression. (205-208)

    In the 1930s, the economy was in a Depression with 25 percent unemployment.
    Economists debated whether the economy would get out of the Depression on its own.
    Classical economists believed that wages would fall and eliminate the unemployment.
    Keynesian economists believed that the economy could remain in a Depression unless government did something to induce people to increase their spending.

2a. The slope of the AD curve is determined by the wealth effect, the interest rate effect, the international effect, and repercussions of these effects. (209-211)

    As the price level falls, the cash people hold is worth more, making people richer, so they buy more (wealth effect). Also, as the price level falls, the value of money rises, inducing people to lend more money, which reduces the interest rate and increases investment expenditures (interest rate effect). Also, as the price level in the United States falls (assuming the exchange rate does not change), the price of U.S. goods relative to foreign goods goes down. U.S. exports increase and U.S. imports decrease. That is, the quantity of U.S. goods demanded rises (the international effect). Repercussions of these effects are called multiplier effects (and make the AD curve flatter than otherwise).

2b. Five important initial shift factors of the AD curve are: (211-213)

● Changes in foreign income.
    A rise in foreign income leads to an increase in U.S. exports and an increase (outward shift to the right) of the U.S. AD curve.

● Changes in expectations.
    Positive (optimistic) expectations about the future state of the economy could cause an outward (rightward) shift of the AD curve.

● Changes in exchange rates.
    A decrease in the value of the dollar relative to other currencies shifts the AD curve outward to the right.

● Changes in the distribution of income.
    Typically, as the real wage increases, the AD curve increases (shifts out to the right).

● Changes in government aggregate demand policy.

    Expansionary macro policy (an increase in government spending and/or a decrease in taxes—fiscal policy; or an increase in the money supply—monetary policy) increases the AD curve, shifting it outward to the right.

    Note: Anything that affects autonomous components of aggregate expenditures (AE or "total spending") is a shift factor of AD (aggregate demand). (Recall that AE = C + I + G + X−M). These components are autonomous consumption (C), investment (I), government spending (G), and net exports (X−M). Any change in these components of total spending is multiplied by the multiplier effect shifting the AD curve by a multiple of the original change in spending.

3a. In the short run, the AS curve is horizontal at the price level in the economy. (214)

    The AS curve is flat because most markets are quantity-adjusting markets. Firms respond to changes in demand primarily by modifying production, instead of changing their prices. (See box on page 216 for reasons why.)

3b. The AS curve shifts in response to changes in the prices of the factors of production. (214-215)

% change in the price level = % change in wages − % change in productivity.

If productivity is constant, increases (decreases) in wages shift the AS curve up (down).

If wages are constant, increases (decreases) in productivity shift the AS curve down (up).

What makes wages change? Whether there is a shortage or surplus in the labor market.

What makes productivity change? Many things: increases in capital, learning by doing, etc.

4. The potential output curve is vertical at potential output. (215)

The potential output curve is vertical because an increase in the price level will not increase potential output. At potential output all resources are fully utilized.

5a. Equilibrium in the short run, is determined by the intersection of the AS curve and the AD curve. (217-221)

Increases (decreases) in aggregate demand increase (decrease) output only. The price level remains constant.

To find the effect of a shift in aggregate demand, start at some point of intersection between the AD curve and the AS curve. Given a shift of either the AD curve or AS curve, simply find the new point of intersection. This is the new short-run equilibrium. However, note that any initial change in the AD curve is magnified because of the multiplier effect.

5b. Equilibrium in the long run is determined by the intersection of the potential output curve and the AD curve. (217-221)

If the economy begins at a long-run equilibrium, increases in aggregate demand will lead to changes in the price level only.

If an economy is in short-run equilibrium, but not long-run equilibrium, the AS curve will shift up or down.

If short-run equilibrium output is below long-run equilibrium output, the economy is in a recessionary gap. The price level will fall and the AS curve will shift down. (See the figure below.)

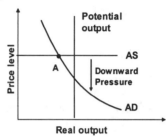

If short-run equilibrium output is above long-run equilibrium output, the economy is in an inflationary gap. The price level will rise and the AS curve will shift up. (See the figure below)

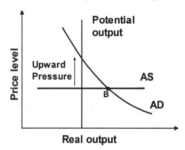

6. Knowing where potential output is just one reason why macro policy is more complicated than the model makes it look. (222-223)

Knowing potential output is important to knowing whether changes in aggregate demand will affect output or the price level. Economists have divided the economy into three ranges: the Keynesian range (the economy is far below potential and the price level is fairly fixed), the intermediate range (between low and high potential output where the price level is somewhat flexible), and the Classical range (above high potential output where the price level is very flexible). We have no way of precisely determining for sure what range the economy is in, or precisely where the correct target level of potential output is, and therefore of precisely knowing by how much we should shift the AD curve (with the use of macro—fiscal and monetary—policy).

● SHORT-ANSWER QUESTIONS

1. How does the Keynesian explanation of the Great Depression differ from the Classical explanation?

2. What effects determine the slope of the AD curve?

3. List some of the important shift factors of the AD curve.

4. What is the slope of the AS curve? Why does it have this shape?

5. What will shift the AS curve up or down?

6. What is the slope of the potential output curve? Why does it have this shape?

7. Show graphically the effect of increased government expenditure on real output when (a) the economy is far below potential output and (b) the economy is at potential output.

8. Why is the AS/AD model more complicated than it looks?

MATCHING THE TERMS
Match the terms to their definitions

____1.   aggregate demand curve
____2.   aggregate supply curve
____3.   inflationary gap
____4.   interest rate effect
____5.   international effect
____6.   multiplier effect
____7.   potential output curve
____8.   quantity-adjusting markets
____9.   recessionary gap
____10.   wealth effect

a.   As the price level falls the interest rate falls which leads to greater investment expenditures.

b.   A curve that shows the amount of goods and services an economy can produce when both labor and capital are fully employed.

c.   A curve that shows how a change in the price level will change aggregate expenditures.

d.   Markets in which firms modify their supply to bring about equilibrium instead of changing prices.

e.   A curve that tells us how changes in aggregate demand will affect real output and the price level.

f.   Amount by which equilibrium output is below potential output.

g.   As the price level falls, people are richer, so they buy more.

h.   As the price level in a country falls the quantity of that country's goods demanded by foreigners and residents will increase.

i.   Amplification of initial changes in expenditures.

j.   Amount by which equilibrium output is above potential output.

● PROBLEMS AND APPLICATIONS

1.   What will likely happen to the shape or position of the *AD* curve in the following circumstances?

    a.   A rise in the price level does not make people feel poorer.

    b.   Income is redistributed from poor people to rich people.

    c.   The country's currency depreciates.

    d.   The exchange rate changes from fixed to flexible.

    e.   Expectations of future rises in the price level develop without any current change in the price level.

2.   State what range of the price/output path you think the economy is in, given the following information:

    a.   The economy is significantly below potential. Downward shifts in aggregate demand do not result in falls in the price level.

b. Increases in aggregate demand result in little change in real output and large increases in the price level.

c. Increases in aggregate demand seem to be split roughly equally between increases in real output and increases in the price level.

3. What will happen to the position of the *AS curve* in the following circumstances?

a. Productivity rises by 3 percent and wages rise by 3 percent.

b. Productivity rises by 3 percent and wages rise by 5 percent.

c. Productivity rises by 3 percent and wages rise by 1 percent.

4. Graphically demonstrate the effect of each of the following on either the AS curve or the potential output curve. Be sure to label all axes.

a. Businesses find that they are able to produce more output without having to pay more wages nor increase their costs of capital.

b. A severe snow storm paralyzes most of the United States.

c. The country's currency appreciates dramatically.

5. The government of Germany wants to expand its economy through increased spending. Show the likely effects of an activist policy in the short run and in the long run in the following three cases.

a. The economy is far below potential output.

b. The economy is close to, but still below, potential output.

c. The economy is at potential output.

6. Demonstrate the following two cases using the AS/AD model. What will happen in the long run if the government does nothing?

a. Inflationary gap.

b. Recessionary gap.

c. What could government do (a) and (b) to keep the price level constant?

● A BRAIN TEASER

1. Suppose the economy has been experiencing a recession for a couple of years with no apparent relief in sight. Currently the unemployment rate is 10%. In response to political pressure to "to put America back to work" government policy makers have recently reduced taxes significantly and have dramatically increased government spending on public works projects to rebuild the nation's crumbling infrastructure (roads, bridges, airports...). During a recent press conference the President of the United States remarked that the new government policy of tax cuts and spending programs will be successful in reducing unemployment and there should be no reason to fear inflation either. As a student in an economics course one of your friends has asked you to evaluate the likely success of these recent policy moves. How would you respond?

● MULTIPLE CHOICE

Circle the one best answer for each of the following questions:

1. Classical economists are generally associated with:
   a. laissez faire.
   b. QWERTY.
   c. an activist policy.
   d. their support of low unemployment.

2. Keynesian economics focuses on
   a. the long run.
   b. the short run.
   c. both the long run and the short run.
   d. neither the long run nor the short run.

3. In Keynesian economics equilibrium income:
   a. will be equal to potential income.
   b. will be below potential income.
   c. will be above potential income.
   d. may be different than potential income.

4. In the AS/AD model,
   a. price of a good is on the horizontal axis.
   b. price level is on the horizontal axis.
   c. price of a good is on the vertical axis.
   d. price level is on the vertical axis.

5. Which of the following is *not* an explanation of the downward slope of the AD curve?
   a. The wealth effect.
   b. The interest rate effect.
   c. The consumption effect.
   d. The international effect.

6. If the exchange rate becomes flexible so that changes in the price level have little effect on exports and imports:
   a. the AD curve will become steeper.
   b. the AD curve will become flatter.
   c. the AD curve will become unaffected.
   d. the AS curve will become steeper.

7. If the multiplier effect is 2 rather than 3,
   a. the AD curve will be steeper.
   b. the AD curve will be flatter.
   c. the AD curve will be unaffected.
   d. the AS curve will be steeper.

8. If there is a rise in foreign income the AD curve will likely:
   a. shift in to the left.
   b. shift out to the right.
   c. become steeper.
   d. become flatter.

9. If there is a rise in a country's exchange rate, the AD curve will likely:
   a. shift in to the left.
   b. shift out to the right.
   c. become steeper.
   d. become flatter.

10. Expansionary monetary policy will likely:
    a. shift the AD curve in to the left.
    b. shift the AD curve out to the right.
    c. make the AD curve steeper.
    d. make the AD curve flatter.

11. If government spending increases by 40, the AD curve will shift to the
    a. right by 40.
    b. left by 40.
    c. right by more than 40.
    d. right by less than 40.

12. The slope of the AS curve is determined by:
    a. opportunity cost
    b. the law of diminishing marginal returns.
    c. institutional realities.
    d. the wealth effect, the international effect and the interest rate effect.

13. If productivity rises by 2% and wages rise by 6%, the AS curve will
    a. likely shift up.
    b. likely shift down.
    c. become flatter.
    d. become steeper.

14. The potential output curve is:
    a. another name for the AD curve.
    b. another name for the AS curve.
    c. a vertical line.
    d. a horizontal line.

15. Refer to the graph below. The graph demonstrates the expected short-run result if:

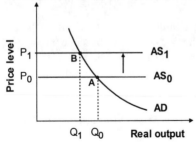

a. productivity increases by less than wages.
b. the government increases the money supply.
c. the exchange rate value of a country's currency falls.
d. there are suddenly expectations of a rising price level.

16. The graph below demonstrates the expected short-run result if:

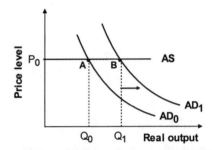

a. productivity increases by less than wages
b. the government increases the money supply
c. a country's exchange rate appreciates (gains value).
d. wages rise by less than the increase in productivity.

17. The graph below demonstrates the expected short-run result if:

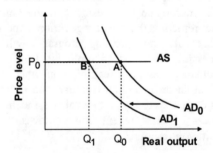

a. productivity increases by less than wages
b. the government increases the money supply
c. a country's exchange rate appreciates (gains value).
d. wages rise by less than the increase in productivity.

18. Assume the economy is initially at potential B. The graph below correctly demonstrates an economy moving to point C if:

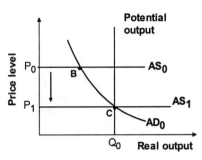

a. productivity increases by less than the increase in wages.

b. the government increases the money supply.

c. a country's exchange rate appreciates (gains value).

d. wages rise by less than the increase in productivity.

19. Assume the economy is initially at point B. The graph below correctly demonstrates an economy moving to point C if:

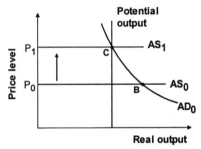

a. productivity increases by less than the increase in wages.

b. the government decreases the money supply.

c. a country's exchange rate appreciates (gains value).

d. wages rise by less than the increase in productivity.

20. Which of the following distances in the graph below is the inflationary gap?

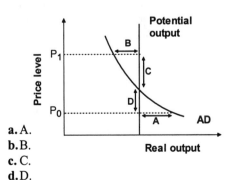

a. A.

b. B.

c. C.

d. D.

21. In the Keynesian range the price level is:

a. flexible.

b. somewhat flexible.

c. indeterminate.

d. fixed.

22. The Classical range is shown by range:

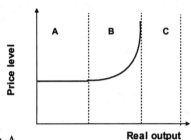

a. A.

b. B.

c. C.

d. The Classical range is not shown.

23. If the target rate of unemployment falls, potential income will:

a. first decrease, then increase.

b. increase.

c. decrease.

d. first increase, then decrease.

● POTENTIAL ESSAY QUESTIONS

You may also see essay questions similar to the "Problems & Applications" and "Brain Teasers" exercises.

1. Why is the AS/AD model more complicated than the model makes it look?

2. What was the Keynesian's main argument against the Classical view that the economy will get itself out of the Depression?

3. What is the paradox of thrift and how does it relate to the AS/AD model?

ANSWERS

SHORT-ANSWER QUESTIONS

1. Classical economists focused on the real wage. They explained that unemployment would decline if the real wage were allowed to decline. Political and social forces were keeping the real wage too high. Keynesians focused on insufficient aggregate expenditures that resulted in a downward spiral. The economy was at a below-potential-income equilibrium. (205-208)

2. The wealth effect, the interest rate effect, international effect, and the repercussions these effects cause, i.e., the multiplier effect, determine the slope of the AD curve. (209-210)

3. Five important initial shift factors of the AD curve are: 1. Changes in the world income. 2. Changes in expectations. 3. Changes in exchange rates. 4. Changes in the distribution of income. 5. Changes in government aggregate demand policy. (211-212)

4. The AS curve specifies how a shift in the aggregate demand curve affects the price level and real output. A standard AS curve is horizontal. That is, increase in aggregate demand lead to increases in output and no change in the price level. Institutional realities about how firms set prices determines the shape of the AS curve. Firms adjust production, not prices, to changes in aggregate demand in the short run. (213-214)

5. The AS curve will shift up or down when input prices rise or fall or if productivity rises or falls. The change in the AS curve (the price level) is determined by the following: % change in price level = % change in wages − % change in productivity. (214-215)

6. The potential output curve is vertical. It has this shape because potential output is output when all inputs are fully employed. Changes in the price level do not affect potential output. (215)

7. If the economy begins at point A, increased government expenditures shifts the AD out to the right from AD_0 to AD_1. If the economy begins below potential output, the price level would remain the same at P_0 but real output would increase from Y_0 to Y_1. I've drawn it so that the AD curve shifts out enough so that the economy is in both long-run and short run equilibrium at potential output at point B. (218)

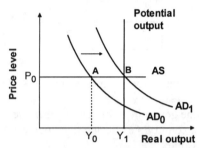

Now suppose the economy begins at point C in both short run and long-run equilibrium. In the short run, when the aggregate demand curve shifts from AD_0 to AD_1, real output rises from Y_1 and Y_2. Since the economy is now above potential output, however, input prices begin to rise and the AS curve shifts up. The AS curve continues to shift up to AS_1 where the economy returns to a long-run equilibrium at a higher price level, P_1, but the same output level as before, Y_1. (218)

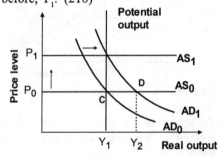

8. The AS/AD model is more complicated than it looks because we do not know the level of potential output, which is the key to knowing whether an increase in aggregate demand will lead to an increase in output, the price level, or a combination of the two. Economists have no sure way of estimating potential output. One method is to estimate the unemployment rate where inflation begins to rise. Unfortunately, this is also difficult to predict. Another way is to add a historical growth factor of 3% to previous levels of real output. This can be problematic if the economy is moving to a lower or higher growth rate. (222-223)

━━━━ ANSWERS ━━━━

MATCHING

1-c; 2-e; 3-j; 4-a; 5-h; 6-i; 7-b; 8-d; 9-f; 10-g.

━━━━ ANSWERS ━━━━

PROBLEMS AND APPLICATIONS

1. **a.** This would cause the wealth effect to become inoperative and the AD curve will become steeper. (209)
   b. Assuming the marginal propensity to consume of rich people is less than that of poor people, the AD curve will shift to the left. (212)
   c. As the exchange rate depreciates, exports will rise and imports will fall. This shifts the AD curve out. (211)
   d. If the exchange rate was originally fixed and became flexible, increases in the price level will be offset by changes in the exchange rate and the international effect becomes inoperative. The *AD* curve will be steeper. (210)
   e. Expectations of future price increases without changes in the current price level will tend to cause the *AD* curve to shift to the right. (211-212)

2. **a.** Keynesian range. (222)
   b. Classical range. (222)
   c. Intermediate range. (222)

3. **a.** The AS doesn't shift at all because rises in input prices are completely offset by increases in productivity. (214-215)
   b. The AS curve shifts up because the rise in input prices exceed the rise in productivity. (214-215)
   c. The AS curve shifts down because the rise in input prices are less than the rise in productivity. (214-215)

4. **a.** The potential output curve shifts to the right as shown below because businesspeople are finding that their productive capacity is larger than they had thought. (215-216)

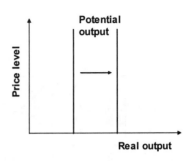

b. The potential output curve shifts to the left as shown below because bad weather will hinder production. Because the storm is temporary, however, the shift in the potential output curve is also temporary. (215-216)

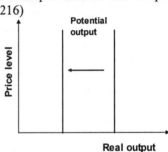

c. The aggregate supply curve shown below shifts down from AS$_0$ to AS$_1$, because businesses will benefit from the declining import prices to the extent that imports are used in production. The fall in input prices is passed through to the goods market. (215-216)

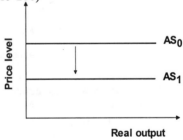

5. **a.** The economy is far below potential output at point A in the graph below. As the AD curve shifts out, the economy moves to point B—the price level remains unchanged at P$_0$, and output increases to Y$_1$. Government activism in this range is very effective. As I have drawn it, Y$_1$ is potential output, and point B is both a short-run and a long-run equilibrium. (217-219)

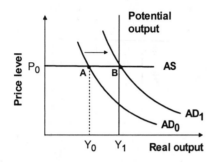

b. The economy is close to potential output at point A in the graph below. The AD curve shifts to AD_1 and real output rises to Y_1, beyond potential. Point B is a short-run equilibrium. Since output is above potential, input prices begin to rise which shifts the AS curve up. As the AS curve shifts up, real output declines and the price level rises. The AS curve will continue to shift up until the economy is at potential output Y_2 and a new price level P_1—point C. Expansionary fiscal policy will increase both real output and the price level when the economy begins at close to potential. Real output rises by less than in (a) and the economy experiences some inflation. (217-219)

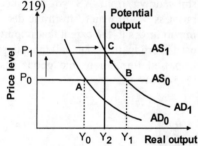

c. The economy is at potential output at point A in the graph below. As the AD curve shifts out, real output rises to Y_1 in the short run where the price level is fixed at P_0—point B. Since the economy is above potential however, eventually input prices will rise and the AS curve will shift up. The AS curve shifts up until real output falls back to potential output—Y_0—but the price level is now at P_1. In the long run, real output remains unchanged at Y_0 and only the price level increases from P_0 to P_1. Government activism in this range is ineffective in the long run. (217-219)

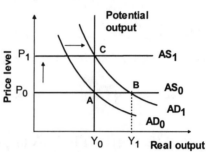

6. a. The graph below demonstrates an inflationary gap—short-run equilibrium output is above potential at existing prices—point A. If government does nothing, eventually wages will be bid up as firms try to hire more workers. This will shift the AS curve up to AS_1. Real output will fall to potential and the price level will rise—to point B. (217-219)

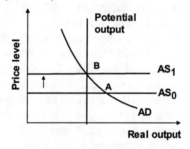

b. The graph below demonstrates a recessionary gap—short-run equilibrium output is below potential at existing prices—point A. Given the excess supply in the labor market firms will be able to offer workers lower wages. Input prices will fall and the AS curve will shift down to AS_2. Real output will rise to potential and the price level will fall—to point B. Generally, government intervenes to increase expenditures (shifting the AD curve) before the price level declines. (217-219)

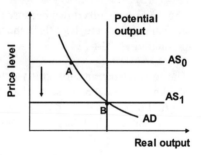

━━━━ ANSWERS ━━━━

A BRAIN TEASER

1. My response depends on where I believe the economy is along the price/output path. If we are in the Keynesian range then the President is right—the policy moves will increase the AD curve and the real output (employment) level will rise without creating any inflation. However, if we are in the intermediate range, then wages will rise pushing the AS curve up and the price level may rise some—the extent to which is difficult to predict. Moreover, it is also very difficult to determine which of the two ranges we would currently find ourselves in. (We know we are not in the Classical range because we are not at full employment—the potential output level.) (221-222)

━━━━ ANSWERS ━━━━

MULTIPLE CHOICE

1. a   Laissez faire is the non-activist policy that Classical economists generally support. See page 206.

2. b   The essence of Keynesian economics was its focus on the short run. See pages 206-207.

3. d   Because of coordination problems equilibrium income could be different than potential income in Keynesian economics; it could be higher, lower or equal to it. See page 207.

4. d   The AS/AD model is different than the micro supply/demand model. It has price *level* on the vertical axis and *total* output on the horizontal axis. See page 208.

5. c   No consumption effect is discussed in the book. See pages 209-210.

6. a   This question refers to the international effect; if the international effect is reduced, the change in the price level will have less effect on AD and the AD curve will be steeper. See page 210.

7. a   The multiplier effect increases the effect of the other effects and hence a smaller multiplier makes the AD curve steeper. See page 210.

8. b   The rise in foreign income will increase demand for exports shifting the AD curve to the right. See page 211.

9. a   The rise in the country's exchange rate will decrease demand for its exports shifting the AD curve in to the left. See page 211.

10. b   Expansionary monetary policy will increase aggregate demand, shifting the AD curve out to the right. See page 212.

11. c   The multiplier effect would increase the effect, so the rightward shift would by more than 40. See page 213.

12. c   The AS curve is not a derived curve; it is an empirical curve determined by institutional realities. See page 214.

13. a   Because wages are rising by more than productivity costs, the AS curve will shift up. Since it is flat it cannot become flatter or steeper. See pages 213-215.

14. c   The potential output curve shows the amount of goods and services an economy can produce when both labor and capital are fully employed. It is a vertical line since price level does not affect potential output. See pages 213-215.

15. a   The aggregate supply curve shifts upward when wages rise by more than increases in productivity. Real output will decline and the price level will rise. See pages 217-218.

16. b   An increase in the money supply will shift the AD curve to the right. In the short run, real output will rise and the price level will remain constant. See pages 217-218.

17. c   Demand for domestic goods will decline if one's currency appreciates because foreign goods will be less expensive compared to domestic goods. Real output will decline as the price level remains constant in the short run. (217-218)

18. d   Since at point B, the economy is below potential, there will be downward pressure on wages. Or at least wages will rise by less than the increase in productivity. The AS curve will shift down until the economy reaches point C. See pages 217-218.

19. a   Since at point B, the economy is above potential, there will be upward pressure on wages. Wages will rise by more than the increase in productivity. The AS curve will shift up until the economy reaches point C. See pages 217-218.

20. a   The inflationary gap occurs when the price level is such that the quantity of aggregate demand exceeds the quantity of potential income. See pages 218-219.

21. d   Fixed prices are the key characteristic of the Keynesian range. See page 222.

22. c   The Classical range is where increases in aggregate demand result only in increases in the price level and no increase in aggregate output. This is where the price/output path is vertical. See page 222.

23. b   Potential income varies inversely with unemployment. See pages 222-223.

■■■ ANSWERS ■■■

POTENTIAL ESSAY QUESTIONS

The following are annotated answers. They indicate the general idea behind the answer.

1.   Knowing where potential output is why macro policy is more complicated than the model makes it look. That is, we have no way of precisely determining for sure what range the economy is in, or precisely where the correct target level of potential output is, and therefore of precisely knowing by how much we should shift the AD curve (with the use of macro—fiscal and monetary—policy). However, most economists see the economy in the intermediate range.

2.   The Classical prescription for the Great Depression was to do nothing (except remove the obstacles which they argued kept wages and prices artificially high) and wait for the market (the downward movement in wages and prices) to work its magic over time (in the long run). But, Keynes was concerned that "in the long run, we're all dead!"

   Keynes believed that equilibrium income was not the same as potential income. He disagreed with Say's law. He argued that supply does *not* create its own demand. That is, there is no guaranteed equality between savings and investment. This is because households or banks may hoard funds. If they do then savings will exceed investment, aggregate expenditures will be insufficient to clear total output off the market, inventories will rise, and output, employment, and incomes would fall creating a further decline in total spending, etc... Note also that Keynes doubted whether falling prices could stop this downward spiral. So, we get stuck in a rut.

   The policy implications are that insufficient total spending in the economy could result in *an equilibrium* level of output, employment, and income *below the potential* full employment output level. Therefore, the Keynesian recommendation for a recession: activist expansionary macro policy. That is, increase government spending, reduce taxes (fiscal policy), and increase the money supply (monetary policy) to stimulate aggregate expenditures. (This would shift the AD curve to the right and increase real output, employment and income.)

3.   The paradox of thrift is that when people collectively decide to save more and consume less, consumption expenditures fall. If that saving is not immediately transferred into investment, total expenditures falls. Faced with excess supply, firms cut production and income falls. As people's income falls, consumption and saving both fall. It is the paradox of thrift that leads to the multiplier effect. This multiplier effect makes the AD curve flatter than it otherwise would have been and accounts for the multiplied effect of shift factors of aggregate demand.

THE MULTIPLIER MODEL

● CHAPTER AT A GLANCE

This review is based upon the learning objectives that open the chapter.

1. Autonomous expenditures are unrelated to income; induced expenditures are directly related to income. (232)

   E₀ (autonomous expenditures) can change (shift the AE curve) if there is an autonomous change in any component of aggregate expenditures (AE).

   Note: AE = C + I + G + (X−M).

   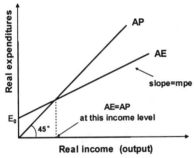

2. To determine income graphically in the multiplier model, you find the income level at which aggregate expenditures equal aggregate production. (235-236)

   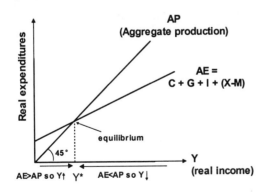

3. To determine income using the multiplier equation, determine the multiplier and multiply it by the level of autonomous expenditures (236)

   multiplier = 1/(1−mpc) = 1/mps.

   Y = (multiplier)(Autonomous expenditures)

   ΔY = (multiplier)(ΔAutonomous expenditures)

   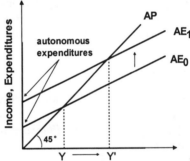

4. The multiplier process works because when expenditures don't equal production, businesspeople change planned production, which changes income, which changes expenditures, which.... (237-239)

   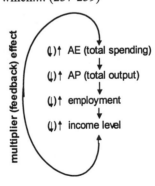

   This is the income adjustment process—the multiplier effect on income given a change in spending.

5. While the multiplier model is a mechanistic multiplier model, it should be used as a guide to one's common sense. The multiplier model has limitations: (243-245)

- The multiplier is not a complete model of the economy.
  The multiplier is best used as a guide for the direction and rough sizes of shifts in aggregate demand on income.

- Shifts are not as great as intuition suggests.
  Because some saving is brought back into the expenditures flow, a change in autonomous expenditures has less of an effect than the model suggests.

- The price level will often change in response to shifts in demand.
  The multiplier model assumes prices are fixed.

- People's forward-looking expectations make the adjustment process much more complicated.
  Business decisions are forward looking.

- Shifts in expenditures might reflect desired shifts in supply and demand.

- Expenditures depend on much more than current income.
  People also base their expenditure decisions on future income.

See also, Appendix A: "An Algebraic Presentation of the Expanded Multiplier Model" and Appendix B: "The Multiplier Model and the AS/AD Model"

● SHORT-ANSWER QUESTIONS

1. What is the difference between induced and autonomous expenditures?

2. Draw an AP and AE curve and show how the level of income is graphically determined in the multiplier model. Describe the forces that are set in motion when income levels are above and below equilibrium?

3. In the multiplier model, if autonomous expenditures were $200 and the *mpc* were 0.75, what is equilibrium income?

4. Explain the process by which the economy reaches a new equilibrium income if autonomous expenditures increase by $100. The marginal propensity to consume is 0.5.

5. True or false: The multiplier model is a complete model of the economy. Explain your answer.

MATCHING THE TERMS
Match the terms to their definitions

___1. aggregate expenditures

___2. aggregate expenditures curve

___3. aggregate production curve

___4. autonomous expenditures

___5. expenditures function

___6. induced expenditures

___7. marginal propensity to consume

___8. marginal propensity to save

___9. multiplier

___10. multiplier equation

___11. permanent income hypothesis

___12. rational expectations model

___13. real business cycle theory

a. The hypothesis that expenditures are determined by permanent or lifetime income.

b. Expenditures that change as income changes.

c. The theory that fluctuations in the economy reflect real phenomena—simultaneous shifts in supply and demand, not simply supply responses to demand shifts.

d. Equation that tells us that income equals the multiplier times autonomous expenditures.

e. A number that tells us how much income will change in response to a change in autonomous expenditures.

f. $AE = C + I + G + (X-M)$.

g. In the multiplier model, the 45° line on a graph with real income measured on the horizontal axis and real production on the vertical axis. Alternatively called the aggregate income curve.

h. The ratio of a change in consumption to a change in income.

i. Expenditures that are unaffected by changes in income.

j. Representation of the relationship between expenditures and income as a mathematical function ($E = E_0 + mpcY$, where E = expenditures, E_0 = autonomous expenditures, mpc = marginal propensity to consume, Y = income).

k. Graphical representation of the expenditures function.

l. Ratio of the change in saving, to a change in income.

m. Model of the economy in which all decisions are based upon expected equilibrium in the economy.

PROBLEMS AND APPLICATIONS

1. Answer the following questions about the aggregate production curve.

   a. Draw an aggregate production curve. Label all axes.

   b. What is the slope of the aggregate production function?

   c. Why is the slope as you have drawn it?

2. You are given the following information about the economy:

Income	Expenditures
0	100
500	500
1000	900
2000	1700
3000	2500
4000	3300

a. What is the level of autonomous expenditures?

b. What is the marginal propensity to consume? Explain why it is important.

c. What expenditures function (an equation) corresponds to the table?

d. What is the *mps*?

3. Putting expenditures and production together:

a. Graph the expenditures function from question 2 on the aggregate production curve from question 1.

b. What is the slope of the expenditures function?

4. Given the following equation, answer the questions: $AE = C_0 + .6Y + I + G + (X - M)$ where $C_0 = 1000$, $I = 500$, $G = 300$, $X = 300$, $M = 400$.

a. Draw the aggregate expenditures curve.

b. What is the slope of the curve?

c. What is the vertical axis intercept?

d. Add the aggregate production curve on the graph.

e. What is the multiplier?

f. What is equilibrium income? Label that point A on the graph.

g. What is the effect of an increase in autonomous consumption of $200 on equilibrium income? Demonstrate your answer graphically.

h. What is the effect on equilibrium income of a change in the *mpc* from .6 to .8? Demonstrate your answer graphically. How does your answer to (g) change with the new *mpc*?

5. Calculate the multiplier in each case.

    a. *mpc* = .7

    b. *mps* = .4

6. For each of the following, state what will happen to equilibrium income.

    a. The *mpc* is 0.9 and autonomous government expenditures just rose $200 billion. Graph your analysis.

b. The *mpc* is 0.65 and autonomous investment just fell $70 billion. Graph your analysis.

A1. You've just been appointed chairman of the Council of Economic Advisers in Textland. The *mpc* is .8, and all nonconsumption expenditures and taxes are exogenous.

    a. How can the government increase output by $400 through a change in expenditures?

    b. Oops! There's been a mistake. Your research assistant tells you that taxes are actually not exogenous, and that there is a marginal tax rate of .1. How can the government change expenditures to increase income by $400?

c. There's more new news which your research assistant just found out. She tells you that not only is there a marginal tax rate of .1; there's also a marginal propensity to import of .2. You have to change your solutions now. How can the government change expenditures to increase income by $400?

A2. What happens to output in the AP/AE model if there is perfect price-level flexibility when the AE curve shifts up due to a shift in autonomous expenditures?

● A BRAIN TEASER

1. We have all heard about the extent to which local communities go to in attracting and recruiting new businesses, conventions, trade shows, professional meetings, etc. into their area. Sometimes they seem to "give away the farm." They may offer a commitment not to impose property taxes for so many years or offer land at no charge if a company will build a production facility in the area, and so forth. Why do local governments offer lucrative tax incentives, etc., to attract new businesses into their area–especially considering that there are relatively only a few number of modestly higher paying jobs created?

● MULTIPLE CHOICE

Circle the one best answer for each of the following questions:

1. In the multiplier model,
   a. production is assumed to be fixed.
   b. planned expenditures are assumed to equal actual production.
   c. the price level is assumed to be fixed.
   d. the price level is assumed to be flexible.

2. Autonomous expenditures are expenditures that:
   a. are automatically created by income.
   b. are unrelated to income.
   c. change as income changes.
   d. automatically change as income changes.

3. The marginal propensity to consume is:
   a. the change in consumption expenditures times the change income.
   b. the change in consumption expenditures divided by the change in income.
   c. the change in consumption expenditures divided by income.
   d. consumption expenditures divided by the change in income.

4. *Mpc* plus *mps* equals
   a. zero.
   b. one.
   c. ten.
   d. unknown (cannot be determined).

5. If the mpc is .8, what is the size of the multiplier in the multiplier model?
   a. .5.
   b. 5.
   c. 1.
   d. 10.

6. As the *mpc* rises, the multiplier
   a. increases.
   b. decreases.
   c. remains the same.
   d. sometimes rises and sometimes falls.

7. Which of the following expenditures function is depicted in the graph below?

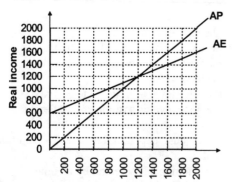

a. AE = $600 + .5Y.
b. AE = .5Y.
c. AE = $600.
d. AE = $600Y/.5.

8. Refer to the graph for Question #7. Planned expenditures exceed production at:
a. income levels above $1,200.
b. income levels below $1,200.
c. income level of $1,200.
d. no income level since planned expenditures equals production.

9. If consumer confidence suddenly falls, you would expect:
a. the aggregate production curve to shift down.
b. the aggregate expenditures curve to rotate to the right and equilibrium income to fall.
c. the aggregate expenditures curve to shift up and equilibrium income to rise.
d. the aggregate expenditures curve to shift down and equilibrium income to fall.

10. In the multiplier model, if autonomous expenditures are $5,000 and the *mpc* equals .9, what is the level of income in the economy?
a. $5,000.
b. $10,000.
c. $20,000.
d. $50,000.

11. In the multiplier model if autonomous exports falls by 40 and the *mpc* is .5, what happens to the income?
a. Income rises by 20.
b. Income falls by 20.
c. Income rises by 80.
d. Income falls by 80.

12. In the multiplier model if autonomous consumption increases by 100 and the AE curve is upward sloping, income:
a. will rise by 100.
b. will rise by more than 100.
c. will fall by 100.
d. may rise or fall. We cannot tell without more information.

13. In the multiplier model if autonomous consumption increases by 10 and the *mpc* is .8, what happens to the income?
a. Income rises by 8.
b. Income falls by 8.
c. Income rises by 50.
d. Income falls by 50.

14. In the multiplier model if autonomous exports fall by 40 and government spending increases by 20, and the *mpc* is .8, what happens to the income?
a. Income rises by 300.
b. Income falls by 300.
c. Income rises by 100.
d. Income falls by 100.

15. In the multiplier model, if people begin to save more of their income:
a. leakages out of the circular flow will rise and equilibrium income will fall.
b. because leakages from the circular flow will still equal injections from the circular flow, equilibrium income will not change.
c. injections into the circular flow will rise and equilibrium income will rise.
d. the flow of income and expenditures will no longer be circular.

16. The term *paradox of thrift* refers to the process by which individuals attempted to save:
a. less, but in doing so spent less and caused income to decrease, ending up saving even lesser.
b. less, but in doing so spent more and caused income to decrease, ending up saving even lesser.
c. more, but in doing so spent less and caused income to decrease, ending up saving less.
d. more, but in doing so spent more and caused income to decrease, ending up saving less.

17. The multiplier model:
 a. determines equilibrium from scratch.
 b. determines the direction the economy might take in response to changes in the economy.
 c. is best applied to an economy with rapidly rising prices.
 d. reflect the complicated adjustment process that results from people's forward-looking expectations.

18. The hypothesis that expenditures are determined by permanent or lifetime income (making the *mpc* close to zero) implies that the AE curve will be
 a. a flat line.
 b. a vertical line.
 c. an upward sloping 45⁰ line.
 d. something economists cannot determine.

19. The interpretative Keynesian macro model differs from the mechanistic Keynesian model in that
 a. the interpretative multiplier model is essentially a Classical model.
 b. the interpretative model sees the Keynesian model as a guide, not a definitive result.
 c. the interpretative multiplier model integrates the quantity theory into the *AE/AP* model.
 d. the interpretative multiplier model integrates the quantity theory into both the Keynesian *AS/AD* and the *AE/AP* models.

20. If there is some price level flexibility
 a. the multiplier model is no longer relevant.
 b. the results of the multiplier model will be reversed.
 c. the results of the multiplier model will be modified but the central point will remain the same.
 d. the multiplier model will turn into a Classical model.

21. In the real business cycle theory, business cycles occur because of:
 a. changes in the real price level.
 b. changes in real income.
 c. technological and other natural shocks.
 d. changes in the money supply.

A1. If the marginal tax rate increases, what would happen to the general expenditures multiplier?
 a. It would increase.
 b. It would decrease.
 c. It would remain the same.
 d. One cannot say.

A2. In the multiplier model, if a country has a very large marginal propensity to import
 a. expansionary fiscal policy would be extremely effective in expanding domestic income.
 b. expansionary fiscal policy would not be very effective in expanding domestic income.
 c. The size of the marginal propensity to import has no effect on the effectiveness of expansionary fiscal policy.
 d. The multiplier model is not relevant to a country with a very large marginal propensity to import.

A3. Assuming the marginal propensity to import is .1, the tax rate is .2, and the marginal propensity to consume is .6, the multiplier will be approximately
 a. 0.
 b. 1.2.
 c. 1.6.
 d. 2.6.

A4. Assume the marginal propensity to import is .1, the tax rate is .25, the marginal propensity to consume is .8, and that the government wants to increase income by 100. In the multiplier model you would suggest increasing government spending by
 a. 10.
 b. 35.7.
 c. 50.
 d. 100.

A5. Assume the marginal propensity to import is .3, the tax rate is .2, the marginal propensity to consume is .5, and that the government wants to increase income by 200. In the multiplier model you would suggest increasing government spending by
 a. 87.5.
 b. 100.
 c. 180.
 d. 200.

B1. When the price level falls
  a. the aggregate expenditures curve remains constant.
  b. the aggregate expenditures curve shifts down.
  c. the aggregate expenditures curve shifts up.
  d. the slope of the aggregate expenditures curve changes.

B2. To derive the aggregate demand curve from the multiplier model, one must
  a. relate the initial autonomous shifts caused by price level changes on the *AE* curve to the *AD* curve.
  b. relate the *AE/AP* equilibria at different price levels to the *AD* curve.
  c. relate the *AE/AP* equilibria at different quantity levels to the *AD* curve.
  d. relate the initial autonomous shifts caused by price level changes on the *AP* curve to the *AD* curve.

B3. If there is partial price-level flexibility
  a. the multiplier model is no longer relevant.
  b. the results of the multiplier model will be reversed.
  c. the results of the multiplier model will be modified but the central point will remain the same.
  d. the multiplier model will turn into a Classical model.

● POTENTIAL ESSAY QUESTIONS

You may also see essay questions similar to the "Problems & Applications" and "Brain Teasers" exercises.

1. In the multiplier model, can macroeconomic equilibrium exist below full employment? Why, or why not?

2. Why does the multiplier process exist? What does the multiplier do to the income level given any change in aggregate expenditures?

3. What is meant by "the paradox of thrift" and how did it help perpetuate the Great Depression?

5. What is the major contribution of the multiplier model to the AS/AD model?

ANSWERS

SHORT-ANSWER QUESTIONS

1. Induced expenditures depend upon the level of income. Autonomous expenditures are independent of income. (232)

2. The *AP* curve is a 45-degree line through the origin. At all points on the *AP* curve, output equals income. The *AE* curve is an upward-sloping line with a slope less than one that intersects the expenditures axis at the level of autonomous expenditures. These curves are shown in the graph below. Equilibrium income is where the two curves intersect. At points to the left, aggregate expenditures exceed aggregate production and businesses find their inventories are being depleted. They increase production, which increases income and expenditures, moving income toward equilibrium. At points to the right, aggregate expenditures are less than aggregate production and businesses see their inventories accumulating. They cut production, which reduces income and expenditures, moving income toward equilibrium. (235-236, 239-241)

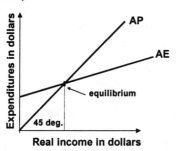

3. To determine equilibrium income, multiply the sum of all autonomous expenditures by the multiplier. In this case the multiplier is $1/(1-.75) = 4$, so equilibrium income is $800. (236)

4. The initial shock is $100. This increase in expenditures causes aggregate production to increase also by $100, which creates an additional $100 in income. Consumers spend $50 of this additional income on additional goods. Once again aggregate production rises by the same amount as the $50 increase in aggregate expenditures. Subsequent increases

in aggregate expenditures and aggregate production are determined in a similar fashion, each time getting smaller and smaller. Equilibrium income is $200 higher at the end of this multiplier process. This is determined by calculating the multiplier, $1/(1-mpc) = 2$ and multiplying it by the initial rise in aggregate expenditures of $100. (239-241)

5. The multiplier model is not a complete model of the economy. Although it purports to determine equilibrium from scratch, it doesn't because it does not tell us where those autonomous expenditures come from. The multiplier model is best used as a guide for the direction and rough size of the effects of changes in autonomous expenditures on income. (243)

ANSWERS

MATCHING

1-f; 2-k; 3-g; 4-i; 5-j; 6-b; 7-h; 8-l; 9-e; 10-d; 11-a; 12-m; 13-c.

ANSWERS

PROBLEMS AND APPLICATIONS

1. **a.** The aggregate production curve is a 45-degree line as shown below. Production is on the vertical axis and real income is on the horizontal axis. (230-231)

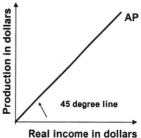

   b. The slope is 1. (230-231)
   c. The slope is one because the aggregate production curve represents the identity that aggregate production must equal aggregate income. That can only be represented by a straight line through the origin with a slope of one. (230-231)

2. **a.** Autonomous expenditures are $100. It is that amount that is independent of income. (232-237)

b. The marginal propensity to consume is 0.8: This is calculated as the change in expenditures/change in disposable income = 400/500. It is important because it tells us how much of any additional income is respent as the economy expands. It is because of the mpc that income changes by a multiple of a change in autonomous expenditures. (232-238)

c. The expenditures function that corresponds to the table is $E = 100 + .8Y$. The 100 comes from the level of expenditures when income is zero and the .8 is the *mpc*. (232-237)

d. The *mps* is 0.2. The *mps* = 1 − *mpc*. (238-239)

3. **a.** The graph of the expenditure function from question 2 and the aggregate production from question 1 are shown together on the graph below. (235)

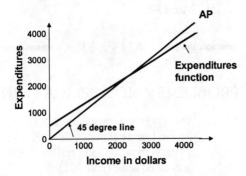

b. The slope of the expenditure function is the *mpc*, or 0.8. (233-234)

4. **a.** The aggregate expenditures curve is drawn below. The slope of the *AE* curve is the *mpc* and the vertical intercept is autonomous expenditures. (233)

b. The slope of the curve is .6. It is the *mpc*. (233-234)

c. The vertical axis intercept is 1000+500+300+(300−400) = 1700. The vertical axis intercept is the level of autonomous expenditures. (233-234)

d. The aggregate production curve is shown in the graph below. It is a 45-degree line through the origin. (230)

e. The multiplier is 2.5. It is 1/(1 −*mpc*). (236)

f. Equilibrium income is $4,250: autonomous expenditures × multiplier, $1,700/(1 −.6). This is shown as point A on the graph below. (236-237)

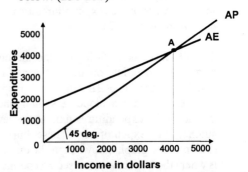

g. An increase in autonomous expenditures of $200 will increase equilibrium income by $500. This is calculated by multiplying $200 by the multiplier, 2.5. The new equilibrium income is $4,750. This is shown below as an upward shift in the AE curve by 200. The new equilibrium income is point B on the graph below. (236-237)

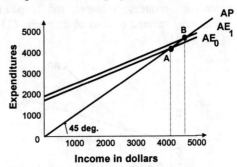

h. The *AE* curve becomes steeper with a slope of .8. The multiplier is now 5 and equilibrium income is now $8,500. This is shown as point C in the graph below. Equilibrium income is calculated by multiplying autonomous expenditures, $1,700, by the multiplier. Since the multiplier is larger, an increase of $200 in autonomous expenditures now increases equilibrium income by $1,000, up to $9,500. (237)

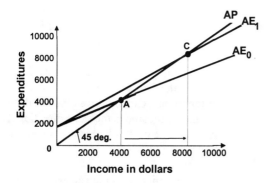

5.　a.　The multiplier is 3.33: 1/(1−.7). (236)
　　b.　The multiplier is 2.5: 1/(.4). (236)

6.　a.　Income rises by $2 trillion: 200/(1−0.9). In this case the aggregate expenditures curve has a slope of 0.9 as shown in the graph below. The increase in government expenditures shifts the AE curve up from AE_0 to AE_1 and income increases by a multiple of that amount, in this case by a multiple of 10. (238-240)

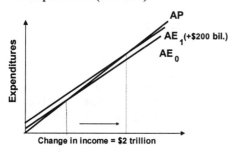

Change in income = $2 trillion

Income in dollars

　　b.　Income falls by $200 billion: $70/.35. In this case the aggregate expenditures curve has a slope of .65 as shown in the graph below. The decrease in investment shifts the AE curve down from AE_0 to AE_1 and income decreases by a multiple of that amount, in this case by a multiple of 2.86. (238-240)

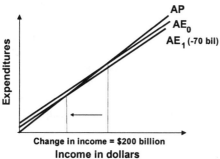

Change in income = $200 billion
Income in dollars

A1.　Given an *mpc* of .8:
　　a.　Increase expenditures by $80. The multiplier is $1/(1-mpc) = 1/(1-.8) = 5$. Therefore, to increase GDP by $400, government spending has to increase $80. (248-249)
　　b.　Increase expenditures by $112. The multiplier is $1/(1-mpc + t\times mpc) = 1/(1-.8+.1\times.8) = 3.57$. Therefore, to increase GDP by $400, government spending has to increase by $112. (248-249)
　　c.　Increase expenditures by $193. The multiplier is $1/(1-mpc + t\times mpc + mpm) = 1/(1-.8+.1\times.8+.2) = 2.08$. Therefore, to increase GDP by $400, government spending has to increase by $192. (248-249)

A2.　In the multiplier model, a change in autonomous expenditures will be offset entirely by a change in the price level that shifts the AE curve in a direction opposite to the initial shift. If the initial shift causes the AE curve to shift up, prices will rise sufficiently to shift the AE curve back to its initial position. (249-251)

■■■■　ANSWERS　■■■■

A BRAIN TEASER

1.　It may appear that the benefits do not outweigh the costs to the community of "giving away the farm"–especially when one considers that the tax breaks offered new businesses will likely result in higher property tax rates imposed on other members of the community if the same quantity and quality of local government services are to be provided. However, even though a relatively few number of modestly higher paying jobs are created, because of the multiplier effect, this *can* translate into still more jobs and even more income, etc.–creating "significant growth and opportunities within the community." Next time you read a headline indicating the amount of jobs (or income) created in the city by having the "Pigs are Beautiful" convention in town you'll know what they mean. (237-238)

ANSWERS

MULTIPLE CHOICE

1.   c   The multiplier model assumes that the price level remains constant and asks how much aggregate equilibrium income will change when aggregate expenditures change. During the adjustment to equilibrium, planned expenditures will not equal actual production. See page 229.

2.   b   Autonomous expenditures are expenditures that exist even when income is zero. They do not change as income changes. See page 232.

3.   b   The marginal propensity to consume is the fraction of additional income that is consumed. It can be calculated by dividing the change in consumption expenditures by the change income. See page 233.

4.   b   This is true by definition. Income that is not spent it saved. See page 239.

5.   b   The multiplier equals $1/(1-.8) = 1/.2 = 5$. See page 236.

6.   a   You can determine this by substituting into the formula. See page 236.

7.   a   The graph shows that the y-axis intercept is $600 and the slope is .5. Calculate the slope as rise over run. For example, beginning at the y-intercept, increasing expenditures by 600 means income rises by 1200 (600/1200 = .5). Substitute these values in the equation for a straight line: $y = (slope)x + (intercept)$. See page 233-234.

8.   b   Planned expenditures exceed production where the AE curve is above the AP curve. This occurs at income levels below $1,200. See page 235.

9.   d   A drop in consumer confidence would be expected to reduce consumption expenditures. This shifts the AE curve down and leads to a reduction in equilibrium income (output). See pages 236, 241-242.

10.   d   The multiplier is 10 so the answer is 10 times $5,000. See page 236.

11.   d   The multiplier is 2 so the answer is 2 times −40. See pages 240-241.

12.   b   In the multiplier model, as long as the mpc is greater than zero, a change in autonomous expenditures will lead to a change in income in the same direction that is a multiple of the change in expenditures. See pages 240-241.

13.   c   The multiplier is 5 so the answer is 5 times 10. See pages 240-241.

14.   d   The multiplier is 5 so the answer is 5 times (−40 + 20) or minus 100. See pages 240-241.

15.   a   If people save more of their income, the mps will rise. Because more income leaks from the circular flow, less returns in the form of expenditures and equilibrium income falls. See pages 238-239.

16.   c   The paradox of thrift is that if individuals increase saving, total income will decline, resulting in lower saving. See page 243.

17.   b   The multiplier model is best used as a historical model that suggests the direction an economy might take given a shock. See page 243.

18.   a   If the *mpc* were close to zero the slope of the AE curve would also be close to zero (flat). See page 245.

19.   b   The interpretative multiplier model views the multiplier model as an aid in understanding. It might integrate the multiplier model with other models but that is not what is distinctive about it. See page 245.

20.   c   The multiplier model assumes that the price level is constant. If, however, the price level is not constant, the multiplier model is modified. The central point, however, that an increase in expenditures has a multiplied effect on equilibrium output is still relevant. See page 244.

21.   c   Real business cycle theory suggests that fluctuations in output are the result of shifting aggregate supply resulting from changes in technology. See page 244.

A1. b This is a hard question since it requires some deduction. The marginal tax rate is one of the components of the marginal propensity to consume. It is a leakage from the circular flow, so it makes the multiplier smaller. See pages 248-249.

A2. b A large marginal propensity to import reduces the size of the multiplier since the marginal propensity to import is one of the components of the marginal propensity to consume. See pages 248-249.

A3. c The multiplier for the full model is $1/(1-c+ct+m)$. Substituting in gives $1/(1-.6+.1+.12)$ or $1/.62$ or a multiplier of about 1.6. See pages 248-249.

A4. c First you determine the multiplier. The multiplier for the full model is $1/(1-c+ct+m)$. Substituting in gives $1/(1-.8+.1+.2)$ or $1/.5$ or a multiplier of 2. Dividing 100 by 2 gives an increase of government spending of 50. See pages 248-249.

A5. c First you determine the multiplier. The multiplier for the full model is $1/(1-c+ct+m)$. Substituting in gives $1/(1-.5+.3+.1)$ or $1/.9$ or a multiplier of about 1.11. Dividing 200 by 1.11 gives an increase of government spending of about 180. The multiplier is very small because the *mpc* is low and the *mpm* is high. See pages 248-249.

B1. c Since a lower price level makes the cash people hold worth more, people feel wealthier and the *AE* curve shifts up. See pages 249-251.

B2. b As discussed on pages 249-251, especially Figure B26-1, one considers the effect of different price levels on the *AE* curve to derive an *AD curve*.

B3. c If you could follow that complicated Figure B10-1 on page 250 you would see that the results are modified. If you are following that, you're doing great. Have you thought of becoming an economist?

■■■■　ANSWERS　■■■■

POTENTIAL ESSAY QUESTIONS

The following are annotated answers. They indicate the general idea behind the answer.

1. Yes, because equilibrium exists *wherever* AE = AP. That is, planned expenditures need not equal production at full employment. If there is inadequate spending then the income adjustment process moves the economy to an equilibrium below full employment.

2. Because a change in spending changes people's incomes, which changes their spending, which changes people's incomes... Because of the induced effects within the income adjustment process, the multiplier magnifies any changes in spending into much larger changes in income. However, given an increase in expenditures, real income increases by a smaller amount when prices are flexible.

3. The paradox of thrift indicates that when people decide to save more this may end up causing people to save less. The increased savings (reduced spending) due to the panic following the stock market crash of 1929 did help perpetuate the Great Depression. This is because when people decided to save more (spend less) businesses responded by cutting back on production and laying off workers. (Businesses were also doing their share of causing a reduction in aggregate expenditures. They were cutting back on investment spending because they were pessimistic about the future as well.) The lower aggregate expenditures in the economy contributed to a multiple decline in income well below full employment. At the lower income levels during the Great Depression savings was much lower than before–hence, the paradox of thrift.

4. The major contribution of the multiplier model to the AS/AD model is that it provides an exact number for the shift in the AD curve when autonomous expenditures change and provides the reasoning behind the multiplier effects needed to derive an AD curve.

DEMAND MANAGEMENT POLICY

CHAPTER AT A GLANCE

This review is based upon the learning objectives that open the chapter.

↓ taxes ↑ Govnt. Spen.

1a. Expansionary fiscal policy involves decreasing taxes or increasing government spending. Contractionary fiscal policy involves increasing taxes or decreasing the government spending. (252)

↑ taxes
↓ Govnt.

Use expansionary fiscal policy to combat cyclical unemployment and slow growth during a recession (a downturn in the business cycle). Use contractionary fiscal policy to combat inflation during an upturn in the business cycle.

1b. Expansionary fiscal policy shifts the aggregate demand curve to the right. The effect on prices and output depends upon how close the economy is to potential output. (255-256)

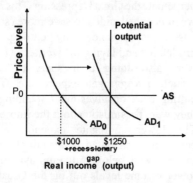

If the multiplier is 5 and there is a recessionary gap of $250, government must increase expenditures by $50 (since $50 × multiplier of 5 = $250) to arrive at potential income. If the recessionary gap was less than $250, the effect of the shift in the AD curve (and the multiplier effect) would be split between increases in real output and increases in the price level.

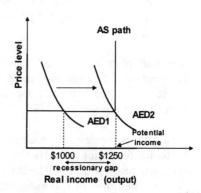

Here is the story using the AP/AE model: In the graph above, initial autonomous AE is $200 and the mpc is 0.8. The multiplier is 1/(1−0.8) = 5. Equilibrium income is $1000. Since there is a recessionary gap of $250, government increases expenditures by $50 (since $50 × multiplier of 5 = $250). This depends upon the price level being fixed..

2. Three alternatives to fiscal policy are directed investment policies, trade policies, and autonomous consumption policies. (258)

Anything which government can do to alter components of AE (C, I, G, and X−M) will have a multiple impact on Y (the income-output level in the macro economy) because of the multiplier. For example, rosy scenarios, bank guarantees, reduction in interest rates, export-led growth policies, and increases in consumer credit availability could increase AE and stimulate the economy.

3a. During the Depression of the 1930s, the economy was far below potential. World War II spending increased aggregate expenditures and output. (262)

The economy exceeded its potential output during World War II, but price controls kept inflation low.

3b. In the late 1990s, the U.S. deficit turned into a surplus. (263)

The surplus was the result of a booming economy driven by consumer and investment spending. The surplus helped to keep the economy from inflation.

4. Six assumptions of the model that could lead to problems with fiscal policy are: (263-268)

1. Financing the deficit doesn't have any offsetting effects.
In reality, it often does (e.g., the crowding-out effect).

2. The government knows what the situation is.
In reality the government must estimate what the situation is.

3. The government knows the economy's potential income.
In reality the government may not know what this level is.

4. The government has flexibility in terms of spending and taxes.
In reality, the government cannot change them quickly.

5. The size of the government debt doesn't matter.
In reality, the size of the debt often does matter.

6. Fiscal policy doesn't negatively affect other government goals.
In reality, it often does.

5. Crowding out is the offsetting effect on private expenditures caused by the government's sale of bonds to finance expansionary fiscal policy. (264)

Increases in the deficit financed by borrowing (selling bonds) leads to increases in interest rates (which increases the cost of borrowing). This leads to lower investment (business spending on capital) which offsets the rise in government spending.

So, increased deficit spending may be partially or totally offset by decreases in other spending components.

The size of the crowding-out effect is debatable.

6. An automatic stabilizer is any government program or policy that will counteract the business cycle without any new government action. (269)

Automatic stabilizers include:
- Welfare payments
- Unemployment insurance, and
- Income tax system.

Assume a recession that is caused by too little total spending. Government expenditures automatically rise (because of increased welfare payments and unemployment claims). Taxes automatically decrease (because fewer people are earning income). The budget deficit increases and AE (total spending) increases. The opposite occurs during an upturn in the business cycle. <u>Automatic stabilizers help smooth out the business cycle.</u>

● SHORT-ANSWER QUESTIONS

1. The initial policy proposal by U.S. Keynesian economists was to introduce public works programs. How did that proposal work and what was added to that policy by subsequent Keynesian policymakers?

2. Suppose you are the featured speaker at a primer for the first-year Congresspeople. You have been asked to speak about fiscal policy. A Congressperson asks what fiscal policy tools Congress has to affect the economy, and what effect they have on the level of output. You tell her.

3. What are contractionary and expansionary fiscal policies?

4. How does fiscal policy affect the economy? Demonstrate an expansionary fiscal policy graphically using the AS/AD model.

5. The first-year Congresspeople are worried about how your answer to question 2. They feel they are politically unable to implement those policies. What three alternatives to fiscal policy can you offer?

6. How do the six problems of fiscal policy limit its use?

7. You are speaking at the Congressional conference. A Congressperson wonders whether financing deficit spending will change the direct effect of fiscal policy. You tell her that it might and explain how.

8. Some economists argue that crowding out totally undermines the activist view of fiscal policy. Explain their argument.

9. A country has just removed its unemployment insurance program and is experiencing a recession. How will this recession differ from earlier recessions?

MATCHING THE TERMS
Match the terms to their definitions

h **1.** aggregate demand management
b **2.** automatic stabilizer
i **3.** contractionary fiscal policy
g **4.** crowding out
e **5.** exchange rate policy
j **6.** expansionary fiscal policy
a **7.** export-led growth policy
c **8.** fine tuning
d **9.** fiscal policy
f **10.** Rosy Scenario policy

a. A policy that increases autonomous exports thereby increasing autonomous expenditures.
b. Any government program or policy that will counteract the business cycle without any new government action.
c. Countercyclical fiscal policy designed to keep the economy always at its target or potential level of income.
d. Deliberate change in either government spending or taxes to stimulate or slow down the economy.
e. Deliberately affecting a country's exchange rate in order to affects its trade balance.
f. Government policy of making optimistic predictions and never making gloomy predictions.
g. The offsetting effect on private expenditures caused by the government's sale of bonds to finance expansionary fiscal policy.
h. Policy aimed at changing the level of income in the economy by a combination of a change in autonomous expenditures and the multiplied induced expenditures resulting from that change.
i. Increase taxes or decrease government spending.
j. Decrease taxes or increase government spending.

PROBLEMS AND APPLICATIONS

1. You are hired by the president who believes that the economy is operating at a level $300 billion beyond potential output. You are told that the marginal propensity to consume is 0.5.

a. The president wants to use taxes to close the gap. What do you advise? Show your answer using the AP/AE model. (Read the box on page 610 for a hint).

b. The president wants to compare your plan in (a) to a plan using spending to close the inflationary gap. What do you advise? Show your answer graphically using the AS/AD model.

c. Advisers from the council realize that the marginal propensity to consume is 0.75. Recalculate your answer to (b) and show using the AS/AD model.

2. You are called by the president to raise equilibrium income by $1,000. You are told that the mpc is 0.

a. You estimate that the economy has a recessionary gap of $1000. Make a proposal to increase short-run equilibrium income as desired by the president. What will happen to the economy in the long run?

b. You've re-estimated potential output. The economy has a recessionary gap of only $500. The president still wants to raise equilibrium income by $1,000. Make a proposal to increase short-run equilibrium income as desired by the president. What will happen to the economy in the long run?

3. Suppose the government wants to increase income by $250 billion. The *mpc* is .6.

   a. Assuming the economy is far below potential output, by how much must government increase spending to reach its goal? Show the effect of this action, using the AS/AD model.

   b. Suppose government finances this increase in spending with the sale of bonds. As a result, interest rates increase. How does this affect the analysis? Demonstrate using the multiplier model.

4. Congratulations. You have just been appointed economic adviser to Dreamland. For each of the following, advise the president.

   a. The president wants to reduce unemployment from 8 to 6 percent. Income is $40,000 and the *mpc* is .4. What spending policy would you advise? (Hint: Use Okun's rule of thumb from a previous chapter.)

   b. The president wants to reduce unemployment from 8 to 6 percent. Income is $50,000 and the *mpc* is .75. What fiscal spending policy would you advise?

5. In 1999, national income was $9 trillion and unemployment was 4%.

   a. Suppose the Chairman of the Council of Economic Advisers believed that the natural rate of unemployment was 4% while the Chairman of the Fed believed that natural rate was 5%. Calculate the difference in the underlying estimates of potential income.

   b. What spending policy would each recommend to close the recessionary gap, assuming the *mpc* is .5?

● A BRAIN TEASER

1. Do the problems associated with implementing activist fiscal policy in practice mean that the multiplier model is wrong? Or, that fiscal policy ought to be eliminated?

● MULTIPLE CHOICE

Circle the one best answer for each of the following questions:

1. Expansionary fiscal policy involves
   a. increasing taxes.
   b. increasing the money supply.
   c. increasing government spending.
   d. changing the exchange rate.

2. According to the multiplier model, government has a role in getting an economy out of recession because
   a. individuals collectively don't have the spending power to make a difference.
   b. government spending will increase income and induce individuals to spend more.
   c. the economy could never be expected to return to potential output on its own.
   d. only the government knows when the economy is in a recession.

3. The macro policy that follows from the multiplier and AS/AD model is generally called
   a. aggregate supply management.
   b. aggregate demand management.
   c. price-level policy.
   d. exchange rate policy.

4. In the graph below, actual income is below potential income. The government is planning to use expansionary fiscal policy. This will:

   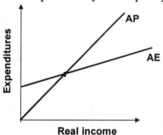

   a. shift the *AP* curve up.
   b. shift the *AE* curve up.
   c. shift the *AP* curve down.
   d. shift the *AE* curve down.

5. In the graph below, autonomous imports have just increased. In the short run, this will cause:

   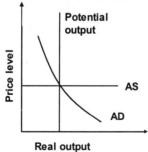

   a. the aggregate supply curve to shift down.
   b. the aggregate supply curve to shift up.
   c. the aggregate demand curve to shift out to the right.
   d. the aggregate demand curve to shift in to the left

6. The economy has a fixed price level, an *mpc* of .5, and a recessionary gap of 240. Using the Keynesian *multiplier model*, an economist would advise government to
   a. increase autonomous expenditures by 120.
   b. increase autonomous expenditures by 240.
   c. increase autonomous expenditures by 480.
   d. increase autonomous expenditures by 620.

7. The economy is in the Keynesian range, has an *mpc* of .8, and is in a recessionary gap of 600. Using the multiplier model, an economist would advise government to
   a. increase autonomous expenditures by 120
   b. increase autonomous expenditures by 480.
   c. increase autonomous expenditures by 600.
   d. increase autonomous expenditures by 3000.

8. The economy has a fixed price level, an *mpc* of .66, and a recessionary gap of 900. Using the multiplier model, an economist would advise government to increase autonomous expenditures by about:
   a. 30.
   b. 300.
   c. 600.
   d. 2700.

9. The economy has an inflationary gap, the government should use fiscal policy to shift:
   a. the *AS* path up.
   b. the *AS curve* down.
   c. the *AD* curve out to the right.
   d. the *AD* curve in to the left.

10. If an economy has an inflationary gap and the government does nothing, the multiplier model predicts that:
    a. the AS curve will shift up as input prices increase, and output will decline.
    b. the AS curve will shift down as input prices decline, and output will rise.
    c. the AD curve will shift out to the right as individuals collectively decide to increase expenditures, and output will rise.
    d. the AD curve will shift in to the left as individuals collectively decide to reduce expenditures, and output will decline.

11. Which of the following is true today?
    a. Keynesian economists support fine tuning.
    b. Classical economists support fine tuning.
    c. Both Keynesian and Classical economists generally support fine tuning.
    d. Both Keynesian and Classical economists generally oppose fine tuning.

12. Expansionary aggregate demand policy includes all of the following except
    a. increasing government spending.
    b. increasing autonomous expenditures.
    c. increasing imports.
    d. decreasing taxes.

13. Contractionary aggregate demand policy includes all of the following except
    a. decreasing autonomous investment.
    b. lowering the value of one's currency by buying foreign currencies.
    c. increasing the value of one's currency by selling foreign currencies.
    d. decreasing government spending.

14. During World War II,
    a. expansionary fiscal policy pushed the economy beyond potential and the price level rose tremendously.
    b. expansionary fiscal policy pushed the economy beyond potential, but the price level was controlled by legislation.
    c. contractionary monetary policy pushed the economy into a depression.
    d. increased taxes to finance the war pushed the economy into recession.

15. Exchange rate policy is
    a. increasing the size of the government deficit.
    b. deliberately affecting the country's exchange rate in order to affect its trade balance.
    c. deliberately affecting the country's money supply in order to affect its trade balance.
    d. deliberately affecting the country's tax rate in order to affect its trade balance.

16. The economy in the late 1990s:
    a. expanded because government spending on Social Security rose tremendously.
    b. was definitely beyond potential, creating inflationary pressures.
    c. expanded as consumption and investment expenditures rose, but inflation did not rise.
    d. slowed from its rapid pace in the mid-1990s because of a growing budget surplus.

17. Crowding out occurs when
    a. the government runs a deficit and sells bonds to finance that deficit.
    b. the government prints money.

c. the government runs a surplus and sells bonds and the people who buy those bonds sell their older bonds to the government.
d. the tendency for new workers to replace more expensive older workers is a factor.

18. If potential output is 2 percent higher than forecasted, the target rate of unemployment is probably:
    a. 1 percentage point lower than expected.
    b. 1 percentage point higher than expected.
    c. 2 percentage points lower than expected.
    d. 2 percentage points higher than expected.

19. Automatic stabilizers:
    a. are government programs to employ workers during recessions.
    b. create government budget surpluses during economic recessions.
    c. are designed to reduce the price level directly.
    d. counteract both recessions and expansions through changes in spending without government action.

● POTENTIAL ESSAY QUESTIONS

You may also see essay questions similar to the "Problems & Applications" and "Brain Teasers" exercises.

1. According to the multiplier model, what is appropriate fiscal policy over the course of the business cycle?

2. How do the automatic stabilizers add stability to the business cycle? Are there any time lag (delay) problems associated with the use of the automatic stabilizers?

3. What is the crowding-out effect? What impact does this have on the effectiveness of fiscal policy in stimulating the economy during a recession? How large is the crowding-out effect according to the Keynesians? The Classicals? What does the empirical evidence suggest about the size of the crowding-out effect?

ANSWERS

SHORT-ANSWER QUESTIONS

1. Keynesian economists' policy proposals worked by starting the multiplier process that got the economy in a low-income equilibrium to work in reverse. It increases aggregate expenditures. Businesses produce more to meet the additional demand, which creates additional income. The additional income results in a further increase in expenditures. The process continues until a new, higher equilibrium level of income is reached. Later Keynesians added to that policy: (1) another way to stimulate the economy by reducing taxes, (2) a way to slow down the economy when called for by decreasing spending or increasing taxes, (3) policies to change the money supply as a way of controlling the economy, and (4) general policies to influence components of aggregate expenditures. (253-254)

2. The tools of fiscal policy are changing taxes and changing government spending. Increasing taxes and lowering spending contract the economy; decreasing taxes and expanding spending expand the economy. (252)

3. Contractionary fiscal policies involve increasing taxes or decreasing government spending. Expansionary fiscal policies involve decreasing taxes or increasing government spending. (252)

4. Fiscal policy affects the economy by changing aggregate expenditures, which changes people's incomes, which increases people's spending even more. Expansionary fiscal policy shifts the aggregate demand curve to the right by a multiple of the increase in government spending, as shown in the diagram below. The change in income equals the multiplier times the change in government expenditures. (254-256)

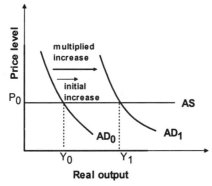

5. Three alternatives to fiscal policy are directed investment policies, trade policies, and autonomous consumption policies. Directed investment policies include talking up the economy so that businesses will invest in expectation of better days and protecting the financial system by guarantees. Trade policies would include government assistance to promote exports. Autonomous consumption policies would include creating institutions conducive to easy credit. (258-262)

6. The six problems with fiscal policy limit its use in the following ways: (1) Financing the deficit might have offsetting effects, reducing the net effect. (2) The government doesn't always know the current state of the economy and where it is headed, meaning these must be forecast; if you don't know the state of the economy you don't know what fiscal policy to use. (3) The government doesn't know what potential income is, meaning it must be estimated; if you estimated it wrong, you get the wrong fiscal policy. (4) The government cannot implement policy easily; if you can't implement it you can't use it. (5) The size of the debt might matter and since deficits create debt, you might not want to use it. Finally, (6) fiscal policy often negatively affects other government goals; if it does you might not use the policy even though it would change the economy in the direction you want. The bottom line is: In extreme cases, the appropriate fiscal policy is clear, but in most cases, the situation is not extreme. (264-268)

7. This first-year Congressperson is sharp! What she has described is crowding out. Crowding out is the offsetting effect on private expenditures caused by the government's sale of bonds to finance expansionary fiscal policy. If the government finances expansionary fiscal policy through the sale of bonds, interest rates will tend to rise. This will cause investment to decline, offsetting the initial stimulus. (264)

8. If crowding out is so strong that the reduced investment totally offsets the expansionary effect of fiscal spending, the net effect of fiscal policy can be zero. (264)

9. Unemployment insurance is an automatic stabilizer, a government program that counter-

acts the business cycle without any new government action. If income falls, automatic stabilizers will increase aggregate expenditures to counteract that decline. Likewise with increases in income: when income increases, automatic stabilizers decrease the size of the deficit. Eliminating unemployment insurance will eliminate this stabilization aspect of the policy and will contribute to making the recession more severe than it otherwise would have been. However, it would also make people more likely to accept lower wages and search harder for a job, thereby reducing the amount of unemployment. As usual, the answer depends. (269)

ANSWERS

MATCHING

1-h; 2-b; 3-i; 4-g; 5-e; 6-j; 7-a; 8-c; 9-d; 10-f.

ANSWERS

PROBLEMS AND APPLICATIONS

1. **a.** The spending multiplier is 2, 1/(1-.5), but only a fraction of the increase in taxes reduces spending. Taxes must be increased by $300 billion to reduce income by $300 billion. We calculate this by solving the following for change in taxes: change in taxes$\times mpc \times 1/(1-mpc))$ = $300 billion. (255-258)

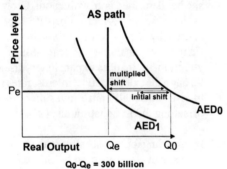

$Q_0 - Q_e = 300$ billion

b. The spending multiplier is 2. Spending must be decreased by $150 billion to reduce income by $300 billion. We calculate this by solving the following for change in

government spending: change in government spending$\times(1/(1-mpc))$ =−300 billion. This is shown in the graph below. (255-258)

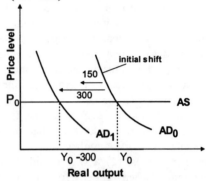

c. The spending multiplier is now 4, 1/(1-.75). Government spending must be decreased by $75 billion to reduce income by $300 billion. We calculate this by solving the following for change in government spending: change in government spending$\times 4$ = −300 billion. This is shown in the graph below. Notice that the initial shift in the AD curve is smaller than in (b). If (b) and (c) had been shown using the multiplier model, the *AE* curve in (c) would be steeper than the AD curve for (b). (255-258)

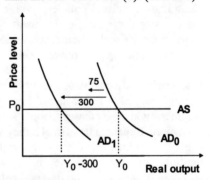

2. **a.** To close the recessionary gap, government expenditures need to rise by the full amount of the gap because the multiplier is 1. This is shown as a shifting from AD_0 to AD_1. In the short run, output rises by $1,000 and the price level remains constant. This is also a long-run equilibrium since short-run equilibrium output equals potential output. (255)

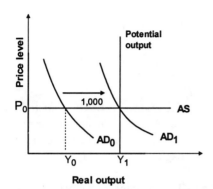

b. An increase in expenditures of $1,000 shifts the AD curve to the right by $1,000. In the short run, output rises by $1,000 and the price level remains constant. This time, however, short-run equilibrium output exceeds potential output. As long as output exceeds potential, wages will continue to rise, the AS curve will continue to shift up. In the long run, the AS curve will shift up to AS_1 and real output will decline by $500 to potential output. (255)

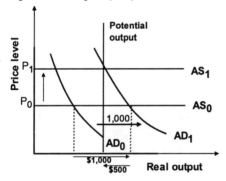

3. The spending multiplier is 2.5 ($1/(1-.4)$). (255-259)

   a. Assuming the economy is far below potential output the government must increase spending on goods and services by $100 billion to increase income by $250 billion. This is shown below as a rightward shift in the AD curve of $100 billion from AD_0 to AD_1. Income increases by a multiple of that amount, by $2.5 \times 100 = \$250$ billion. (255-259)

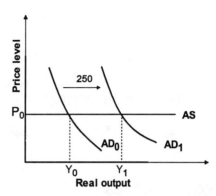

   b. Since interest rates have risen, investment declines and the AE curve shifts down, partially offsetting the initial increase in aggregate expenditures. The net effect of the spending increase is smaller than $250 billion. This is shown by a shift down in the AE curve from AE_1 to AE_2 resulting in income Y_2, lower than Y_1. (264)

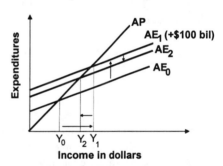

4. **a.** Increase spending by $1,200. According to Okun's Law, to decrease unemployment by 2 percent income must rise 4 percent, which in this case is $1,600. With an *mpc* of .4 and thus a multiplier of 1.67, the government needs to increase spending by $1,600/1.67 or $960 (266-267)

   b. Increase spending $500. According to Okun's Law to decrease unemployment by 2 percent income must rise 4 percent, which is $2,000. With an *mpc* of .75 and thus a multiplier of 4, the government needs to increase spending by $2,000/4 or $500. (266-267)

5. **a.** A 1 percent increase in the unemployment rate means a decrease in income of 2%, or, in 1999, $180 billion. The Chairman of the CEA believed potential income was $9 trillion while the Chairman of the Fed believed potential income was $8.820 trillion. (266-267)

b. The spending multiplier is $(1/(1-mpc)) = 2$. The Chairman of the CEA would suggest no change in spending since the economy is at potential while the Chairman of the Fed would suggest a decrease in spending of $180/2 = $90 billion. (266-267)

ANSWERS

A BRAIN TEASER

1. Although a number of important problems arise, which makes the actual practice of fiscal policy difficult, these problems don't mean that the model is wrong; they simply mean that for fiscal policy to work, the policy conclusions drawn from the model must be modified to reflect the real world problems. Unless, of course, you are a committed ("hard-core") Classical economist. (264-269)

ANSWERS

MULTIPLE CHOICE

1. c   Expansionary fiscal policy is the deliberate change in either government spending or taxes to stimulate the economy. Increasing government spending will increase expenditures and increase income. Changing the money supply is monetary policy, not fiscal policy. See page 252.

2. b   With fiscal policy, government provides the needed increased spending that increases individuals' incomes, inducing them to spend more. The multiplier takes over and income increases by more than the government stimulus. Individuals collectively do have the spending power to get an economy out of recession, but do not act collectively because individuals do not take into account the effect of their spending on aggregate income. See pages 253-254.

3. b   Aggregate demand management is government's attempt to control the aggregate level of spending in the economy. See page 253.

4. b   Expansionary fiscal policy increase aggregate expenditures which is shown by a shift up in the AE curve. See Figure 11-1. See page 255.

5. d   See Figure 11-1. Also remember from earlier chapters that an increase in imports is a decrease in autonomous expenditures. See page 255.

6. a   To determine how much to increase expenditures in the *multiplier model* to reach potential income, you divide the recessionary gap of 240 by the multiplier of 2. See pages 255-256.

7. a   To determine how much to increase expenditures in the AS/AD model when the AS curve is flat, divide the recessionary gap, 600, by the multiplier, 5. See pages 255-256.

8. b   To determine how much to increase expenditures in the Keynesian *multiplier model* to reach potential income, you divide the recessionary gap of 900 by the multiplier of 3. See pages 255-256.

9. d   Aggregate demand management policies do not affect AS, so a and b are out. With an inflationary gap you want to decrease output, so the answer is d. See Figure 11-2. See page 257.

10. a   Inflation results in higher input prices which shifts the AS curve up. See page 257.

11. d   As discussed on page 257, while earlier Keynesian economists supported fine tuning, modern Keynesian economists do not.

12. c   Increasing imports is contractionary. See pages 253-255.

13. b   Decreasing imports and increasing exports is expansionary. See pages 253-255.

14. b   During World War II, taxes rose, but spending rose even more so that the net result was expansionary. Although the economy exceeded potential, inflation was avoided by price controls. See page 262.

15. b   By changing the value of one's currency, government can affect the level of exports and imports and thus affect aggregate output. See page 261.

16. c   In the 1990s, the economy expanded beyond the potential forecasted by economists, but did not result in accelerating inflation.   The expansion was led by consumption and investment expenditures. See page 253.

17. a   Crowding out is the offsetting of a change in government expenditures by a change in private expenditures in the opposite direction. Answer c, if you could follow it, is nonsensical. See page 264.

18. a   Okun's law says that a 1 percentage point fall in the unemployment rate is associated with a 2 percent rise in income.   An economist who underpredicts potential output by 2 percent is overpredicting the target rate of unemployment rate by 1 percentage point. See pages 266-267.

19. d   Automatic stabilizers are welfare payments, unemployment insurance and taxes that raise income during recessions and lower income during expansions. See page 269.

ANSWERS

POTENTIAL ESSAY QUESTIONS

The following are annotated answers. They indicate the general idea behind the answer.

1.   Recall that a downturn in the business cycle is caused by a decline in aggregate expenditures (AE–or, total spending). So, government needs to stimulate AE. Therefore, it should use expansionary fiscal policy to combat a recession. Use contractionary fiscal policy to combat the inflation during the expansionary phase of the business cycle. Note that it is appropriate for government to run a deficit during a recession but to move in the direction of a surplus when the economy is expanding.

2.   When the economy is in a recession and total spending is too low then government spending automatically rises while tax collections automatically fall (the government automatically incurs a deficit). This helps to stimulate total spending and cushion the downturn in the economy. The opposite is true when the economy is expanding. Note that these changes take place while the income level falls and expands. Therefore, there are no time lag problems accompanying the automatic stabilizers.

3.   The crowding-out effect states that deficit spending financed by borrowing will increase interest rates and therefore crowd out private spending. Any "crowding out" associated with deficit spending renders fiscal policy less effective in stimulating total spending and therefore the economy during a recession. The Keynesians argue that the crowding out effect is relatively small. Committed Classicals argue that there is a total crowding out effect, which renders fiscal policy impotent in stimulating total spending. Some Classicals have argued that the effect of deficit spending may even be negative on the economy if private spending is more productive than government spending. The empirical evidence on the size of the crowding-out effect is mixed and has not resolved the debate. However, everyone agrees that the closer the economy comes to its potential income level, the greater is the crowding-out effect.

POLITICS, SURPLUSES, DEFICITS, AND DEBT

CHAPTER AT A GLANCE

This review is based upon the learning objectives that open the chapter.

1a. A surplus is an excess of revenues over payments. A deficit is a shortfall of revenues under payments. (Surpluses are negative deficits and vice versa.) (275)

Surpluses and deficits are flow concepts; all deficits must be financed.

1b. Surpluses and deficits are simply summary measures of the financial health of the economy. To understand that summary you must understand the methods that were used to calculate it. (276-277)

Different accounting procedures yield different figures for surpluses and deficits.

2. The real deficit is the nominal deficit adjusted for inflation.

Real deficit = Nominal deficit − (Inflation × Total debt.) (277)

Inflation wipes out debt. Inflation also causes the real deficit to be less than the nominal deficit. However, inflation means a higher percentage of the deficit (or spending) will be devoted to debt service (paying interest on the debt). Moreover, creditors who do not anticipate the inflation pay the cost of eliminating the debt through inflation.

3. A structural deficit or surplus is that part of a budget deficit or surplus that would exist even if the economy were at its potential level of income. A passive (also called cyclical) surplus or deficit is that part that exists because the economy is operating below or above its potential income. (278-279)

Passive (cyclical) deficits or surpluses are largely due to the automatic stabilizers.

4a. Debt is accumulated deficits minus accumulated surpluses. It is a <u>stock</u> concept. (279)

Debt is a summary measure of a country's financial situation.

GDP serves the same function for government as income does for an individual. The greater the GDP (income) the greater the ability to handle debt. However, government debt is different than an individual's debt. Government is ongoing; government can pay off the debt by printing money; and much of the government debt is internal—owed to its citizens.

4b. Since in a growing economy a continual deficit is consistent with a constant ratio of debt to GDP, and GDP serves as a measure of the government's ability to pay off the debt, a country can run a continual deficit. (283)

The more you earn the more debt you can handle.

5. Since World War II, until recently, the U.S. government ran almost continual deficits. Recently the government has begun running surpluses. (282-283)

But, we still have debt.

6. Because of accounting conventions the surpluses in the early 2000s are less of a surplus than meets the eye. Regardless of whether there is, or is not, a trust fund, real output must match real expenditures when the baby boomers retire. (289)

Always watch out for political spin when discussing the government budget.

● SHORT-ANSWER QUESTIONS

1. How much importance do most economists give to the budget deficit or surplus?

2. If the nominal interest rate is 6%, the inflation rate is 4%, the nominal deficit is $100 billion, and the debt of the country is $2 trillion, what is the real deficit?

3. If the nominal interest rate is 5%, the inflation rate is 5%, the real deficit is $100 billion, and the debt of the country is $1 trillion, what is the nominal deficit?

4. If the U.S. economy is below potential and the surplus is $40 billion, is the structural surplus greater or less than $40 billion?

5. In an expanding economy a government should run a continual deficit. True or false? Why?

6. If a politician presents you with a plan that will reduce the nominal budget deficit by $40 billion, but will not hurt anyone, how would you in your capacity as an economist likely respond?

7. President Clinton has claimed that the budget surplus came about because of his policies. How would you likely respond?

8. In what way is the trust fund not a real solution to the Social Security problem?

--- MATCHING THE TERMS ---

Match the terms to their definitions

____ 1. Budget Enforcement Act of 1990

____ 2. cash flow accounting system

____ 3. deficit

____ 4. external debt

____ 5. internal debt

____ 6. nominal deficit or surplus

____ 7. Passive deficit or surplus

____ 8. pay as you go system

____ 9. real deficit

____ 10. Social Security system

____ 11. structural deficit

____ 12. surplus

a. An accounting system entering expenses and revenues only when cash is received or paid out.

b. A partially unfunded pension system of the U.S.

c. A shortfall per year of incoming revenue under outgoing payments.

d. A federal law establishing a pay-as-you-go test for new spending and tax cuts, along with additional spending limits for government.

e. An excess of revenues over payments

f. Government debt owed to individuals in foreign countries.

g. Pension system in which pensions are paid from current revenues.

h. That portion of the surplus or deficit that results from fluctuations in the economy.

i. The deficit or surplus determined by looking at the difference between expenditures and receipts.

j. Government debt owed to its own citizens.

k. The deficit that would remain when the cyclical or passive elements have been netted out.

l. The nominal deficit adjusted for inflation's effect on the debt.

PROBLEMS AND APPLICATIONS

1. Calculate the debt and deficit in each of the following:

   a. Your income has been $30,000 per year for the last five years. Your expenditures, including interest payments, have been $35,000 per year for the last five years.

   b. Your income is $50,000 per year; $15,000 of your $65,000 expenditures are for the purchase of the rights to an invention.

   c. Your wage income is $20,000 per year. You have a bond valued at $100,000, which pays $10,000 per year. The market value of that bond rises to $110,000. Expenses are $35,000 per year. Use the opportunity cost approach in your calculations.

2. For each of the following calculate the real deficit:

   a. Inflation is 5%. Debt is $2 trillion. Nominal deficit is $100 billion.

   b. Inflation is -3%. Debt is $500 billion. Nominal deficit is $20 billion.

   c. Inflation is 10%. Debt is $3 trillion. Nominal deficit is $100 billion.

   d. Inflation is 8%. Debt is $20 billion. Nominal deficit is $5 billion.

3. Assume a country's nominal GDP is $7 trillion, government expenditures less debt service are $1.5 trillion, and revenue is $1.3 trillion. The nominal debt is $4.9 trillion. Inflation is 2% and real interest rates are 5%. Expected inflation is fully adjusted.

   a. Calculate debt service payments.

   b. Calculate the nominal deficit.

   c. Calculate the real deficit.

   d. Suppose inflation rose to 4%. Again, expected inflation is fully adjusted. Recalculate (a) - (c).

4. Potential income is $8 billion. The income in the economy is $7.2 billion. Revenues do not vary with income, but taxes do; they increase by 20% of the change in income. The current deficit is $400 million.

   a. What is the economy's structural deficit?

   b. What is the economy's passive deficit?

● A BRAIN TEASER

1. How could deficit spending actually reduce the debt burden of future generations?

● MULTIPLE CHOICE

Circle the one best answer for each of the following questions:

1. A deficit is:
   a. the total amount of money that a country owes.
   b. the shortfall of payments under revenues in a particular time period.
   c. the shortfall of revenues under payments in a particular time period.
   d. accumulated debt.

2. If the U.S. government raised the retirement age to 72 starting in 2010, the current budget deficit would be:
   a. reduced.
   b. increased.
   c. unaffected.
   d. eliminated.

3. The nominal deficit is $100 billion; inflation is 4 percent; total debt is $2 trillion. The real deficit is:
   a. zero.
   b. $20 billion.
   c. $80 billion.
   d. $100 billion.

4. If the nominal surplus is $200 billion, inflation is 10 percent, and total debt is $2 trillion,
   a. the real surplus is zero.
   b. the real deficit is $100 billion
   c. the real surplus is $400 billion.
   d. the real surplus is $2.2 trillion.

5. The real deficit is $100 billion; inflation is 4 percent; total debt is $2 trillion. The nominal deficit is
   a. zero.
   b. $120 billion.
   c. $180 billion.
   d. $200 billion.

6. If creditors are able to forecast inflation perfectly and there are no institutional constraints on interest rates,
   a. the government will not have to make interest payments.
   b. interest payments will rise by the amount that the real debt declines.
   c. the real deficit will equal the nominal deficit.
   d. the government will be unable to finance the debt.

7. Country A has a debt of $10 trillion. Country B has a debt of $5 trillion.
   a. Country A is in a better position than Country B.
   b. Country B is in a better position than Country A.
   c. One cannot say what relative position the countries are in.
   d. Countries A and B are in equal positions.

8. As a percentage of GDP, since World War II,
   a. debt in the United States has been rising.
   b. debt in the United States has been falling.
   c. debt in the United States has been sometimes rising and sometimes falling.
   d. the U.S. government has had no debt.

9. The portion of the budget deficit or surplus that would exist even if the economy were at its potential level of income is called the:
   a. structural deficit or surplus.
   b. passive deficit or surplus.
   c. primary deficit or surplus.
   d. secondary deficit or surplus.

10. If an economy is $100 billion below potential, the tax rate is 20 percent, and the deficit is $180 billion, the passive deficit is:
    a. $20 billion.
    b. $160 billion.
    c. $180 billion.
    d. $200 billion.

11. Government debt is different from individual debt because:
    a. government does not pay interest on its debt.
    b. government never really needs to pay back its debt.
    c. all government debt is owed to other government agencies or to its own citizens.
    d. the ability of a government to pay off is debt is unrelated to income.

12. If there is growth and a country with a debt of $1 trillion has decided it wants to keep its ratio of debt-to-GDP ratio constant:
    a. it should run a deficit.
    b. it should run a surplus.
    c. it should run a balanced budget.
    d. the deficit has no effect on debt.

13. Payroll taxes for social security:
    a. reduce the reported deficit and increase the reported surplus.
    b. increase the reported deficit and reduce the reported surplus.
    c. do not affect the budget since it is an off-budget item.
    d. are offset by future obligations in the budget.

14. The "real" problem of 2020 will be caused by:
    a. an unfunded Social Security Trust Fund.
    b. not enough people producing goods for the people wanting them.
    c. baby boomers having children, which creates what's called a boomlet.
    d. the rising number of workers as the population grows.

● POTENTIAL ESSAY QUESTIONS

You may also see essay questions similar to the "Problems & Applications" and "Brain Teasers" exercises.

1. What are three reasons why government debt is different from individual debt?

2. How can a growing economy reduce the concern over deficits and the debt?

ANSWERS

SHORT-ANSWER QUESTIONS

1. While there are differences of opinion, most economists are hesitant to attach too much importance to a deficit or a surplus. The reason why is that the deficit and surplus depends on the accounting procedures used, and these can vary widely. Only with much more additional information will an economist attribute importance to a surplus or deficit. It is financial health—by which is meant the ability to cover costs over the long term—of the economy that most economists are concerned with. (276-277)

2. To calculate the real deficit you multiply inflation times the total debt (4% $\times$ $2 trillion), giving $80 billion; then subtract that from the nominal deficit of $100 billion. So in this example the real deficit equals $20 billion. The interest rate does not enter into the calculations. (277-278)

3. To calculate the nominal deficit you multiply inflation times the total debt (5% $\times$ $1 trillion), giving $50 billion, and add that to the real deficit of $100 billion. So in this example the nominal deficit equals $150 billion. The interest rate does not enter into the calculation. (277-278)

4. Since the economy is below potential, the structural surplus is larger than the nominal surplus. (278-279)

5. It depends. In an expanding economy with no deficits the ratio of debt to GDP will be falling; if the government wants to hold the debt-to-GDP constant it will need to run a continual deficit. If it wants to reduce that ratio, then it need not run a continual deficit. (283-284)

6. TANSTAAFL. I would check to see what accounting gimmick the politician was proposing and what the plan would do to the long-run financial health of the country. (276)

7. The budget surplus came about because the U.S. economy grew at a much faster rate than economists had thought possible. It also came about because of the laws that made it harder to increase spending when there was a surplus. To the degree that he played a role in these he deserves credit, but none of his policy initiatives can be seen as the cause of the budget surplus. (286)

8. Ultimately, real expenditures must equal real output in each period. The trust fund provides a financial solution to the Social Security problem, but it does not directly see to it that real expenditures will equal real output in the future, and thus may "solve" the problem through inflation as recipients of the trust fund spend and workers at the time spend more than there are goods to go around. (290-291)

ANSWERS

MATCHING

1-d; 2-a; 3-c; 4-f; 5-j; 6-i; 7-h; 8-g; 9-l; 10-b; 11-k; 12-e.

ANSWERS

PROBLEMS AND APPLICATIONS

1. a. Deficit is $5,000 per year; Debt is $25,000. On page 275, deficit is defined as income less expenditures and debt is defined as accumulated deficits minus accumulated surpluses. For each of the past 5 years, you have incurred an annual deficit of $5,000. Total debt is $5,000 times five years, or $25,000. (275, 279)

    b. Deficit is $15,000; Debt is $15,000. Page 276 tells you that what is included as expenses is ambiguous. If you count the purchase of the rights to the invention as a current expenditure, the deficit is $15,000. If you had no previous debt, debt is also $15,000. If, however, you count the purchase of the invention as an investment and include it in your capital budget, then your expenses are only $50,000 and your current account will be in balance. (276, 279)

    c. Surplus of $5,000. Using an opportunity cost approach, a person holding bonds should count the rise in the bonds' market value as revenue. Here, wage income is $20,000 per year, interest income is

$10,000 and the bond's value has increased by $10,000. Total income is $40,000. Income of $40,000 less expenses of $35,000 per year yields a budget surplus of $5,000. (276)

2. As discussed on page 277, the real deficit is the nominal deficit adjusted for inflation's effect on the debt. The definition of real deficit states: Real deficit = Nominal deficit − (Inflation × Total debt).
    a. $0: $100 billion − .05 × $2 trillion. (277)
    b. $35 billion: $20 billion − (−.03) × $500. (277)
    c. Surplus of $200 billion: $100 billion − .10 × $3 trillion. (277)
    d. $3.4 billion: $5 billion − .08 × $20 billion. (277)

3. a. $343 billion: Debt service payment = nominal interest rate × nominal debt. The nominal interest rate when expected inflation is fully adjusted is the real interest rate plus inflation (5+2). Debt service payment = .07 × $4.9 trillion. (283-284)
    b. $543 billion deficit: The nominal deficit is revenues less government expenditures (including debt service), $1.3 trillion − ($1.5 trillion + $.343 trillion). (277-278)
    c. $445 billion deficit: The real deficit = Nominal deficit −(Inflation × Total debt) = $.543 trillion − .02 × $4.9 trillion). (277-278)
    d. Since bondholders must be compensated for the loss in the value of their bonds, they demand a nominal interest rate of 9% (5 + 4). Debt service payment is now $441 billion (.09 × $4.9 trillion). The nominal deficit is higher at $641 billion. ($1.3 trillion − ($1.5 trillion + $.441 trillion)). The real deficit has not changed. It is still $445 billion (The real deficit = Nominal deficit − (Inflation × Total debt) = $.641 trillion − (.04 × $4.9 trillion)). (277-278, 283-284)

4. a. If the economy were at potential, government would collect $160 million more in taxes, reducing the deficit by that amount. There would a structural deficit of $400 − $160 = $240 million. (278-279)
    b. The passive deficit is the deficit that occurs because the economy is below potential. The passive deficit is $800 million × 20 percent, or $160 million. (278-279)

━━━━ ANSWERS ━━━━

A BRAIN TEASER

1. If the deficit spending is used to increase the productivity of the nation, enabling the nation to experience much higher rates of economic growth, then the income of the nation could expand faster than its debt. If this happens, then the debt-to-GDP ratio gets smaller, the interest expense is less burdensome, and the debt will be easier to pay off. (282)

━━━━ ANSWERS ━━━━

MULTIPLE CHOICE

1. c   A country has a budget deficit if it does not collect sufficient revenue to cover expenditures during the year. See page 275.

2. c   The U.S. uses a cash flow accounting method, so changes affecting the future are not seen in the current budget. See page 276.

3. b   Real deficit = nominal deficit −(inflation ×total debt). See page 277.

4. c   Real surplus = nominal surplus + (inflation × total debt). See page 277.

5. c   Real deficit = nominal deficit −(inflation × total debt). See page 277.

6. b   If creditors can forecast inflation perfectly, the interest rate will rise when inflation rises and the subsequent increase in interest payments will match the decline in the real debt due to higher inflation. See pages 277-278.

7. c   Debt must be judged relative to assets and to total GDP. See page 280.

8. c   See Figure 12-2 on page 283.

9. a   The passive deficit or surplus is the deficit or surplus that exists because the economy is below potential. The structural deficit or surplus is the deficit or surplus that exists because the economy is at potential. The text doesn't define primary or secondary deficits or surpluses. See page 278.

10. a   The passive deficit is the deficit that exists because the economy is below potential. The government would collect $20 billion more in revenue if the economy were at potential, so the passive deficit is $20 billion. See page 278.

11. b   Because government goes on forever it doesn't ever need to pay back its debt. Only about 75 percent of government debt is owed to other government agencies or to its own citizens. The other government debt is owed to foreign individuals. Government is better able to pay off debt when income rises. Both government and individuals pay interest on debt. See pages 281-282.

12. a   Real growth will reduce the ratio of existing debt to GDP so to hold the ratio constant a continual deficit is necessary. See page 283-284.

13. a   While payroll taxes for social security represent future obligations by government to pay social security, they are counted as current revenue today and reduce the reported deficit (increase the reported surplus). See pages 287-288.

14. b   The trust fund is a financial solution to the obligation of government to provide social security payments. The real problem is the mismatch between real demand and real supply of goods as the baby boomers retire and the demand for goods and services by retirees outstrips the supply by workers in 2020. See pages 288-289.

POTENTIAL ESSAY QUESTIONS

The following are annotated answers. They indicate the general idea behind the answer.

1.   First, the government's life is unlimited and therefore it never has to settle its accounts. Second, it can pay off debt by creating money (which is not recommended however). Third, much of the government's debt is internally held and therefore, on average as a group, people are neither richer nor poorer because of the debt (even though it may redistribute income to upper-income individuals).

2.   When a society experiences real growth (growth adjusted for inflation), it becomes richer, and, being richer, it can handle more debt. Moreover, since in a growing economy a continual deficit is consistent with a constant ratio of debt to GDP, and GDP serves as a measure of the government's ability to pay off debt, a country can run a continual deficit. Deficits should be viewed relative to GDP to determine their importance.

Pretest
Chapters 6 - 12

Take this test in test conditions, giving yourself a limited amount of time to complete the questions. Ideally, check with your professor to see how much time he or she allows for an average multiple choice question and multiply this by 35. This is the time limit you should set for yourself for this pretest. If you do not know how much time your teacher would allow, we suggest 1 minute per question, or 35 minutes.

1. Inflation and unemployment are
    a. best studied in the long-run framework.
    b. best studied in the short-run framework.
    c. fall within both the short-and long-run frameworks.
    d. are not problems of today and therefore are not studied.

2. The secular trend growth rate in the United States is approximately
    a. 1 to 1.5 percent per year.
    b. 2.5 to 3.5 percent per year.
    c. 5 to 5.5 percent per year.
    d. 7 to 7.5 percent per year.

3. Keynesians
    a. generally favor activist government policies.
    b. generally favor laissez-faire policies.
    c. believe that frictional unemployment does not exist.
    d. believe that all unemployment is cyclical unemployment.

4. Using Okun's rule of thumb, if unemployment rises from 5 to 6 percent, one would expect total output of $5 trillion to
    a. rise by $5 billion.
    b. rise by $100 billion.
    c. fall by $100 billion.
    d. fall by $5 billion.

5. If the price level rises by 20 percent and real output remains constant, by how much will nominal output rise?
    a. 1 percent.
    b. 5 percent.
    c. 20 percent.
    d. 40 percent.

6. To move from GDP to GNP, one must:
    a. add net foreign factor income.
    b. subtract inflation.
    c. add depreciation.
    d. subtract depreciation.

7. There are two firms in an economy, Firm A and Firm B. Firm A produces 100 widgets and sells them for $2 apiece. Firm B produces 200 gadgets and sells them for $3 apiece. Firm A sells 30 of its widgets to Firm B and the remainder to consumers. Firm B sells 50 of its gadgets to Firm A and the remainder to consumers. What is GDP in this economy?
    a. $210.
    b. $590.
    c. $600.
    d. $800.

8. The largest component of expenditures in GDP is
    a. consumption.
    b. investment.
    c. net exports.
    d. government purchases of goods and services.

9. Gross investment differs from net investment by:
    a. net exports.
    b. net imports.
    c. depreciation.
    d. transfer payments.

10. If nominal GDP rises:
    a. welfare has definitely increased.
    b. welfare has definitely decreased.
    c. welfare may have increased or decreased.
    d. welfare most likely has increased.

11. If the growth rate is 6%, how many years will it take for output to double?
    a. 4.
    b. 8.
    c. 12.
    d. 16.

12. Suppose output grew at 4% in China and 2% in the United States.
    a. Per capita income grew faster in China
    b. Per capita income grew faster in the U.S.
    c. We cannot say in which country per capita income grew faster.
    d. Per capita output grew faster in China.

13. If there are increasing returns to scale:
    a. as inputs rise, outputs fall.
    b. as inputs rise, output rises by a smaller percentage.
    c. as inputs rise, output rises by a larger percentage.
    d. as one input rises, output rises by a larger percentage.

14. New growth theories are theories that emphasize:
    a. technology.
    b. human capital.
    c. physical capital.
    d. entrepreneurship.

15. Patents create:
    a. incentives to innovate and hence are a good thing.
    b. barriers to entry and hence are a bad thing.
    c. both barriers to entry and incentives to innovate and hence are both a bad and good thing.
    d. common knowledge and hence are a good thing.

16. In the AS/AD model,
    a. price of a good is on the horizontal axis.
    b. price level is on the horizontal axis.
    c. price of a good is on the vertical axis.
    d. price level is on the vertical axis.

17. If there is a rise in foreign income the AD curve will likely:
    a. shift in to the left.
    b. shift out to the right.
    c. become steeper.
    d. become flatter.

18. If productivity rises by 2% and wages rise by 6%, the AS curve will
    a. likely shift up.
    b. likely shift down.
    c. become flatter.
    d. become steeper.

19. The graph below demonstrates the expected short-run result if:

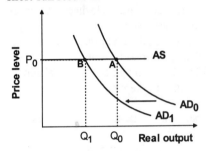

    a. productivity increases by less than wages
    b. the government increases the money supply
    c. a country's exchange rate appreciates (gains value).
    d. wages rise by less than the increase in productivity.

20. If the target rate of unemployment falls, potential income will:
    a. first decrease, then increase.
    b. increase.
    c. decrease.
    d. first increase, then decrease.

21. *Mpc* plus *mps* equals
    a. zero.
    b. one.
    c. ten.
    d. unknown (cannot be determined).

22. If the mpc is .8, what is the size of the multiplier in the multiplier model?
    a. .5.
    b. 5.
    c. 1.
    d. 10.

23. In the multiplier model, if autonomous expenditures are $5,000 and the *mpc* equals .9, what is the level of income in the economy?
    a. $5,000.
    b. $10,000.
    c. $20,000.
    d. $50,000.

24. In the multiplier model if autonomous exports fall by 40 and government spending increases by 20, and the *mpc* is .8, what happens to the income?
    a. Income rises by 300.
    b. Income falls by 300.
    c. Income rises by 100.
    d. Income falls by 100.

25. In the real business cycle theory, business cycles occur because of:
    a. changes in the real price level.
    b. changes in real income.
    c. technological and other natural shocks.
    d. changes in the money supply.

26. Expansionary fiscal policy involves
    a. increasing taxes.
    b. increasing the money supply.
    c. increasing government spending.
    d. changing the exchange rate.

27. In the graph below, actual income is below potential income. The government is planning to use expansionary fiscal policy. This will:

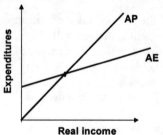

    a. shift the *AP* curve up.
    b. shift the *AE* curve up.
    c. shift the *AP* curve down.
    d. shift the *AE* curve down.

28. The economy has a fixed price level, an *mpc* of .66, and a recessionary gap of 900. Using the multiplier model, an economist would advise government to increase autonomous expenditures by about:
    a. 30.
    b. 300.
    c. 600.
    d. 2700.

$$1 - .66 = .34$$
$$\frac{1}{.34} = 2.94 = 306 -$$

29. Which of the following is true today?
    a. Keynesian economists support fine tuning.
    b. Classical economists support fine tuning.
    c. Both Keynesian and Classical economists generally support fine tuning.
    d. Both Keynesian and Classical economists generally oppose fine tuning.

30. Crowding out occurs when
    a. the government runs a deficit and sells bonds to finance that deficit.
    b. the government prints money.
    c. the government runs a surplus and sells bonds and the people who buy those bonds sell their older bonds to the government.
    d. the tendency for new workers to replace more expensive older workers is a factor.

31. The nominal deficit is $100 billion; inflation is 4 percent; total debt is $2 trillion. The real deficit is:
    a. zero.
    b. $20 billion.
    c. $80 billion.
    d. $100 billion.

32. If creditors are able to forecast inflation perfectly and there are no institutional constraints on interest rates,
    a. the government will not have to make interest payments.
    b. interest payments will rise by the amount that the real debt declines.
    c. the real deficit will equal the nominal deficit.
    d. the government will be unable to finance the debt.

33. If an economy is $100 billion below potential, the tax rate is 20 percent, and the deficit is $180 billion, the passive deficit is:
    a. $20 billion.
    b. $160 billion.
    c. $180 billion.
    d. $200 billion.

34. If there is growth and a country with a debt of $1 trillion has decided it wants to keep its ratio of debt-to-GDP ratio constant:
    a. it should run a deficit.
    b. it should run a surplus.
    c. it should run a balanced budget.
    d. the deficit has no effect on debt.

35. The "real" problem of 2020 will be caused by:
   a. an unfunded Social Security Trust Fund.
   b. not enough people producing goods for the people wanting them.
   c. baby boomers having children, which creates what's called a boomlet.
   d. the rising number of workers as the population grows.

ANSWERS

1.	c	(6:1)		**19.**	c	(9:17)
2.	b	(6:4)		**20.**	b	(9:7)
3.	a	(6:12)		**21.**	b	(10:4)
4.	c	(6:16)		**6.**	b	(10:5)
5.	c	(6:20)		**7.**	d	(10:10)
6.	a	(7:2)		**8.**	d	(10:14)
7.	b	(7:5)		**9.**	c	(10:21)
8.	a	(7:9)		**10.**	c	(11:1)
9.	c	(7:11)		**11.**	b	(11:4)
10.	c	(7:17)		**12.**	b	(11:8)
11.	c	(8:3)		**13.**	d	(11:11)
12.	c	(8:5)		**14.**	a	(11:17)
13.	c	(8:10)		**15.**	b	(12:3)
14.	a	(8:16)		**16.**	b	(12:6)
15.	c	(8:21)		**33.**	a	(12:10)
16.	d	(9:4)		**17.**	a	(12:12)
17.	b	(9:8)		**35.**	b	(12:14)
18.	a	(9:13)				

Key: The figures in parentheses refer to multiple choice question and chapter numbers. For example (1:2) is multiple choice question 2 from chapter 1.

MONEY, BANKING, AND THE FINANCIAL SECTOR

13

CHAPTER AT A GLANCE

This review is based upon the learning objectives that open the chapter.

1. The financial sector is central to almost all macroeconomic debates because behind every real transaction, there is a financial transaction that mirrors it. (296)

   If the interest rate does not perfectly translate saving (flows out of the spending stream) into investment (flows into the spending stream), then the economy will either expand or contract.

2. Money is a highly liquid, financial asset that is generally accepted in exchange for goods and services, is used as a reference in valuing other goods and can be stored as wealth. (298)

   Money is any financial asset that serves the functions of money.

3. The three functions of money are: (299)

   - Medium of exchange;
     As long as people are confident that the purchasing power of the dollar will remain relatively stable over time (by the Fed controlling the money supply) then people will continue to swap real goods, services, and resources for money and vice versa.

   - Unit of account; and
     Money acts as a measuring stick of the relative value (relative prices) of things. Therefore, the value of money itself must remain relatively stable over time.

   - Store of wealth.
     Money's usefulness as a store of wealth also depends upon how well it maintains its value. The key is for the Fed to keep the purchasing power of money (and therefore prices) relatively stable over time. Inflation can be a problem!

4a. M1 is the component of the money supply that consists of cash in the hands of the public plus checking accounts and traveler's checks. (301)

   M1 is the narrowest measure of the money supply. It is also the most liquid.

4b. M2 is the component of the money supply that consists of M1 plus savings deposits, small-denomination time deposits and money market mutual funds. (302)

   M2 is the measure of the money supply most used by the Fed to measure the money supply in circulation. This is because M2 is most closely correlated with the price level and economic activity.

   Anything which changes M2 changes the money supply!

4c. The broadest measure of the money supply is L (which stands for liquidity). It consists of almost all short-term financial assets. (302)

5. Banks "create" money because a bank's liabilities are defined as money. So when a bank incurs liabilities it creates money. (304)

   Banks "create" money (increase the money supply) whenever they make loans. Whenever a person borrows from a bank they are swapping a promissory note to repay the loan (which is really an IOU; and an individual's IOU is not money because it doesn't meet the criteria of serving the functions of money) in exchange for cash or funds put in his/her checking account. Cash and checking account balances are money! Therefore, the money supply increases. Also Note: When a loan is repaid, the money supply (M2) decreases.

6a. The money multiplier is the measure of the amount of money ultimately created by the banking system per dollar deposited. When people hold no cash it equals 1/r, where r is the reserve ratio. (304)

A single bank is limited in the amount of money it may create. The limit is equal to its excess reserves–the maximum amount of funds, which it can legally loan out. However, when considering an entire banking system, where any bank's loans, when spent, may end up being deposited back into that bank or another bank, then the entire banking system ends up being able to increase the money supply by a multiple of its initial excess reserves (the initial maximum amount of funds which can legally be loaned out) because of the money multiplier.

Simple money multiplier = 1/r.

(Initial change in money supply) × (money multiplier) = change in the money supply

6b. When people hold cash the approximate money multiplier is 1/ (r + c). (309)

Approximate real-world money multiplier = 1/ (r+c), where c is the ratio of money people hold in currency to the money held as deposits.

The approximate real-world money multiplier is less than the simple money multiplier because some of the funds loaned out are held as cash and therefore do not return to the banks as deposits.

7. Financial systems are based on trust that expectations will be fulfilled. Banks borrow short and lend long, which means that if people lose faith in banks, the banks cannot keep their promises. (310)

It is important to maintain the public's confidence in the banking system.
Government guarantees of financial institutions can have 2 effects:
- *They can prevent unwarranted fear that causes financial crises.*
- *They can also eliminate warranted fears and hence eliminate a market control of bank loans.*

See also, Appendix A: "A Closer Look at Financial Institutions and Financial Markets." Appendix B: "Creation of Money Using T-Accounts."

● SHORT-ANSWER QUESTIONS

1. At lunch you and your friends are arguing about the financial sector. One friend says that real fluctuations are measured by real economic activity in the goods market and therefore the financial sector has nothing to do with the business cycle. You know better and set him straight.

2. You are having another stimulating lunchtime conversation, this time about money. Your friend says "I know what money is; it's cash, the dollar bills I carry around." What is your response?

3. You continue the conversation and begin to discuss why we have money. Your friend states that the function of money is to buy things like the lunch he has just bought. Another friend says that because she has money she is able to compare the cost of two types of slacks. Still another offers that she holds money to make sure she can buy lunch next week. What is the function of money that each has described? Are there any others?

4. What are the two most liquid measures of money? What are the primary components of each?

5. What is the broadest measure of money? What does it consist of?

6. Your friends are curious about money. At another lunchtime discussion, they ask each other two questions: Is all the money deposited in the bank in the bank's vaults? Can banks create money? Since they are stumped, you answer the questions for them.

7. Using the simple money multiplier, what will happen to the money supply if the reserve ratio is 0.2 and high-powered money is increased by $100?

8. Using the equation for the approximate real-world money multiplier, what will happen to the money supply if the reserve ratio is 0.2, cash to deposit ratio is 0.3, and high-powered money is increased by $100?

9. How does the interest rate regulate the flow of saving into the flow of expenditures during normal times?

10. What would happen if everyone simultaneously lost trust in their banks and ran to withdraw their deposits?

11. What is the potential problem with government guarantees to prevent bank-withdrawal panics?

MATCHING THE TERMS
Match the terms to their definitions

___	1.	approximate real-world money multiplier	**a.** Broad definition of "money" that includes almost all short-term assets.
___	2.	asset management	**b.** Cash that a bank keeps on hand that is sufficient to manage the normal cash inflows and outflows.
___	3.	bond	
___	4.	excess reserves	**c.** Component of the money supply that consists of M_1 plus savings deposits, small-denomination time deposits, and money market mutual fund shares, along with some esoteric relatively liquid assets.
___	5.	Federal Reserve Bank (the Fed)	
___	6.	financial assets	
___	7.	interest rate	**d.** Component of the money supply that consists of cash in the hands of the public, checking account balances, and travelers' checks.
___	8.	L	
___	9.	liability management	**e.** Assets whose benefit to the owner depends on the issuer of the asset meeting certain obligations.
___	10.	M_1	
___	11.	M_2	**f.** How a bank attracts deposits and what it pays for them.
___	12.	money	**g.** How a bank handles its loans and other assets.
___	13.	reserve ratio	**h.** Measure of the amount of money ultimately created by the banking system, per dollar deposited, when cash holdings of individuals and firms are treated the same as reserves of banks. The mathematical expression is $1/(r+c)$.
___	14.	reserves	
___	15.	simple money multiplier	

i. Measure of the amount of money ultimately created by the banking system per dollar deposited, when people hold no cash. The mathematical expression is $1/r$.

j. Ratio of cash or deposits a bank holds at the central bank to deposits a bank keeps as a reserve against withdrawals of cash.

k. Reserves above what banks are required to hold.

l. The U.S. central bank. Its liabilities serve as cash in the United States.

m. A highly liquid financial asset that is generally accepted in exchange for other goods and is used as a reference in valuing other goods and as a store of wealth.

n. A promise to pay a certain amount of money plus interest in the future.

o. Price paid for the use of a financial asset.

● PROBLEMS AND APPLICATIONS

1. For each, state whether it is a component of M_1 or M_2, both, or neither:

   a. Money market mutual funds.

   b. Savings deposits.

   c. Travelers' checks.

   d. Stocks.

   e. Twenty-dollar bills.

2. Assuming individuals hold no cash, calculate the simple money multiplier for each of the following reserve requirements:

    a. 15% $\frac{15}{100} = \cdot 15 = \frac{1}{\cdot 15} = 6 \cdot 67 \cdot$

    b. 30% $\frac{30}{100} = 3 \cdot 3$

    c. 60% $\frac{60}{100} = 1 \cdot 67$

    d. 80% $\frac{80}{100} = 1 \cdot 25$

    e. 100% $\frac{100}{100} = 1$

3. Assuming individuals hold 10% of their deposits in the form of cash, recalculate the *approximate* real-world money multipliers from question 2.

    a. 15% $\frac{1}{\cdot 10 + \cdot 15} = \frac{1}{\cdot 25} = 4$

    b. 30% $\frac{1}{\cdot 30 + \cdot 10}$

    c. 60% $\frac{1}{\cdot 60 + \cdot 10}$

    d. 80% $= \frac{1}{\cdot 80 + \cdot 10}$

    e. 100% $= \frac{1}{\cdot 110} = \cdot 91 \cdot$

4. While Jon is walking to school one morning, a helicopter flying overhead drops $300. Not knowing how to return it, Jon keeps the money and deposits it in his bank. (No one in this economy holds cash.) If the bank keeps only 10 percent of its money in reserves and is fully loaned out, calculate the following:

    a. How much money can the bank now lend out?

        $= 300 \cdot 30 = 270$

b. After this initial transaction, by how much has the money in the economy changed?

c. What's the money multiplier?

d. How much money will eventually be created by the banking system from Jon's $300?

A1. For each, state whether a financial asset has been created. What gives each financial asset created its value?

    a. Your friend promises to pay you $5 tomorrow and expects nothing in return.

    b. You buy an apple at the grocery store.

    c. The government sells a new bond with a face value of $5,000, a coupon rate of 8%, and a maturity date of 2006.

    d. A firm issues stock.

    e. An existing stock is sold to another person on the stock market.

A2. For each of the following financial instruments, state for whom it is a liability and for whom it is an asset. Also state, if appropriate, whether the transaction occurred on the capital or money market and whether a financial asset was created.

    a. First Bank grants a mortgage to David.

    b. First Bank sells David's mortgage to Financial Services, Inc.

    c. Broker McGuill sells existing stocks to client Debreu.

    d. An investment broker sells 100 shares of new-issue stock to client Debreu.

    e. U.S. government sells a new three-month T-bill to Corporation X.

    f. Corporation X sells a 30-year government bond to Sally Quinn.

B1. Assume that Textland Bank Balance Sheet looks like this:

Assets		Liabilities	
Cash	30,000	Demand Deposits	150,000
Loans	300,000	Net Worth	350,000
Phys. Assets	170,000		
Total Assets	500,000	Total Liabilities and Net Worth	500,000

    a. If the bank is not holding any excess reserves, what is the reserve ratio?

    b. Show the first three steps in money creation using a balance sheet if Jane Foundit finds $20,000 in cash and deposits it at Textland.

Step #1

Step #2

Step #3

    c. After the first three steps, how much in excess reserves is the bank holding?

    d. Show Textland's balance sheet at the end of the money creation process.

● A BRAIN TEASER

1. Whenever new loans are made the money supply expands. Whenever loans are repaid the money supply decreases. During any given period of time new loans are being made and old loans are being repaid. On balance, what happens to the money supply depends upon the

magnitude of these conflicting forces. We also know that making loans is the principle source of profits to banks. Having said this, how can bankers' collective lending decisions (whether to give loans or not to give loans in order to maximize their profits, or to avoid losses) destabilize the business cycle–cause recessions to get worse and upturns to become more pronounced?

● MULTIPLE CHOICE

Circle the one best answer for each of the following questions:

1. For every financial asset
    a. there is a corresponding financial liability.
    b. there is a corresponding financial liability if the financial asset is financed.
    c. there is a real liability.
    d. there is a corresponding real asset.

2. Using economic terminology, when an individual buys a bond, that individual
    a. is investing.
    b. is saving.
    c. is buying a financial liability.
    d. is increasing that individual's equities.

3. Which of the following is not a function of money?
    a. Medium of exchange.
    b. Unit of account.
    c. Store of wealth.
    d. Equity instrument.

4. Which of the following is not included in the M_1 definition of money?
    a. checking accounts.
    b. currency.
    c. traveler's checks.
    d. savings accounts.

5. Which of the following components is not included in the M_2 definition of money?
    a. M_1.
    b. savings deposits.
    c. small-denomination time deposits.
    d. bonds.

6. In an advertisement for credit cards, the statement is made, "Think of a credit card as smart money." An economist's reaction to this would be
    a. a credit card is not money.
    b. a credit card is dumb money.
    c. a credit card is simply money.
    d. a credit card is actually better than money.

7. Using a credit card creates
    a. a financial liability for the holder and a financial asset for the issuer.
    b. a financial asset for the holder and a financial liability for the issuer.
    c. a financial liability for both the holder and issuer.
    d. a financial asset for both the holder and issuer.

8. Modern bankers
    a. focus on asset management.
    b. focus on liability management.
    c. focus equally on asset management and liability management.
    d. are unconcerned with asset and liability management and instead are concerned with how to make money.

9. Assuming individuals hold no cash, the reserve requirement is 20 percent, and banks keep no excess reserves, an increase in an initial $100 of money will cause an increase in total money of
    a. $20.
    b. $50.
    c. $100.
    d. $500.

10. Assuming individuals hold no cash, the reserve requirement is 10 percent, and banks keep no excess reserves, an increase in an initial $300 of money will cause an increase in total money of
    a. $30.
    b. $300.
    c. $3,000.
    d. $30,000.

11. Assuming the ratio of money people hold in cash to the money they hold in deposits is .3, and the reserve requirement is 20 percent, and that banks keep no excess reserves, an increase in an initial $100 of money will cause an increase in total money of _____. (Use the approximate real world money multiplier.)
    a. $50.
    b. $100.
    c. $200.
    d. $500.

12. If banks hold excess reserves whereas before they did not, the relative money multiplier
    a. will become larger.
    b. will become smaller.
    c. will be unaffected.
    d. might increase or might decrease.

13. A sound bank will
    a. always have money on hand to pay all depositors in full.
    b. never borrow short and lend long.
    c. never borrow long and lend short.
    d. keep enough money on hand to cover normal cash inflows and outflows.

14. FDIC is an acronym for
    a. major banks in the United States.
    b. major banks in the world.
    c. U.S. government program that guarantees deposits.
    d. types of financial instruments.

15. The textbook author's view of government guarantees of deposits is
    a. they don't make sense.
    b. stronger ones are needed.
    c. it depends.
    d. it should be a private guarantee program.

A1. A secondary financial market is a market in which
    a. minor stocks are sold.
    b. minor stocks and bonds are sold.
    c. previously issued financial assets can be bought and sold.
    d. small secondary mergers take place.

A2. If you are depositing money at a bank, the bank is likely
    a. an investment bank
    b. a commercial bank.
    c. a municipal bank.
    d. a government bank.

A3. Liquidity is
    a. a property of water stocks.
    b. the ability to turn an asset into cash quickly.
    c. the ability to turn an asset into liquid quickly.
    d. a property of over-the-counter markets.

A4. A financial market in which financial assets having a maturity of more than one year are bought and sold is called a
    a. money market.
    b. capital market.
    c. commercial paper market.
    d. commercial bank market.

B1. The demand deposits in a bank would go on
    a. the asset side of its balance sheet.
    b. the liabilities side of its balance sheet.
    c. the net worth part of its balance sheet.
    d. on both sides of its balance sheet.

B2. The cash that a bank holds would go on
    a. the asset side of its balance sheet.
    b. the liabilities side of its balance sheet.
    c. the net worth part of its balance sheet.
    d. on both sides of its balance sheet.

● POTENTIAL ESSAY QUESTIONS

You may also see essay questions similar to the "Problems & Applications" and "Brain Teasers" exercises.

1. Why is it important for the macroeconomy that the financial sector operate efficiently?

2. Why aren't credit cards money? What is the difference between money and credit?

3. What is the major benefit and problem of government guarantees associated with financial institutions?

━━━ ANSWERS ━━━

SHORT-ANSWER QUESTIONS

1. The financial sector is important to the business cycle because the financial sector channels the flow of savings out of the circular flow back into the circular flow either as consumer loans, business loans, or government loans. If the financial sector did not translate enough of the savings out of the spending stream back into the spending stream, output would decline and a recession might result. Likewise, if the financial sector increased flows into the spending stream (loans) that exceeded flows out of the spending stream (savings), an upturn or boom might result and inflation might rise. It is this role of the financial sector that Keynesians focused on to explain why production and expenditures might not be equal, resulting in fluctuations in output. (296-298).

2. In one sense your friend is right; cash is money. But money is more than just cash. Money is a highly liquid financial asset that is accepted in exchange for other goods and is used as a reference in valuing other goods. It includes such things as CDs and traveler's checks. (298-301)

3. The first friend has described money as a medium of exchange. The second has described money as a unit of account. And the third has described money as a store of wealth. These are the three functions of money. There are no others. (299-300)

4. The two most liquid measures of money are M_1 and M_2. M_1 consists of currency, checking accounts, and traveler's checks. M_2 consists of M_1 plus savings deposits, small-denomination time deposits, and money market mutual funds. (301-302)

5. The broadest measure of money is L. L consists of almost all short-term financial assets. (302-303)

6. No, banks do not hold all their deposits in their vaults. They keep a small percentage of it for normal withdrawal needs and lend the remainder out. Banks' maintenance of checking accounts is the essence of how banks create money. You count your deposits as money since you can write checks against them and the money that is lent out from bank deposits is counted as money. Aha! The bank has created money. (304-309)

7. The equation for the simple money multiplier is $(1/r)$ where r is the reserve ratio. Plugging in the values into the equation, we see that the money multiplier is 5, so the money supply increases by $500. (307)

8. The equation for the approximate real-world money multiplier is $1/(r+c)$ where r is the reserve ratio and c is the ratio of cash to deposits. Plugging the values into the equation, we see that the money multiplier is 2, so the money supply increases by $200. (309)

9. Just as price equilibrates quantity supplied and demanded in the real sector, interest rates equilibrate quantity supplied and demanded for saving. The supply of saving comes out of the spending stream. The financial sector transforms those savings back into the spending stream in the form of loans that are then used to purchase consumer or capital goods. (297-298)

10. If everyone lost their trust in banks, a financial panic could occur. The bank holds only a small portion of total deposits as reserves so that if everyone withdraws their money, the bank cannot meet its promises. (310-313)

11. The potential problem with government guarantees to prevent bank-withdrawal panics is that guarantees might lead to unsound lending and investment practices by banks. Also, depositors have less of a reason to monitor the practices of their banks. (311-312)

━━━ ANSWERS ━━━

MATCHING

1-h; 2-g; 3-n; 4-k; 5-l; 6-e; 7-o; 8-a; 9-f; 10-d; 11-c; 12-m; 13-j; 14-b; 15-i.

━━━━ ANSWERS ━━━━

PROBLEMS AND APPLICATIONS

1. **a.** M_2. (302)
   b. M_2. (302)
   c. Both. (302)
   d. Neither. (302)
   e. Both. (302)

2. **a.** 6.67. multiplier = $(1/.15)$. (307)
   b. 3.33. multiplier = $(1/.30)$. (307)
   c. 1.67. multiplier = $(1/.6)$. (307)
   d. 1.25. multiplier = $(1/.8)$. (307)
   e. 1. multiplier = $(1/1)$. (307)

3. **a.** $4 = 1/(.10+.15)$. (309)
   b. $2.5 = 1/(.1+.3)$. (309)
   c. $1.43 = 1/(.1+.6)$. (309)
   d. $1.11 = 1/(.1+.8)$. (309)
   e. 0.91. In reality a multiplier less than one would be highly unlikely. Recall that this is the approximate real-world multiplier. See page 309, especially footnote 4 for the precise money multiplier.

4. **a.** $270. (306-307)
   b. $570: the initial $300 in new deposits plus $.9 \times 300$ in loans that are then deposited. (306-307)
   c. 10: $1/r = 1/.1$. (306-307)
   d. $3,000: money multiplier×initial deposit = 10×300. (306-307)

A1. a. A financial asset has been created. Your friend's promise to pay you $5 is what gives that asset its value. (316)
   b. No, a financial asset has not been created, although a financial transaction did occur. (316)
   c. Yes, a financial asset has been created. The government's promises to pay you $5,000 at maturity and $400 each year until then are what give that asset its value. (316)
   d. Yes, a financial asset has been created. A claim to future profits is what gives that asset its value. (316)
   e. No, a financial asset has not been created. The financial asset sold already existed. (316)

A2. a. The mortgage is an asset for First Bank and a liability for David. The transaction occurred on the capital market. A financial asset was created. (316)
   b. The mortgage is an asset for Financial Services, Inc., and a liability for David. The transaction occurred on the capital market. A financial asset was not created. (316)
   c. The stocks are an asset for client Debreu and a liability for the broker's firm. The transaction occurred on the capital market. A financial asset was not created. (316)
   d. The stocks are an asset for client Debreu and a liability for the firm. The transaction occurred on the capital market. A financial asset was created. (316)
   e. The T-bill is a liability for the U.S. government and an asset for Corporation X. The transaction occurred on the money market. A financial asset was created. (316)
   f. The bond is a liability for the U.S. government and an asset for Sally Quinn. The transaction occurred on the capital market. A financial asset was not created. (316)

B1. a. .2: cash/deposits = 30,000/150,000. (325-327)
   b. Step 1: Increase of $20,000 in demand deposits and cash:

Assets		Liabilities	
Cash	30,000	Demand Deposits	150,000
Cash from Jane	20,000	Jane's deposit	20,000
Total cash	50,000	Total deposits	170,000
Loans	300,000	Net Worth	350,000
Phys. Assets	170,000		
Total Assets	520,000	Total Liabilities and net worth	520,000

Step 2: Assuming the reserve ratio is .2 as calculated in (a), the bank can now lend out 80% of the $20,000 received in cash. It lends $16,000 to another person, Sherry: (325-327)

Assets		Liabilities	
Cash	50,000	Demand Deposits 170,000	
Cash to Sherry	16,000		
Total cash	34,000		
Begin. Loans	300,000	Net Worth	50,000
Loan to Sherry	16,000		
Total loans	316,000		
Phys. Assets	170,000		
Total Assets	520,000	Total Liabilities 520,000 and net worth	

Step 3: Sherry uses the loan to purchase a car from John. John deposits the cash in the bank (325-327):

Assets		Liabilities	
Cash	34,000	Demand Deposits 70,000	
Cash from John	16,000	Deposit from John 16,000	
Total cash	50,000	Total Deposits	186,000
Begin. Loans	316,000	Net Worth	350,000
Phys. Assets	170,000		
Total Assets	536,000	Total Liabilities 536,000 and net worth	

    c. The bank is holding $12,800 in excess reserves. Required reserves for $186,000 in deposits is $.2 \times 186,000 = \$37,200$. The bank has $50,000 in reserves, $12,800 higher than required. (325-327)

    d. The ending balance sheet will look like this (325-327):

Assets		Liabilities	
Cash	50,000	Demand Deposits 250,000	
Loans	380,000	Net Worth	350,000
Phys. Assets	170,000		
Total Assets	600,000	Total Liabilities 600,000 and net worth	

━━━ ANSWERS ━━━

A BRAIN TEASER

1. An uncontrolled private banking system (where government is not involved in trying to control the money supply) is destabilizing to the business cycle. Why? Because during reces-sions, bankers are reluctant to grant loans due to the greater probability of default on loans (bankers are simply wishing to avoid losses). Fewer loans made during a recession coupled with the concurrent repayment of old loans (most likely given during the previous upturn in the economy) means that, on balance, the money supply decreases. Less money means less spending. Less spending means the recession gets worse–unemployment rises further and the economy grows even more slowly. Conversely, during an economic expansion, banks make more loans than old loans are being repaid (bankers are happy to make loans when there is a low probability of default–after all, workers are not likely to lose their jobs and businesses' markets and profits are expanding). Therefore, the money supply expands and total spending increases–people spend their loans. The economy expands even more. (304-311)

━━━ ANSWERS ━━━

MULTIPLE CHOICE

1. **a** The very fact that it is a financial asset means that it had a financial liability, so the qualifier in b is unnecessary. See page 296.

2. **b** In economic terminology, buying a financial asset, which is what buying a bond is, is a form of saving. Investing occurs when a firm or an individual buys a real asset. See pages 296-298.

3. **d** Money is not a type of stock so it is not an equity instrument. See page 298.

4. **d** See page 301 and Figure 13-2 on page 303.

5. **d** See page 302 and Figure 13-2 on page 303.

6. **a** A credit card is not money and thus *a* would be the best answer. A credit card replaces money, making the same amount of money able to handle many more transactions. See page 303.

7. **a** One is borrowing money when one uses a credit card, thereby incurring a financial liability. See page 303.

8. c   As discussed on page 304, banks are concerned with both asset management and liability management. The second part of answer d is obviously true, but it's through management of assets and liabilities that they make money, so the first part is wrong.

9. d   The simple money multiplier is $1/r=1/.2=5$, which gives an increase in total money of $500. See page 307.

10. c   The simple money multiplier is $1/r=1/.1=10$ which gives an increase of total money of $3,000. See pages 307-309.

11. c   The approximate real-world money multiplier is $1/(r+c)=1/.5=2$, which gives an increase in total money of $200. See page 309.

12. b   Holding excess reserves would be the equivalent to increasing the reserve requirement, which would decrease the multiplier. See page 309.

13. d   Banks earn income by managing their assets and liabilities. To follow any policy other than d would cost them income. See pages 309-310.

14. c. FDIC stands for Federal Deposit Insurance Corporation. See page 311.

15. c   For this textbook author, just about everything depends; you can't get him to take a firm position on anything. See pages 311-312.

A1. c   See page 319.

A2. b   Investment banks don't take deposits, and who knows what the last two types of banks are; we certainly don't. See pages 316-317.

A3. b   Answers a and c are total gifts to you — water stocks; give us a break — and it's unclear what d means. The b option is the definition given on page 320.

A4. b   See page 321.

B1. b   Demand deposits at banks are liabilities for those banks and hence go on the liability side. See page 326.

B2. a   The cash that banks hold is an asset for them; hence it goes on the asset side. See page 326.

─────────── ANSWERS ───────────

POTENTIAL ESSAY QUESTIONS

The following are annotated answers. They indicate the general idea behind the answer.

1. Recall that for every real transaction there is a financial transaction that mirrors it. The financial sector's role is to ensure the smooth flow of savings out of the spending stream back into the economy. Whenever the financial sector is not operating efficiently then it is quite possible that the flow of savings out of the spending stream could be greater than the amount of money going through the financial sector and back into the economy. If this happens, we will experience a recession. The opposite would create inflationary (demand-pull inflation) problems.

2. Money is a financial asset of individuals and a financial liability of banks. Credit card balances cannot be money since they are assets of a bank and a liability of the nonbanking public. In a sense, credit card balances are the opposite of money. Credit is savings made available to be borrowed. Credit is not an asset for the holder of the card. However, ready availability of credit through the use of credit cards does reduce the amount of money people need or wish to hold.

3. The benefit is that they prevent unwarranted fears that causes financial crises. People are less likely to create a run on a bank when they know they will be able to get all of their money back even if the bank fails. The problem is that these guarantees can eliminate warranted fears. A bank manager may be more reckless when depositors are less concerned about the financial well-being of the bank.

MONETARY POLICY AND T
ABOUT MACRO POLI

CHAPTER AT A GLANCE

This review is based upon the learning objectives that open the chapter.

1a. Monetary policy is a policy that influences the economy through changes in the money supply and available credit. (328)

Monetary policy is undertaken by the Fed. Expansionary (contractionary) monetary policy shifts the AD curve to the right (left). The effect on real income depends upon the range of the AS curve the economy is operating in.

1b. The Fed is a semiautonomous organization composed of 12 regional banks. It is run by the Board of Governors. (330)

The Fed (Federal Reserve Bank) is in charge of monetary policy (changing the money supply, credit availability, and interest rates).

1c. Congress gave the Fed six explicit duties. The most important is conducting monetary policy. (332)

6 Functions of the Fed:

1. *Conducting monetary policy (influencing the supply of money and credit in the economy).*
2. *Supervising and regulating financial institutions.*
3. *Serving as a lender of last resort to financial institutions.*
4. *Providing banking services to the U.S. government.*
5. *Issuing coin and currency.*
6. *Providing financial services (such as check clearing) to commercial banks, savings and loan associations, savings banks, and credit unions.*

2. The three tools of monetary policy are: (334)

1. Changing the reserve requirement;
   This is the least-used tool. It is a potentially very powerful tool (could be a case of overkill) because it changes (1) banks' excess reserves and (2) the money multiplier.

2. Changing the discount rate; and
   The discount rate is the interest rate the Fed charges banks for loans. It is the least powerful tool.
   Banks don't usually like to borrow from the Fed any more than we do from our parents.

3. Executing open market operations.
   Open market operations are the Fed's buying and selling of U.S. government securities. This is the most frequently used and most important tool to change the money supply.

   If the economy is in a recession, the Fed should increase the money supply (pursue an expansionary monetary policy) by doing any one or more of the following:
   - *Decrease the reserve requirement.*
   - *Decrease the discount rate.*
   - *Buy government securities.*

3. The Federal funds rate is the interest rate banks charge one another for overnight bank reserve loans. The Fed determines whether monetary policy is loose or tight depending upon what's happening to the Fed funds rate. The Fed funds rate is an important intermediate target. (339)

The Fed targets a range for the Fed funds rate. If the Fed funds rate goes above (below) that target range, it buys (sells) bonds. These are "defensive" actions by the Fed.

4. The Taylor rule states: (340)
For every percentage point inflation is above (below) the Fed's inflation target, the Fed funds rate will rise (fall) by 1.5 percentage points;

For every percentage point the economy's total output is above (below) its potential output, the Fed funds rate will rise (fall) by half a percentage point.

This rule described Fed policy in the late 1990s.

5. In the AS/AD model, monetary policy works as follows: (341)

Contractionary monetary policy shifts the AD curve to the left:
$M\downarrow \Rightarrow i\uparrow \Rightarrow I\downarrow \Rightarrow Y\downarrow$

Used during an upturn in the economy to close an inflationary gap.

Expansionary monetary policy shifts the AD curve to the right:
$M\uparrow \Rightarrow i\downarrow \Rightarrow I\uparrow \Rightarrow Y\uparrow$

Used during a downturn in the economy to close a recessionary gap.

To increase the money supply (M2), the Fed must first increase banks' excess reserves and therefore bank loans.

6. Five problems of monetary policy: (343)

● Knowing what policy to use.
Need to know the potential income level first.

● Understanding what policy you're using.
Fed only indirectly controls M.

● Lags in monetary policy.
It takes time to work.

● Political pressure.
Fed is not totally insulated from political pressures.

● Conflicting international goals.
We live in a global economy. The desired domestic policy may adversely affect the exchange rate value of the dollar and our trade balance.

See also, Appendix A: "The Effect of Monetary Policy Using T-Accounts."

● SHORT-ANSWER QUESTIONS

1. You have been asked to speak to the first-year Congresspeople. Your talk is about the Fed. They want to know what monetary policy is. You tell them.

2. To clarify your answer to question 1 you tell them when the Fed was created and what its specific duties are.

3. Another Congressperson asks what monetary policy actions the Fed can take. You answer.

4. You are asked to elaborate on your answer to question 3. Now that you have listed each of the tools of monetary policy, how does each work?

5. One Congressperson realizes that the Fed does not have complete control over the money supply. She states that people could demand more cash, which will reduce the money supply. How does the Fed know whether its buying and selling of bonds is having the desired effect? You answer by explaining the Fed's intermediate target.

6. Another Congressperson asks whether there are any rules that they could use to predict what the Fed will do to the Fed's intermediate target. You explain the rule that has described Fed policy in the 1990s.

7. Another Congressperson asks how monetary policy can keep the economy from overheating. You reply from the perspective of the AS/AD model.

8. Suppose the economy is below potential output. Now how can monetary policy boost output? You reply again from the perspective of the AS/AD model.

9. You take one final question at the conference and it is a difficult one: "It doesn't seem that the Fed is doing a good job. I read in the paper that the Fed has followed too contractionary a policy and has caused a recession or that it is not even sure what policy it is following." How do you respond to those concerns?

MATCHING THE TERMS
Match the terms to their definitions

___ 1. central bank

___ 2. contractionary monetary policy

___ 3. discount rate

___ 4. expansionary monetary policy

___ 5. Federal Open Market Committee (FOMC)

___ 6. Federal funds rate

___ 7. monetary base

___ 8. monetary regime

___ 9. nominal interest rate

___ 10. open market operations

___ 11. real interest rate

___ 12. reserve requirement

___ 13. Taylor rule

a. Interest rate you actually see and pay.

b. Interest rate adjusted for expected inflation.

c. Rate of interest the Fed charges on loans it makes to banks.

d. The Fed's day-to-day buying and selling of government securities.

e. The percentage the Federal Reserve System sets as the minimum amount of reserves a bank must have.

f. A banker's bank; it conducts monetary policy and supervises the financial system.

g. Currency in circulation, vault cash plus reserves that banks have at the Fed.

h. Monetary policy aimed at raising the money supply and raising the level of aggregate demand.

i. Monetary policy aimed at reducing the money supply and reducing the level of aggregate demand.

j. The Fed's chief policy making body.

k. The interest rate banks charge one another for Fed funds.

l. For every percentage point inflation is above (below) the Fed's inflation target, the Fed funds rate will rise (fall) by 1.5 percentage points; for every percentage point the economy's total output is above (below) its potential output, the Fed funds rate will rise (fall) by ½ percentage point.

m. A predetermined statement of the policy that will be followed in various situations.

● PROBLEMS AND APPLICATIONS

1. The Fed wants to change the reserve requirement in order to change the money supply (which is currently $3,000). For each situation below, calculate the current reserve requirement and the amount by which the Fed must change the reserve requirement to achieve the desired change in the money supply. Assume no cash holdings.

    a. Money multiplier is 3 and the Fed wants to increase money supply by $300.

    b. Money multiplier is 2.5 and the Fed wants to increase the money supply by $300.

    c. Money multiplier is 4 and the Fed wants to decrease the money supply by $500.

    d. Money multiplier is 4 and the Fed wants to increase the money supply by $1,000.

2. How do your answers change for 1 (a) - (d) if instead of changing the reserve requirement, the Fed wants to use an open market operation to change the money supply? Assume the reserve requirement remains unchanged. What should the Fed do to achieve the desired change? (The multiplier and desired change in money supply for each are listed.)

   a. Money multiplier is 3 and the Fed wants to increase money supply by $300.

   b. Money multiplier is 2.5 and the Fed wants to increase the money supply by $300.

   c. Money multiplier is 4 and the Fed wants to decrease the money supply by $500.

   d. Money multiplier is 4 and the Fed wants to increase the money supply by $1000.

3. Instead of changing the reserve requirement or using open market operations, the Fed wants to change the discount rate to achieve the desired change in the money supply. Assume that for each 1 percentage-point fall in the discount rate, banks borrow an additional $20. How do your answers change to questions 1 (a) - (d)? (The multiplier and desired change in money supply for each are listed below.)

   a. Money multiplier is 3 and the Fed wants to increase money supply by $300.

   b. Money multiplier is 2.5 and the Fed wants to increase the money supply by $300.

   c. Money multiplier is 4 and the Fed wants to decrease the money supply by $500.

   d. Money multiplier is 4 and the Fed wants to increase the money supply by $1,000.

4. Using the Taylor rule, what do you predict will happen to the Fed funds rate in the following situations?

   a. Inflation is at the Fed's target, but output is 1 percent below potential.

   b. Output is at potential, but inflation is 2 percentage points above the Fed's target.

   c. Inflation is 1 percentage point above the Fed's target and output is 1 percent above potential.

   d. Inflation is 2 percentage points above the Fed's target and output is 2 percent below potential.

5. Fill in the blanks in the following table:

	Inflation rate	Nominal Interest rate	Real Interest rate
a.	5%	10%	____
b.	____	15%	7%
c.	-3%	____	9%
d.	4%	____	10%

6. Suppose the Fed decides to pursue an expansionary monetary policy. The money supply is currently $1 billion. Assume people hold no cash, the reserve requirement is 10 percent, and there are no excess reserves.

   a. By how much must the Fed change the reserve requirement to increase the money supply by $100 million?

   b. What would the Fed do to increase the money supply by $100,000 through open market operations?

7. The money supply is currently $1 billion. Assume people hold 25 percent of their money in the form of cash balances, the reserve requirement is 25 percent, and there are no excess reserves.

   a. By how much must the Fed change the reserve requirement to increase the money supply by $200 million?

   b. What would the Fed do to increase the money supply by $200 million through open market operations?

A1. Suppose the money multiplier is 2.5 and there are no cash holdings. Textland Bank is the only bank in the country. The Fed wants to decrease the money supply by $10,000. The initial balance sheet is shown below.

Initial Balance Sheet

Assets		Liabilities	
Cash	20,000	Demand Deposits	50,000
Loans	120,000	Net Worth	100,000
Phys. Assets	10,000		
Total Assets	150,000	Total Liabilities and net worth	150,000

   a. What open market operations must the Fed execute to reduce the money supply by $10,000?

   b. Using T-accounts show the first two steps of the effects of the Fed open market operation reducing the money supply by $10,000.

   Step #1

Assets	Liabilities

   Step #2

Assets	Liabilities

   c. Show the final balance sheet for Textland bank.

   Final Position

Assets	Liabilities

A2. Using T-accounts, show the effect of a decrease in the reserve ratio from .2 to .1 given the following initial position of Textland. Again, Textland is the only bank, no one holds cash, and there are no excess reserves. Show the first two steps and then the final position.

Initial Position

Assets		Liabilities	
Cash	40,000	Demand Deposits	200,000
Loans	230,000	Net Worth	100,000
Phys. Assets	30,000		
Total Assets	300,000	Total Liabilities and net worth	300,000

Step #1

Assets	Liabilities

Step #2

Assets	Liabilities

Final Position

Assets	Liabilities

A BRAIN TEASER

1. Assume the economy is currently experiencing a recessionary gap of $1000. Also assume that the income multiplier is 4, the reserve ratio is 0.1, the ratio of people's cash-to-deposits is 0.4. Investment changes by $100 for every 1% change in the interest rate. The interest rate changes by 1% for every $50 change in the money supply. Generally, what should the Fed do with its three monetary policy tools? By how much would the Fed have to change banks' excess reserves if it wished to close the recessionary gap? (Assume all excess reserves are loaned out.)

MULTIPLE CHOICE

Circle the one best answer for each of the following questions:

1. The central bank of the United States is
   a. the Treasury.
   b. the Fed.
   c. the Bank of the United States.
   d. Old Lady of Threadneedle Street.

2. Monetary policy is
   a. a variation of fiscal policy.
   b. undertaken by the Treasury.
   c. undertaken by the Fed.
   d. the regulation of monetary institutions.

3. There are seven Governors of the Federal Reserve, who are appointed for terms of
   a. 5 years.
   b. 10 years.
   c. 14 years.
   d. 17 years.

4. Explicit functions of the Fed include all the following *except*
   a. conducting monetary policy.
   b. conducting fiscal policy.
   c. providing banking services to the U.S. government.
   d. serving as a lender of last resort to financial institutions.

5. FOMC stands for
   a. Federal Open Money Committee.
   b. Federal Open Market Committee.
   c. Fixed Open Market Commitments.
   d. Federation of Open Monies Committee.

6. Tools of monetary policy include all the following *except*
   a. changing the reserve requirement.
   b. changing the discount rate.
   c. executing open market operations.
   d. running deficits.

7. If expansionary monetary policy increases real income by 4 percent and nominal income by 6 percent, the price level will rise by:
   a. 2 percent.
   b. 4 percent.
   c. 6 percent.
   d. 10 percent.

8. Assuming $c = .2$ and $r = .1$, the approximate real-world money multiplier would be
   a. 1.33.
   b. 2.33.
   c. 3.33.
   d. 4.33.

9. The discount rate refers to
   a. the lower price large institutions pay for government bonds.
   b. the rate of interest the Fed charges for loans to banks.
   c. the rate of interest the Fed charges for loans to individuals.
   d. the rate of interest the Fed charges for loans to government.

10. The primary tool of monetary policy is
    a. open market operations.
    b. changing the discount rate.
    c. changing the reserve requirement.
    d. imposing credit controls.

11. If the Fed wants to increase the money supply, it should:
    a. buy bonds.
    b. sell bonds.
    c. pass a law that interest rates rise.
    d. pass a law that interest rates fall.

12. When the Fed sells bonds, the money supply
    a. expands.
    b. contracts.
    c. Selling bonds does not have any effect on the money supply.
    d. sometimes rises and sometimes falls.

13. An open market purchase
    a. raises bond prices and reduces interest rates.
    b. raises both bond prices and interest rates.
    c. reduces bond prices and raises interest rates.
    d. reduces both bond prices and interest rates.

14. The Federal funds rate is the interest rate
    a. the government charges banks for Fed funds.
    b. the Fed charges banks for Fed funds.
    c. the banks charge individual investors for Fed funds.
    d. the banks charge each other for Fed funds.

15. Assuming the Fed is following the Taylor Rule, if inflation exceeds the target inflation by 1 percent and output is 1 percent above potential, what would you predict would happen to the Fed funds rate?
    a. It will rise by 1 percent
    b. It will rise by 2 percent
    c. It will fall by 2.5 percent
    d. It will fall by 3 percent

16. In the short run if the Fed undertakes expansionary monetary policy the effect will be to
    a. shift the AD curve out to the right.
    b. shift the AD curve in to the left.
    c. shift the AS curve up.
    d. shift the AS curve down.

17. In the short run if the Fed undertakes contractionary monetary policy the effect will be to
    a. shift the AD curve out to the right.
    b. shift the AD curve in to the left.
    c. shift the AS curve up.
    d. shift the AS curve down.

18. Which of the following is the path through which contractionary monetary policy works?
    a. Money down implies interest up implies investment down implies income down.
    b. Money down implies interest down implies investment down implies income down.
    c. Money down implies interest up implies investment up implies income down.
    d. Money down implies interest down implies investment up implies income down.

19. A monetary regime is preferred to a monetary policy because:
    a. a monetary policy is too closely related to fiscal policy.
    b. a monetary regime takes into account feedback effects.
    c. a monetary policy takes into account feedback effects.
    d. One is not preferred to the other; the two a essentially the same thing.

20. Expected inflation is 4 percent; nominal interest rates are 7 percent; the real interest rate is
    a. 1 percent.
    b. 2 percent.
    c. 3 percent.
    d. 7 percent.

21. The real interest rate is 3 percent; the nominal interest rate is 7 percent. It is likely that one could deduce an expected inflation rate of
    a. 1%.
    b. 2%.
    c. 3%.
    d. 4%.

22. The Fed most directly controls
    a. M_1.
    b. M_2.
    c. the monetary base.
    d. the amount of credit in the economy.

2. What are some general problems associated with the implementation of monetary policy?

3. Why do economists keep an eye on the Fed funds rate in determining the state of monetary policy?

4. How does open market operations affect interest rates through the bond market?

● POTENTIAL ESSAY QUESTIONS

You may also see essay questions similar to the "Problems & Applications" and "Brain Teasers" exercises.

1. According to the AS/AD model, what is considered to be appropriate monetary policy over the course of the business cycle? What is the cause-effect chain relationship through which a change in the money supply will effect the level of economic activity? How would this cause-effect relationship be reflected graphically?

━━━━ ANSWERS ━━━━

SHORT-ANSWER QUESTIONS

1. Monetary policy is a policy that influences the economy through changes in the money supply and available credit. The Fed conducts U.S. monetary policy. (328)

2. The Fed was created in 1913. Its six explicit duties are (1) conducting monetary policy, (2) regulating financial institutions, (3) serving as a lender of last resort, (4) providing banking services to the U.S. government, (5) issuing coin and currency, and (6) providing financial services to financial institutions. (330-333)

3. The three tools of monetary policy at the disposal of the Fed are (1) changing the reserve requirement, (2) changing the discount rate, and (3) executing open market operations (buying and selling bonds). (334)

4. Changing the reserve requirement changes the amount of reserves the banks must hold and thus changes the amount of loans they can make. This changes the money supply. Changing the discount rate changes the willingness of banks to borrow from the Fed to meet reserve requirements, thus changing the amount of loans they are willing to make. This changes the money supply. Open market operations change the reserves banks hold by directly increasing or decreasing cash held by banks and simulta- neously decreasing or increasing their holdings of government bonds. This changes the amount of loans banks can make and changes the money supply. (334-337)

5. Economists and policymakers keep a close eye on the Fed funds rate, the rate banks charge one another for loans of reserves, as an intermediate target to determine the effect of an open market operation—whether it indeed was expansionary or contractionary. An expansionary action will lower the Fed funds rate and contractionary action will raise the Fed funds rate. In effect, the Fed chooses a range for the Fed funds rate and buys and sells bonds to keep the Fed funds rate within that range. If the Fed funds rate is below (above) the target, the Fed sells (buys) bonds. (339)

6. The Taylor rule described Fed policy in the late 1990s relatively well. It states: For every percentage point inflation is above (below) the Fed's inflation target, the Fed funds rate will rise (fall) by 1.5 percentage points; for every percentage point the economy's total output is above (below) its potential output, the Fed funds rate will rise (fall) by half a percentage point.

7. The Fed should decrease the money supply by increasing the reserve requirement, increasing the discount rate, or selling U.S. government bonds. This contractionary monetary policy in the AS/AD model increases interest rates, lowers investment. This shifts the AD curve to the left and reduces income. (340)

8. The Fed should increase the money supply by decreasing the reserve requirement, decreasing the discount rate, or buying U.S. government bonds. This expansionary monetary policy in the AS/AD model decreases interest rates, raises investment. This shifts the AD curve to the right and increases income. (340)

9. You tell the Congressperson that conducting monetary policy is difficult. Five problems often encountered in conducting monetary policy are: (1) Knowing what potential income is. No one has the magic number. It must be estimated. (2) Knowing whether the policy you are using is contractionary or expansionary. The Fed does not directly control the money supply. (3) There are significant lags in the effect of monetary policy in the economy. (4) The Fed is subject to political pressure. And (5) often domestic goals differ from international goals when deciding which policy to follow. (343-345)

━━━━ ANSWERS ━━━━

MATCHING

1-f; 2-i; 3-c; 4-h; 5-j; 6-k; 7-g; 8-m; 9-a; 10-d; 11-b; 12-e; 13-l.

ANSWERS

PROBLEMS AND APPLICATIONS

1. **a.** Current $r = 1/3$; New $r = .3$, so it must be reduced by .03. To find the reserve requirement solve $1/r = 3$ for r. $r = 1/3$. These calculations are based on the formula $M = (1/r) \times MB$, where M is the money supply, r is the reserve ratio, and MB is the monetary base (here it equals reserves). We first find out the cash (monetary base) that supports $3,000 money supply with a money multiplier of 3. It is $1,000. We want the money supply to be $3,300. So the multiplier we want is $3,300/1,000 = 3.3$. Again solving $1/r = 3.3$ we find r must be 0.3. (334)

    b. To find the reserve requirement solve $1/r = 5/2$ for r. $r = .4$. Cash must be $1,200 to support money supply of $3,000. The Fed must reduce the reserve requirement to .3636 to increase the money supply by $300. Use the method described in (a) to find the answer. (334)

    c. To find the reserve requirement solve $1/r = 4$ for r. $r = .25$. Cash must be $750 to support money supply of $3,000. The Fed must increase the reserve requirement to .3 to decrease the money supply by $500. Use the method described in (a) to find the answer. (334)

    d. To find the reserve requirement solve $1/r = 4$ for r. $r = .25$. Cash must be $750 to support money supply of $3,000. The Fed must reduce the reserve requirement to .1875 to increase the money supply by $1,000. Use the method described in (a) to find the answer. (334)

2. These calculations are based on the formula $M = (1/r) \times MB$, where M is the money supply, r is the reserve ratio, and MB is the monetary base (here it equals reserves).

    a. The Fed should buy bonds to increase reserves in the system by $100. We find this by dividing the desired increase in the money supply by the money multiplier. (337-338)

    b. The Fed should buy bonds to increase reserves in the system by $120. We find this by dividing the desired increase in the money supply by the money multiplier. (337-338)

    c. The Fed should sell bonds to decrease reserves in the system by $125. We find this by dividing the desired decrease in the money supply by the money multiplier. (337-338)

    d. The Fed should buy bonds to increase reserves in the system by $250. We find this by dividing the desired increase in the money supply by the money multiplier. (337-338)

3. These calculations are based on the formula $M = (1/r) \times MB$, where M is the money supply, r is the reserve ratio, and MB is the monetary base (here it equals reserves). Find out how much reserves must be changed and divide by 20 to find how much the discount rate must be lowered (if reserves are to be raised) or increased (if reserves are to lowered).

    a. To increase reserves in the system by $100, the discount rate should be reduced by 5 points. We find how much reserves must be increased by dividing the desired increase in the money supply by the money multiplier. We find how much the discount rate must be lowered by dividing the desired increase in reserves by 20 (the amount reserves will increase with each percentage point decline in the discount rate). (336-337)

    b. To increase reserves in the system by $120, the discount rate should be reduced by 6 points. See introduction to answer number 3 for how to calculate this. (336-337)

    c. To decrease reserves in the system by $125, the discount rate should be increased by 6.25 points. See introduction to answer number 3 for how to calculate this. (336-337)

    d. To increase reserves in the system by $250, the discount rate should be reduced by 12.5 points. See introduction to answer number 3 for how to calculate this. (336-337)

4. **a.** Since output is 1 percent below potential, the Fed will be expected to reduce the Fed funds rate by ½ percentage point. (339-340)

    b. Since inflation is 2 percentage points above target, the Fed will be expected to raise the Fed funds rate by 3 percentage points. (339-340)

    c. Since inflation is 1 percentage point above its target, the Fed will be expected to raise the Fed funds rate by 1.5 percentage points. In addition, since output is 1 percent above potential, it is expected to raise the Fed funds rate an additional ½ percentage point for a total increase of 2 percentage points. (339-340)

d. Since inflation is 2 percentage points above its target, the Fed will be expected to raise the Fed funds rate by 3.0 percentage points. However, there is an offsetting factor—output is 2 percent below potential. Thus, the Fed will in the end raise the Fed funds rate by only 2 percentage points. (339-340)

5.

	Inflation rate	Nominal Interest rate	Real Interest rate
a.	5%	10%	5% :

Real rate = nominal - inflation. (342)

b.	8%	15%	7%:

Inflation = nominal - real rate. (342)

c.	-3%	6%	9%:

Nominal = inflation + real. (342)

d.	4%	14%	10%:

Nominal = inflation + real. (342)

6. These calculations are based on the formula $M = (1/r) \times MB$, where M is the money supply, r is the reserve ratio, and MB is the monetary base (here it equals reserves).

a. The money multiplier is $1/r = 10$. Reserves must be $100 million to support a money supply of $1 billion. The reserve ratio to support $1.1 billion money supply with $100 million reserves is about 9.1%. We find this by dividing reserves by the desired money supply. (335-339)

b. The Fed would have to buy $10,000 worth of bonds to increase the money supply by $100,000. Calculate this by dividing the desired increase in the money supply by the money multiplier. (335-339)

7. In this case, the approximate real-world money multiplier is $1/(r + c) = 1/(.25+.33) = 1.72$. The cash-to-deposit ratio is .33 since people hold 25% of their money in cash and the remainder, 75%, in deposits.

a. The reserve requirement must be lowered to about 15%. We find this by first calculating the monetary base: $1 billion / 1.72 = $580 million (Money supply/multiplier). For the money supply to increase to $1.2 billion, the money multiplier must be $1.2/.580 = 2.07. To find the new reserve ratio solve $1/(r+c) = 2.07$ for r. We find that $r = .15$. (335-339)

b. The Fed must buy $116,280,000 in bonds to increase the money supply by $200 million Calculate this by dividing the desired increase in the money supply by the money multiplier: $200 million / 1.72. (335-339)

A1. This calculations are based on the formula $M = (1/r) \times MB$, where M is the money supply, r is the reserve ratio, and MB is the monetary base (here it equals reserves).

a. The Fed must sell bonds worth $4,000 to reduce reserves by $4,000. We calculate this by dividing the desired reduction in the money supply by the money multiplier. (348-349)

b. Step 1: An individual or group of individuals buy $4,000 in Treasury bonds from the Fed. Individuals withdraw the funds from the bank. (348-349)

Assets		**Liabilities**	
Cash	20,000	Demand Deposits	50,000
Payment to individuals	(4,000)	Withdrawals	(4,000)
Total cash	16,000	Total demand deposits	46,000
Loans	120,000	Net Worth	100,000
Phys. Assets	10,000		
Total Assets	146,000	Total Liabilities and net worth	146,000

Step 2: Reserves are now too low to meet the reserve requirement of .4. (We calculated the reserve requirement by solving the equation $1/r = 2.5$ for r.) The bank must call in $2,400 in loans (46,0003.4 - 16,000). This shows up as loans repaid. But the individuals repaying the loans must get the money from somewhere. Since no one holds cash and Textland bank is the only bank, the individuals must withdraw the $2,400 from the bank. This is shown as a withdrawal on the liability side and a payment to individuals on the asset side. Again reserves are too low, this time by $1,440. (348-349)

Assets		Liabilities	
Cash	16,000	Demand Deposits	46,000
Loans repaid	$2,400	Withdrawals	(2,400)
Payment to inds.	(2,400)	Total demand deposits	43,600
Total Cash	16,000		
Loans	120,000	Net Worth	100,000
loans called in	(2,400)		
Loans	117,600		
Phys. Assets	10,000		
Total Assets	143,600	Total Liabilities and net worth	143,600

c. Final balance sheet: Banks continue to call in loans to meet reserve requirements until the multiplier process is finished. The money supply is now $10,000 less. At last, the balance sheet is as shown: (348-349)

Assets		Liabilities	
Cash	16,000	Demand Deposits	40,000
Loans	114,000	Net Worth	100,000
Phys. Assets	10,000		
Total Assets	140,000	Total Liabilities and net worth	140,000

A2. Step 1: The bank makes $20,000 in new loans. This money is spent and then deposited into Textland by other individuals. (348-349)

Assets		Liabilities	
Cash	40,000	Demand Deposits	200,000
Payments out	(20,000)	New deposits	20,000
Payments in	20,000	Total deposits	220,000
Total cash	40,000		
Loans	230,000	Net Worth	100,000
New loans	20,000		
Total loans	250,000		
Phys. Assets	30,000		
Total Assets	320,000	Total Liabilities and net worth	320,000

Step 2: Textland still has excess reserves (40,000/220,000 > .1) by $18,000 so it makes $18,000 in new loans. Calculate excess reserves by reserves - total deposits×reserve ratio. (348-349)

Assets		Liabilities	
Cash	40,000	Demand Deposits	220,000
Payments out	(18,000)	New deposits	18,000
Payments in	18,000	Total deposits	238,000
Total cash	40,000		
Loans	250,000	Net Worth	100,000
New loans	18,000		
Total loans	268,000		
Phys. Assets	30,000		
Total Assets	338,000	Total Liabilities and net worth	338,000

Final position: The previous steps continue until the money creation process ends as shown below. (348-349).

Assets		Liabilities	
Cash	40,000	Demand Deposits	400,000
Loans	430,000	Net Worth	100,000
Phys. Assets	30,000		
Total Assets	500,000	Total Liabilities and net worth	500,000

ANSWERS

A BRAIN TEASER

1. The Fed should undertake expansionary monetary policy: 1) Buy government securities on the open market, 2) decrease the discount rate, and/or 3) decrease required reserves. It should do any one or more of these things to increase banks' excess reserves by $75. This is because to close a recessionary gap of $1,000 when the income multiplier is 4 will require an increase in aggregate expenditures of $250. To accomplish this, investment spending will have to increase by $250. This will require the interest rate to decrease by 2.5%. That will require an increase in the money supply of $150. When the money multiplier equals 2, or $[1/(.1 + .4)]$, excess reserves will only have to increase by $75. (334-338)

ANSWERS

MULTIPLE CHOICE

1. b   See pages 330.

2. c   The correct answer is "policy undertaken by the Fed." The last answer, d, involves regulation, which is also done by the Fed, but such regulation generally does not go under the name "monetary policy." Given the accuracy of answer c, answer d should be avoided. See pages 328, 330-334.

3. c   See page 330.

4. b   Fiscal policy is definitely not a function of the Fed. See pages 332-333.

5. b   See the text, Figure 14-2, page 331, and page 334.

6. d   Deficits are a tool of fiscal policy. See page 334.

7. a   The price level rise is the difference between the change in nominal income (6 percent) and real income (4 percent). 6-4=2 percent. See page 329.

8. c   The approximate real-world money multiplier is $1/(r + c) = 1/.3 = 3.33$. See page 335.

9. b.   The Fed makes loans only to other banks, and the discount rate is the rate of interest the Fed charges for these loans. See page 336.

10. a   See pages 337-338.

11. a   The last two answers, c and d, cannot be right, because the Fed does not pass laws. When the Fed buys bonds, it lowers the interest rate but it does not lower interest rates by law. Therefore, only a is correct. See pages 337-338.

12. b   People pay the Fed for those bonds with money—Fed IOUs—so the money supply in private hands is reduced. See page 337.

13. a   As the Fed buys bonds this increases their demand and their prices rise. Since bond prices and interest rates are inversely related, interest rates will fall. See pages 337-338.

14. d   See page 339.

15. b   The Taylor rule states that for every percentage point inflation is above the Fed's inflation target, the Fed funds will rise by 1.5 percent and for every percentage point the economy's total output is above potential, the Fed funds rate will rise by a half a percentage point. Thus, the inflation will cause a 1.5 percent increase in the Fed funds rate and the output exceeding potential will cause the Fed funds rate to increase by .5 percent, making a total increase of 2 percent. See pages 339-340.

16. a   Expansionary monetary policy reduces interest rates as a result of which investment increases. Hence, AD shifts out to the right by a multiple of the increase in investment. See pages 340-341.

17. b   Contractionary monetary policy increases interest rates which reduces investment, a component of aggregate expenditures. The AD curve shifts to the left by a multiple of the decline in investment. See pages 340-341.

18. a   Contractionary monetary policy increases interest rates which decreases investment, thereby decreasing income by a multiple of that amount. See pages 340-341.

19. b   Monetary regimes are predetermined rules of what the Fed will do in certain situations; they take feedback effects into account; a regime presets monetary policy. See page 343.

20. c   To determine real interest rate, you subtract expected inflation from nominal interest rates. 7−4=3. See page 342.

21. d   To determine expected inflation you subtract real interest rates from nominal interest rates. 7−3=4. See page 342.

22. c   The monetary base is the cash in circulation, vault cash and the reserves

banks have at the Fed. It is the one variable the Fed can directly control. See page 344.

ANSWERS

POTENTIAL ESSAY QUESTIONS

The following are annotated answers. They indicate the general idea behind the answer.

1. Use expansionary monetary policy (Fed reduces reserve requirements, reduces the discount rate, or buys government securities.) during a recession; use contractionary policy during an upturn in the business cycle. Expansionary monetary policy will increase the money supply (rightward shift of the supply of money curve), which will reduce the interest rate and increase investment spending (movement down along the investment demand curve). This shifts the AD curve out to the right by a multiple of the initial increase in investment spending and brings about a multiple increase in the income level. (See Figure 14-4, page 340.) Contractionary monetary policy is just the opposite.

2. See the list and the discussion that begins on page 343 of the text.

3. When the Fed funds rate is above its targeted range many banks have shortages of reserves and therefore money must be tight (credit is tight); and vice versa. The Fed will buy (sell) bonds when the Fed funds rate is above (below) its target and monetary policy is too tight (loose).

4. If the Fed buys (sells) bonds this increases the demand for (supply of) bonds and thereby increases (decreases) their price. As the price of bonds goes up (down), the interest rate goes down (up). Hence, the Fed buying (selling) bonds decreases (increases) interest rates.

INFLATION AND ITS RELATIONSHIP TO UNEMPLOYMENT AND GROWTH

● CHAPTER AT A GLANCE

This review is based upon the learning objectives that open the chapter.

1. Inflation redistributes income to those who can raise their prices or wages from those who cannot raise their prices or wages. (351)

   For example, if inflation is unexpected income is redistributed from:

   - *workers to firms if workers have fixed wage contracts but firms raise their prices.*
   - *lenders to borrowers since the real interest rate declines when the nominal interest rate is fixed.*

   On average the winners and losers in an inflation balance out; inflation does not make a nation richer or poorer.

2. Three ways expectations of inflation are formed are: (352)

   1. *Rational expectations* ⇒ *expectations that the economists' model predicts.*

   2. *Adaptive expectations* ⇒ *expectations based in some way on the past.*

   3. *Extrapolative expectations* ⇒ *expectations that a trend will continue.*

   Expectations can change the way an economy operates. Expectations play a key role in policy.

   Policymakers use the following equation to determine whether inflation may be coming:

   Inflation = Nominal wage increase – productivity growth.

3. The quantity theory of money basically states that inflation is directly related to the rise in the money supply. It is based upon the equation of exchange: $MV = PQ$. (353)

   Three assumptions made in the quantity theory of money:

   1. *Velocity (V) is constant.*
   2. *Real output (Q) is independent of the money supply (M).*
   3. *Causation goes from money (M) to prices (P). That is, an increase (decrease) in M causes an increase (decrease) in P.*
   Note: The price level rises because the money supply rises.

   In the 1990s, the close relationship between money and inflation broke down. Economists debate whether this is temporary or permanent. For large inflations, the connection between money and inflation is still evident.

4. The institutional theory believes that institutional and structural aspects of inflation, as well as increases in the money supply, are important causes of inflation. It sees the causation in the equation of exchange going from right to left. That is, changes in price level result in changes in the money supply. (358)

   Firms find it easier to raise wages, profits and rents to keep the peace with employees and other owners of the factors of production. To pay for those increases, firms raise prices. Government then raises the money supply to make sure there is sufficient demand to buy the goods at the higher price.

   The "insider" versus "outsider" situation creates imperfect markets. Imperfect markets provide an opportunity for "insiders" to increase their wages and prices even when unemployment and excess capacity exists in the overall economy, thereby creating inflation.

In a nutshell: According to the quantity theory, $MV \Rightarrow PQ$

According to the institutionalist theory, $PQ \Rightarrow MV$

5a. The long-run Phillips curve is vertical; it takes into account the feedback of inflation on expectations of inflation. (363)
In the long run when expectations of inflation are met, changes in the rates of inflation have no effect on the level of unemployment. This is shown as LR in the accompanying graph.

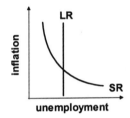

5b. The short-run Phillips curve is downward sloping. Expectations of inflation are constant along the short-run Phillips curve. (363)

The short-run Phillips curve reflects the empirically observed trade-off between inflation and unemployment. It is shown as SR in the graph above. Expectations of inflation are constant along the short-run (SR) Phillips curve. Increases (decreases) in inflationary expectations shift the short-run Phillips curve to the right (left).

In the long run we have more time to adjust our expectations to actual inflation. In the short run we may be fooled—we may expect less (more) inflation than actually occurs when inflation is accelerating (decelerating).

6. Quantity theorists believe that inflation undermines long-run growth. Institutionalists are less sure of a negative relationship between inflation and growth. (367)

According to the quantity theory, the best policy is policy that leads to price stability.

Institutionalists believe that low unemployment is an important goal that must be balanced with the risk of inflation.

● SHORT-ANSWER QUESTIONS

1. Your study partner states that inflation is bad because it makes a nation poorer. How do you respond?

2. What are three ways people form expectations of future inflation?

3. If there is a high inflation, most economists are willing to accept that a rough approximation of the quantity theory holds true. Why?

4. What is the quantity theory of money and how does it relate to long-run growth?

5. How does the institutionalist theory of inflation differ from the quantity theory of inflation?

6. Who is more likely to favor a monetary rule: economists who support the quantity theory or the institutional theory of inflation? Why?

7. Which of the two curves in the graph below is a short-run Phillips curve, and why

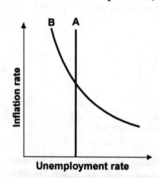

8. Would an economist who supports the quantity theory or one who supports the institutionalist theory of inflation be more likely to see a long-run trade-off between inflation and unemployment? Why?

9. Why would an institutionalist be more likely to support the introduction of an incomes policy than a quantity theorist would be?

MATCHING THE TERMS
Match the terms to their definitions

____ 1. adaptive expectations
____ 2. extrapolative expecta-
       tions
____ 3. incomes policy
____ 4. inflation tax
____ 5. insider/outsider model
____ 6. long-run Phillips curve
____ 7. quantity theory of money
____ 8. rational expectations
____ 9. short-run Phillips curve
____ 10. stagflation
____ 11. velocity of money

a. Expectations based in some way on the past.
b. An institutionalist story of inflation where insiders bid up wages and outsiders are unemployed.
c. A policy placing direct pressure on individuals to hold down their nominal wages and prices.
d. A curve showing the trade-off between inflation and unemployment when expectations of inflation are constant.
e. A curve showing the trade-off (or complete lack thereof) between inflation and unemployment when expectations of inflation equal actual inflation.
f. The price level varies in response to changes in the quantity of money.
g. Combination of high and accelerating inflation and high unemployment.
h. Expectations that a trend will continue.
i. The number of times per year, on average, a dollar goes around to generate a dollar's worth of income.
j. Expectations that the economists' model predicts.
k. An implicit tax on the holders of cash and the holders of any obligations specified in nominal terms.

● PROBLEMS AND APPLICATIONS

1. a. What are the three assumptions that translate the equation of exchange into the quantity theory of money?

    b. State the equation of exchange and show how the three assumptions lead to the conclusion that inflation is always and everywhere a monetary phenomenon.

2. With the equation of exchange, answer the following questions:

    a. GDP is $2,000, the money supply is 200. What is the velocity of money?

    b. The velocity of money is 5.60, the money supply is $1,100 billion. What is nominal output?

    c. Assuming velocity is constant and the money supply increases by 6%, by how much does nominal output rise?

3. Suppose the economy is operating at potential output. Inflation is 3% and expected inflation is 3%. Unemployment is 5.5%.
   a. Draw a long-run Phillips curve and a short-run Phillips curve consistent with these conditions.

   b. The government implements an expansionary monetary policy. As a result, unemployment falls to 4.5% and inflation rises to 6%. Expectations do not adjust. Show where the economy is on the graph you drew for 3(a). What happens to the short-run Phillips curve? Inflation? Unemployment?

   c. Expectations now fully adjust. Show this on the graph drawn for 3(a). What happens to the short-run Phillips curve?

4. Redraw the long-run Phillips curve and a short-run Phillips curve consistent with the conditions of the economy described in question #3 above and explain the effect of the following on inflation and unemployment using the curves you have drawn.

   a. The government implements a contractionary monetary policy. As a result, unemployment rises to 6.5% and inflation falls to 0%. Expectations do not adjust.

b. Expectations now fully adjust.

5. For each of the following points that represents the economy on the Phillips curve, make a prediction for unemployment and inflation.

   a.

   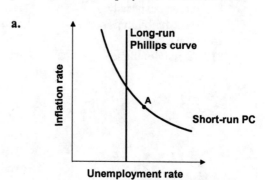

   b.

   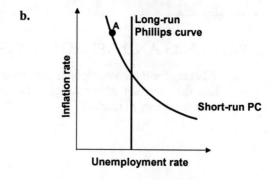

   c.

   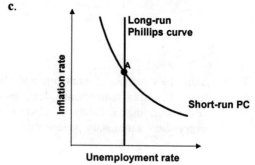

6. Suppose inflation is 12% and unemployment is 5.5% and the natural rate of unemployment is 5.5%. The president believes inflation and unemployment are both too high.

    a. Assume you are a quantity theorist. What policy would you recommend to improve the situation?

    b. Show the short-run effect of this policy on unemployment and inflation using the Phillips curve analysis. Will the president be satisfied? What is your response?

    c. Show the long-run effect of this policy on unemployment and inflation using the Phillips curve analysis. Will the president be satisfied? What is your response? (In that response, discuss the issue of long-run growth).

● A BRAIN TEASER

1. Why do countries increase the money supply enormously even though they know that doing so will lead to high inflation?

● MULTIPLE CHOICE

Circle the one best answer for each of the following questions:

1. In an expected inflation lenders will generally:
    a. gain relative to borrowers
    b. lose relative to borrowers
    c. neither gain nor lose relative to borrowers
    d. The effect will be totally random.

2. In an unexpected inflation lenders will generally
    a. gain relative to borrowers.
    b. lose relative to borrowers.
    c. neither gain nor lose relative to borrowers.
    d. The effect will be totally random.

3. According to the text if individuals base their expectations on the past we say that their expectations are:
    a. rational.
    b. historical.
    c. adaptive.
    d. extrapolative.

4. If productivity growth is 2 percent and inflation is 5 percent, on average nominal wage increases will be:
    a. 2 percent.
    b. 3 percent.
    c. 5 percent.
    d. 7 percent.

5. Assuming velocity is relatively constant and real income is relatively stable, an increase in the money supply of 40 percent will bring about an approximate change in the price level of:
    a. 4 percent.
    b. 40 percent.
    c. 80 percent.
    d. zero percent.

6. According to the quantity theory.
    a. unemployment is everywhere and always a monetary phenomenon.
    b. inflation is everywhere and always a monetary phenomenon.
    c. the equation of exchange does not hold true.
    d. real output is everywhere and always a monetary phenomenon.

7.   The quantity theory is most applicable to:
     a. U.S. type economies.
     b. West European type economies.
     c. developing economies.
     d. Japanese type economies.

8.   The inflation tax is
     a. a tax placed by government on inflators.
     b. a tax placed by god on inflators.
     c. a tax on the holders of cash.
     d. a tax on holders of goods whose price is inflating.

9.   Which central bank(s) have a strict monetary rule against inflation?
     a. The U.S. and the European central banks.
     b. The European and Russian central banks.
     c. The U.S. and New Zealand central banks.
     d. The European and New Zealand central banks.

10. Individuals who hold an institutional theory of inflation argue:
     a. the equation of exchange is incorrect.
     b. the equation of exchange should be read from right to left.
     c. the equation of exchange should be read from left to right.
     d. both the quantity theory and the equation of exchange are incorrect.

11. If an economist focuses on social pressures in his or her discussion of inflation, that economists is likely:
     a. a quantity theory advocate.
     b. an Institutionalist theory of inflation advocate.
     c. an insider theory of inflation advocate.
     d. an outsider theory of inflation advocate.

12. An individual has said that she favors an incomes policy. She
     a. is likely an institutional theory of inflation advocate.
     b. is likely a quantity theory of inflation advocate economist.
     c. could be either a quantity theory or institutionalist theory advocate.
     d. is not an economist, because no economist could ever support an incomes policy.

13. The Phillips curve represents a relationship between
     a. inflation and unemployment.
     b. inflation and real income.
     c. money supply and interest rates.
     d. money supply and unemployment.

14. The short-run Phillips curve shifts around because of changes in:
     a. the money supply.
     b. expectations of employment.
     c. expectations of inflation.
     d. expectations of real income.

15. The slope of the long-run Phillips curve is thought by many economists to be:
     a. horizontal.
     b. vertical.
     c. downward sloping.
     d. backward bending.

16. If the economy is at point A in the Phillips curve graph below, what prediction would you make for inflation?

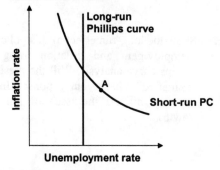

     a. It will increase.
     b. It will decrease.
     c. It will remain constant.
     d. It will explode.

17. If the economy is at Point A in the Phillips curve graph below, what prediction would you make for inflation?

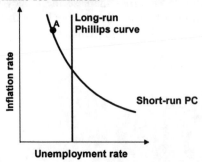

a. It will increase
b. It will decrease.
c. It will remain constant.
d. It will immediately fall to zero.

18. Stagflation is
    a. a combination of low and decelerating inflation and low unemployment.
    b. a combination of low and decelerating inflation and high unemployment.
    c. a combination of high and accelerating inflation and low unemployment.
    d. a combination of high and accelerating inflation and high unemployment.

19. Economists explain the "New Economy" in the last half of the 1990s as:
    a. an example of the stagflation.
    b. an example of the movement from the long run the short run Phillips curve.
    c. an example of the movement from the short run the long run Phillips curve.
    d. a case when productivity grew much faster than expected, negating the standard Phillips curve story.

20. Advocates of the quantity theory are likely to see a tradeoff between inflation and:
    a. unemployment.
    b. distribution.
    c. growth.
    d. money.

● POTENTIAL ESSAY QUESTIONS

You may also see essay questions similar to the "Problems & Applications" and "Brain Teasers" exercises.

1. In what way is inflation a tax? Who pays it?

2. What are the differences between the quantity theorists and the institutionalists with respect to unemployment?

3. What role does government play in the Insider/Outsider model?

ANSWERS

SHORT-ANSWER QUESTIONS

1. Inflation does not make a nation poorer. It redistributes income from those who can and do raise their prices to those who cannot or do not raise their prices. On average, the winners and losers average out. An example is lenders and borrowers. (351)

2. People formulate expectations in a variety of ways. Three types of expectations are adaptive expectations (expectations based in some way on the past), rational expectations (the expectations that the economists' model predicts), and extrapolative expectations (expectations that a trend will continue). (352)

3. The quantity theory is based on the equation of exchange, *MV=PQ*. The quantity theory adds the following assumptions: (1) that velocity is relatively constant; (2) that real output is relatively constant; and (3) that changes in money supply cause changes in prices. In reality, velocity and real output can change sufficiently to make it questionable whether this theory is useful. However, when there is significant inflation—say 100% or more—the relative changes in velocity and real output that are reasonable to assume possible are much smaller than that 100%, leaving a rough correlation between changes in the money supply and changes in the price level.

   The debate between economists does not concern the relationships between money growth and inflation; it concerns the direction of causation. Quantity theorists tend to believe that the causation goes from money to prices, and hence they are willing to accept the existence of a long-run vertical Phillips curve. Institutionalists tend to believe that the causation goes from changes in prices and expectations of prices to changes in the money supply—the government is accommodating the higher prices. Thus they favor more institutionally-oriented theories of inflation. (352-360)

4. The quantity theory of money is best summarized by the phrase "Inflation is everywhere and always a monetary phenomenon." Essentially, it is that increases in the money supply are the cause of inflation, and all other supposed causes are simply diversions from the key monetary cause. According to the quantity theory there is a long-run inverse relationship between inflation and growth. (352-354, 366-367)

5. The institutionalist theory of inflation differs from the quantity theory in that it is more likely to include institutional and social aspects as part of the theory. The insider/outsider model is an institutionalist model of inflation. Another way of stating the difference is that the institutional theory of inflation sees the equation of exchange as being read from right to left, rather than from left to right. (352-360)

6. Economists who support the quantity theory of money are more likely to favor a monetary rule, because they see the economy gravitating toward a natural (or target) rate of unemployment regardless of monetary policy. Thus expansionary monetary policy can lead only to inflation. A monetary rule will limit the government's attempt to expand the economy with monetary policy and hence will achieve the natural rate of unemployment and low inflation. Institutional economists are less likely to see the economy gravitating toward the natural (or target) rate of unemployment, so they would favor some discretionary policy to improve the operation of the macro economy. (357-358, 360-361)

7. Curve B is the short-run Phillips curve. The Phillips curve represents a trade-off between inflation and unemployment. It is an empirically determined phenomenon, and based on that empirical evidence economists generally believe that the downward sloping curve (curve B) represents the short-run Phillips curve: Whenever unemployment decreases, inflation increases, and vice versa. They explain that this empirical occurrence is due to slowly adjusting expectations and institutions. In the long run, expectations and institutions can change and hence the reason for the trade-off is eliminated, making the vertical line represent the long-run Phillips curve—it represents the lack of a trade-off between inflation and unemployment in the long run. (361-364)

8. Institutional economists see institutional and social aspects of the price setting process as more important than do quantity theorists. They also see individuals as having a cost of rationality, so individuals may not notice small amounts of inflation. These aspects of the institutional theory make it more likely that there is a long-run trade-off between inflation and unemployment since, in their absence, we would expect that money is essentially a veil and real forces predominate. (361-364)

9. An incomes policy is a policy designed to put direct downward pressure on the nominal price setting process. Institutional economists see institutional and social aspects of the price setting process as more important than do quantity theorists. It is these social aspects of the price setting process, which place a direct upward pressure on the price level that will require an incomes policy to offset. Therefore, institutionalists are more likely to support an incomes policy. (360-361)

━━━━━ ANSWERS ━━━━━

MATCHING

1-a; 2-h; 3-c; 4-k; 5-b; 6-e; 7-f; 8-j; 9-d; 10-g; 11-i.

━━━━━ ANSWERS ━━━━━

PROBLEMS AND APPLICATIONS

1. **a.** 1. Velocity is constant, 2. Real output is independent of the money supply, 3. Causation goes from money supply to prices. (353-354)
   b. $MV = PQ$ is the equation of exchange. Since V is constant and Q exogenous, the only remaining variables that change within the system are M and P. Since the causation runs from M to P, to keep the equation balanced, a rise in M must lead to a rise in P (and only P since Q is exogenous). (353-354)

2. **a.** $V = 10$: $MV = PQ$; $200V = \$2,000$; $V = 10$. (353-354)
   b. $6,160 billion: $MV = PQ$; $(5.6)(1,100) = \$6,160$ billion. (353-354)
   c. By 6%. (353-354)

3. **a.** The long-run Phillips curve is vertical at the rate of unemployment consistent with potential output, here at 5.5%. The short-run Phillips curve is the downward sloping curve shown in the graph below as PC_1. In this case, we drew a short-run Phillips curve where expected inflation equals 3%, actual inflation. It intersects the long-run Phillips curve at 5.5% unemployment and 3% inflation. The economy is at point A. (361-365)

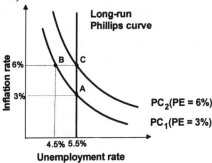

   b. The economy moves along the short-run Phillips curve up and to the left to point B. The short-run Phillips curve does not shift since inflation expectations have not changed. At point B, inflation is 6% and unemployment rate is 4.5%. (361-365)
   c. Now that expectations fully adjust, the short-run Phillips curve shifts to the right to PC_2 so that it intersects the long-run Phillips curve at inflation rate of 6%. The unemployment rate returns to 5.5% and inflation remains at 6%. (361-365)

4. **a.** The economy moves along the short-run Phillips curve down and to the right to point B in the graph below. The short-run Phillips curve does not shift since inflation expectations have not changed. At point B, inflation is 0% and unemployment rate is 6.5%. (361-365)

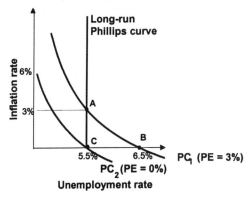

b. Now that expectations fully adjust, the short-run Phillips curve shifts to the left to PC_2 so that it intersects the long-run Phillips curve at inflation rate of 0%. The unemployment rate returns to 5.5% and inflation remains at 0%. (361-365)

5. **a.** Inflation is below expected inflation and unemployment is higher than the natural rate of unemployment. As expectations adjust, the short-run Phillips curve shifts to the left and both unemployment and inflation will fall. (361-365)

   b. Inflation is above expected inflation and unemployment is lower than the natural rate of unemployment. As expectations adjust, the short-run Phillips curve shifts to the right and both unemployment and inflation will rise. (361-365)

   c. Inflation equals expected inflation and unemployment equals the target rate of unemployment. Inflation and unemployment will not change. (361-365)

6. **a.** I assume that in the long run, only inflation can be improved, so I ignore the higher-than-desired rate of unemployment and focus on fighting inflation. A contractionary monetary policy will improve the inflation rate. (357-358)

   b. The economy begins at point A in the graph below, where unemployment is 5.5% and inflation is 12%. Inflation expectations equal actual inflation. With contractionary monetary policy, the economy moves along the short-run Phillips curve down and to the right to point B. The short-run Phillips curve does not shift since inflation expectations have not changed. At point B, inflation is lower than 12% and the unemployment rate is higher than 5.5%. The president will be happy that inflation is lower, but disappointed that unemployment is higher. I tell him that in the short run there is a trade-off between the two. Just wait for expectations of inflation to adjust and we will return to 5.5% unemployment. (361-365)

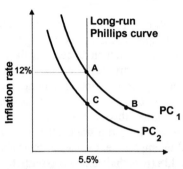

c. Now that expectations fully adjust, the short-run Phillips curve shifts to the left to PC_2 so that it intersects the long-run Phillips curve at inflation rate of below 12% at point C. The unemployment rate returns to 5.5%. The president is now pleased because inflation is lower and unemployment returned to 5.5%. But he wanted the unemployment rate to be below 5.5%. I tell him that 5.5% is the natural rate. If he were to follow an expansionary policy, unemployment would fall in the short run, but would return to 5.5% in the long run and inflation would be higher than it currently is. The higher inflation would undermine the economy's long-term growth. (361-365)

ANSWERS

A BRAIN TEASER

1. The reasons are complicated. If a government does not have the capability of either taxing or borrowing to finance expenditures (and if the central bank is not independent) the government may rely on its ability to print money to finance government expenditures. For some countries the choice is between inflation and allowing an economy and its government to fall apart. (356-357)

ANSWERS

MULTIPLE CHOICE

1. **c**   In an unexpected inflation borrowers gain and lenders lose because the money they

are paying back with will buy less because of the inflation. In an expected inflation the interest rate will have adjusted to compensate lenders for the decrease in the value of money. See page 351.

2. b In an unexpected inflation borrowers gain and lenders lose because the money they are paying back with will buy less because of the inflation. See page 351.

3. c Rational expectations are based on models; extrapolative are based on expectations that a trend will continue. Historical expectations are not mentioned in the text. See page 352.

4. b Nominal wage increases are the difference between inflation and productivity growth. See page 352.

5. b Using the equation of exchange, $MV=PQ$, given these assumptions there is a close relationship between changes in M and changes in P. See page 353.

6. b The quantity theory directly relates money and inflation. See page 353.

7. c The quantity theory is most applicable when there are large increases in the money supply and significant inflation. This is most likely to be the case in developing countries. See pages 355-356.

8. c The inflation tax is a tax on the holders of cash because inflation makes their cash worth less. See page 355-357.

9. d As discussed in the text the European and New Zealand central banks have strict rules against inflation. The U.S. does not; Russia is not mentioned in the text. See page 358.

10. b The equation of exchange is a tautology; it cannot be incorrect; Institutionalists see prices changes causing money and velocity changes so MV=PY should be read from right to left. See page 358.

11. b The book describes two general theories of inflation; social pressures definitely fit with the institutionalist theory. One type of institutionalist theory of inflation is the insider/outsider model, but that is not presented as a choice. See pages 358-360.

12. a As discussed in the text an incomes policy would most likely be favored by an advocate of an institutional theory of inflation. See page 361.

13. a The Phillips curve is drawn with inflation on the vertical axis and unemployment on the horizontal axis. See page 361-362.

14. c The short-run Phillips curve holds expectations of inflation constant. Therefore, it shifts because changes in expectations of inflation cause everybody to build those expectations into their nominal price requests. See page 363.

15. b As discussed in the text, the long-run Phillips curve is vertical. Actually, there is some debate about whether it is downward sloping, but the text focuses on the vertical nature of the curve so that is the answer that should be given. Remember, one is choosing the best answer relative to what is presented in the text. See page 363.

16. b Since Point A is to the right of the long-run Phillips curve, actual unemployment exceeds the natural rate of unemployment. Therefore we would expect inflationary expectations to be decreasing, and hence inflation to be decreasing. See pages 364-365.

17. a Since Point A is to the left of the long-run Phillips curve, actual unemployment is below the natural rate of unemployment. Therefore we would expect inflationary expectations to be increasing, and hence inflation to be increasing. See pages 364-365.

18. d Stagflation is defined as a combination of high and accelerating inflation and high unemployment. See page 365.

19. d The last half of the 1990s was a period of low inflation and low unemployment which

is not consistent with their Phillips curve story. Economist's explanation of this period centered on the higher than expected increases in productivity. See page 365.

20. c   Quantity theory advocates argue that in the long run a non-inflationary environment is conducive to growth and thus there is a long run tradeoff between inflation and growth. See page 366.

ANSWERS

POTENTIAL ESSAY QUESTIONS

The following are annotated answers. They indicate the general idea behind the answer.

1. Inflation can be viewed as a tax because it reduces the value of obligations specified in nominal terms. A simple way to see this is if prices rose at a rate of 5 percent a day, a dollar today will buy only 95 cents worth of goods tomorrow. The holder of the dollar (or any obligation specified in nominal terms) pays the tax.

2. Quantity theorists see a competitive labor market guaranteeing full employment. Institutionalists see an imperfectly competitive labor market. Institutionalists also envision a potential lack of demand for workers because of a lack of aggregate demand for the goods they produce. To institutionalists, this can create some unemployment at any wage.

3. Inflation is a result of *im*perfectly competitive markets. This allows workers and firms (especially "insiders") to raise their nominal wages and prices even during periods of high unemployment and excess production. Other groups, feeling relatively worse off, will push for higher wages and prices too. The government can either ratify this inflation by increasing the money supply or it can refuse to ratify it, causing unemployment (especially for the "outsiders"). In sum, Keynesians emphasize institutional and social causes of inflation.

OPEN ECONOMY MACRO: EXCHANGE RATE AND TRADE POLICY

16

● CHAPTER AT A GLANCE

This review is based upon the learning objectives that open the chapter.

1a. The balance of payments is a country's record of all transactions between its residents and the residents of all foreign countries. (373)
It is broken down into the:
- *current account*
- *capital account*
- *official transactions account.*

   Remember: If it is a minus (plus) sign, money is going out (coming in). Moreover, if foreigners are buying our goods, services, or assets, that represents a demand for the dollar (an inflow) in international exchange rate markets. If we buy foreign goods, services, or assets, that represents a supply of dollars (an outflow).

1b. The balance of trade is the difference between the value of goods and services a nation exports and the value of goods and services it imports. (374)
The balance of merchandise trade is often discussed in the popular press as a summary of how the U.S. is doing in international markets. However, it only includes goods exported and imported—not services. Trade in services is just as important as trade in merchandise, so economists pay more attention to the combined balance on goods and services.

1c. Since the balance of payments consists of both the capital account and the trade account, if the capital account is in surplus and the trade account is in deficit, there can still be a balance of payments surplus. (375-376)
The capital account measures the flows of payments between countries for assets such as stocks, bonds, and real estate. The current (or trade) account measures the flows of payments for goods and services.

1d. A deficit in the balance of payments means that the private quantity supplied of a currency exceeds the private quantity demanded. A surplus in the balance of payments means the opposite. (378)
Whenever the exchange rate is <u>above equilibrium</u> (below equilibrium) then the country will experience a balance of payments <u>deficit</u> (surplus).

2. Three important fundamental determinants of exchange rates are prices, interest rates, and income. (378)
A decrease in the value of a currency can be caused by:

- *<u>An increase in the nation's inflation rate</u>.*
- *<u>A decrease in the nation's interest rates</u>.*
- *<u>An increase in the nation's income</u> .*

3. A country fixes the exchange rate by standing ready to buy and sell its currency any time at the fixed exchange rate. (379)

   It is easier for a country to maintain a fixed exchange rate below equilibrium. All it has to do is to print and sell enough domestic currency to hold the value down.

   However, if a country wants to maintain a fixed exchange rate <u>above long-run equilibrium</u> then it can do so only as long as it has the foreign currency (official) reserves to buy up its currency. Once it runs out of official reserves, it will be unable to intervene, and must either borrow, use indirect methods (domestic fiscal and monetary policies), ask other countries to buy its currency (to sell their currency), or devalue its currency.

In reality, because a country has a limited amount of official reserves, it only uses strategic currency stabilization (not a fixed exchange rate policy).

4. Purchasing power parity is a method of calculating exchange rates such that various currencies will each buy an equal basket of goods and services. Those exchange rates may or may not be appropriate long-run exchange rates. (382)
Long-run equilibrium exchange rates can only be estimated. The PPP (Purchasing Power Parity) is one method of doing so. However, for many economists, it has serious problems. They contend that the current exchange rate is the best estimate of the long-run equilibrium rate.

5a. Three exchange rate régimes are:
- Fixed exchange rate: The government chooses an exchange rate and offers to buy and sell currencies at that rate.
- Flexible exchange rate: Determination of exchange rates is left totally up to the market.
- Partially flexible exchange rate: The government sometimes affects the exchange rate and sometimes leaves it to the market. (384)
Which is best is debatable.

5b. Fixed exchange rates provide international monetary stability and force governments to make adjustments to meet their international problems. (This is *also* a disadvantage.) If they become unfixed, they create monetary instability. (384)
Know these advantages and disadvantages!

5c. Flexible exchange rate régimes provide for orderly incremental adjustment of exchange rates rather than large sudden jumps, and allow governments to be flexible in conducting domestic monetary and fiscal policy. (This is *also* a disadvantage.) They are, however, susceptible to private speculation. (385)
Know these advantages and disadvantages!

5d. Partially flexible exchange rate régimes combine the advantages and disadvantages of fixed and flexible exchange rates. (386)
Most countries have opted for this policy. However, if the market exchange rate is below the rate the government desires, and the

government does not have sufficient official reserves (to buy and increase the demand for its currency), then it must undertake policies that will either increase the private demand for its currency or decrease the private supply. Doing so either involves using traditional macro policy—fiscal and monetary policy—to influence the economy, or using trade policy to affect the level of exports and imports.

6. Some important international trade restrictions include tariffs, quotas, voluntary restraint agreements, and regulatory trade restrictions. (387)
Know the difference between these different trade restrictions as well as embargoes and nationalistic appeals!

7. Economists generally support free trade because trade restrictions lower aggregate output, reduce international competition, and often result in harmful trade wars that hurt everyone. (390)
The costs of trade restrictions (which include, among other things, higher prices domestic consumers must pay) almost always outweigh the benefits (which include protection from foreign competition that provides higher short-run profits and greater short-run job security to the protected domestic industries).

However, strategic trade policies (threats to implement trade restrictions on another country if it doesn't reduce its trade barriers) can be used to promote free trade (if these threats are credible and the other country reduces its trade restrictions).

See also, Appendix A: "History of Exchange Rate Systems."

● SHORT-ANSWER QUESTIONS

1. Distinguish between the balance of payments and the balance of trade.

2. How can a country simultaneously have a balance of payments deficit and a balance of trade surplus?

3. How does each part of the balance of payments relate to the supply and demand for currencies?

4. What are the three fundamental determinants of exchange rates?

5. If the demand and supply for a country's currency depends upon demand for imports and exports, and demand for foreign and domestic assets, how can a country fix its exchange rate?

6. How do market exchange rates differ from exchange rates using the purchasing power parity concept?

7. Define fixed exchange rates.

8. Define flexible exchange rates.

9. Define partially flexible exchange rates.

10. Which are preferable, fixed or flexible exchange rates?

11. What are a few of the most important international trade restrictions?

12. Why do economists generally support free trade?

MATCHING THE TERMS
Match the terms to their definitions

___ **1.** balance of payments
___ **2.** balance of trade
___ **3.** capital account
___ **4.** current account
___ **5.** exchange rate intervention
___ **6.** fixed exchange rate
___ **7.** flexible exchange rate
___ **8.** free trade
___ **9.** official transactions account
___ **10.** partially flexible exchange rate
___ **11.** purchasing power parity
___ **12.** strategic trade policies.
___ **13.** tariffs
___ **14.** voluntary restraint agreement

a. A method of calculating exchange rates that attempts to value currencies at a rate so that each will buy an equal basket of goods.

b. Agreements in which countries voluntarily restrict their exports.

c. A country's record of all transactions between its residents and the residents of all foreign countries.

d. Taxes governments place on internationally traded goods, generally imports.

e. An exchange rate established by a government that sometimes affects the exchange rate and sometimes leaves it to the market.

f. An exchange rate established by a government that chooses an exchange rate and offers to buy and sell currencies at that rate.

g. An exchange rate for which the determination of its value is left up to the market.

h. Threatening to implement tariffs to bring about a reduction in tariffs or some other concession from the other country.

i. Policy of allowing unrestricted trade among countries.

j. Government policy of buying and selling a currency to affect its price.

k. The difference between the value of goods a nation exports and the value of goods it imports.

l. The part of the balance of payments account that records the amount of a currency or other international reserves a nation buys or sells.

m. The part of the balance of payments account that lists all long-term flows of payments.

n. The part of the balance of payments account that lists all short-term flows of payments.

● PROBLEMS AND APPLICATIONS

1. State for each whether the transaction shows up on the balance of payments current account or the balance of payments capital account or neither.

    a. An American buys 100 stocks of Mercedes Benz, a German company.

    b. A Japanese businessperson buys Ameritec, an American bank.

    c. An American auto manufacturer buys $20 million in auto parts from a Japanese company.

    d. An American buys 100 shares of IBM stock.

    e. Saturn exports 10,000 cars to Germany.

    f. Toyota Motor Corporation, a Japanese firm, makes a $1 million profit from its plant in Kentucky, USA.

2. For each of the following, state who is demanding and who is supplying what currency:

    a. A French person buys a set of china from a U.S. firm.

    b. A U.S. tourist in Japan buys a Japanese kimono from a department store.

    c. An Italian exchange rate trader believes that the exchange rate value of the dollar will rise.

    d. A Swiss investor invests in Germany.

3. Draw supply and demand curves for British pounds, showing equilibrium quantity and price. Price is shown by price of pounds in dollars.

    a. What is the demand for dollars in this case?

    b. Explain a movement up along the supply curve.

    c. Explain a movement down along the demand curve.

    d. What would be the effect on the price of pounds of an increase in demand for pounds by the British? Show this graphically.

e. What would be the effect on the price of pounds of an increase in demand for dollars by the British? Show this graphically.

4. For each of the following, show graphically what would happen to the market for British pounds. Assume there are only two countries, the United States and Britain.

    a. Income in the Britain rises.

    b. Income in the United States rises.

    c. The prices of goods in the United States increases.

    d. Interest rates rise in Britain.

    e. The value of the pound is expected to fall.

A BRAIN TEASER

1. What could cause the U.S. to temporarily experience an increase in its balance of payments deficit even though there is downward movement in the exchange rate value of the dollar? (Hint: Think in terms of demand and supply analysis.)

MULTIPLE CHOICE

Circle the one best answer for each of the following questions:

1. An exchange rate is:
    a. the rate the Fed charges commercial banks for loans.
    b. the rate the Fed charges individuals for loans.
    c. the rate at which one country's currency can be exchanged for another country's currency.
    d. the speed at which exchange occurs.

2. If a country has perfectly flexible exchange rates and is running a current account deficit, it is running
    a. a capital account surplus.
    b. a capital account deficit.
    c. an official transactions surplus.
    d. an official transactions deficit.

3. In the balance of payments accounts, net investment income shows up in
    a. the current account.
    b. the capital account.
    c. the official transactions account.
    d. Net investment income is not an entry in the balance of payments.

4. If the official transactions account is significantly in surplus, the country is
    a. trying to hold up its exchange rate.
    b. trying to push down its exchange rate.
    c. trying to have no effect on its exchange rate.
    d. sometimes trying to increase and sometimes trying to decrease its exchange rate.

5. In recent years, the United States has generally
    a. run a balance of trade surplus.
    b. run a balance of trade deficit.
    c. had sometimes a balance of trade surplus and sometimes a balance of trade deficit.
    d. had a balance of trade equality.

6. In recent years, the United States generally
    a. has run a capital account surplus.
    b. has run a capital account deficit.
    c. has sometimes run a capital account surplus and sometimes run a capital account deficit.
    d. has run a capital account equality.

7. If there is a black market for a currency, the country probably has
    a. nonconvertible currency.
    b. a fixed exchange rate currency.
    c. a flexible exchange rate currency.
    d. a partially flexible exchange rate currency.

8. If the French demand for U.S. imports increases, one would expect the price of French francs in terms of dollars to:
    a. rise.
    b. fall.
    c. remain unchanged.
    d. sometimes rise and sometimes fall.

9. If the U.S. demand for French imports increases, one would expect the price of French francs in terms of dollars to:
    a. rise.
    b. fall.
    c. remain unchanged.
    d. sometimes rise and sometimes fall.

Use the following graph to answer Questions 10 – 12:

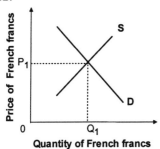

10. If U.S. income increases
    a. the supply curve will shift out to the right.
    b. the supply curve will shift in to the left.
    c. the demand curve will shift out to the right.
    d. the demand curve will shift in to the left.

11. If French interest rates increase relative to world interest rates:
    a. only the supply curve will shift out to the right.
    b. only the demand curve will shift in to the left.

c. the supply curve will shift in to the left and the demand curve will shift out to the right.
d. the supply curve will shift out to the right and the demand curve will shift in to the left.

12. If French inflation increases relative to world interest rates:
    a. only the supply curve will shift out to the right.
    b. only the demand curve will shift in to the left.
    c. the supply curve will shift in to the left and the demand curve will shift out to the right.
    d. the supply curve will shift out to the right and the demand curve will shift in to the left.

13. If a country runs expansionary monetary policy, in the short run one would expect the value of its exchange rate to
    a. rise.
    b. fall.
    c. be unaffected.
    d. sometimes rise and sometimes fall.

14. Refer to the graph below.   If the U.S. government wants to fix its convertible currency at exchange rate P_1, it will have to:

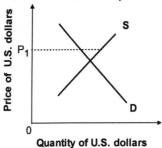

    a. supply official reserves in exchange for dollars.
    b. supply dollars in exchange for official reserves.
    c. disallow currency conversion except at the official rate P1.
    d. supply both official reserves and dollars because excess supply of dollars is so large.

15. Say the Bangladeshi taka is valued at 42 taka to $1. Also say that you can buy the same basket of goods for 10 taka that you can buy for $1. In terms of dollars the purchasing power parity of the taka is
    a. overvalued.
    b. undervalued.
    c. not distorted.
    d. non convertible.

16. Compared to a fixed exchange rate system, a flexible exchange rate system
    a. allows countries more flexibility in their monetary policies.
    b. allows countries less flexibility in their monetary policies.
    c. has no effect on monetary policies.
    d. allows countries more flexibility in their industrial policies.

17. Tariffs are
    a. quantity limits placed on imports.
    b. agreements in which countries voluntarily restrict their exports.
    c. taxes governments place on internationally traded goods—generally imports.
    d. an all-out restriction on the import or export of a good.

18. Which of the following is *not* generally a reason for economists' opposition to trade restrictions?
    a. they lower aggregate output.
    b. they reduce international competition.
    c. they often result in harmful trade wars that hurt everyone.
    d. they increase output of foreign countries relative to the domestic country.

A1. The gold standard is a type of
    a. fixed exchange rate.
    b. partially flexible exchange rate.
    c. flexible exchange rate.
    d. nonconvertible exchange rate.

A2. The gold specie flow mechanism works primarily by flows of
    a. money from one country to another.
    b. services from one country to another.
    c. merchandise from one country to another.
    d. exchange rates from one country to another.

A3. Under the gold standard, if a country has a balance of payments deficit
    a. gold would flow out of the country.
    b. gold would flow into the country.
    c. the country's exchange rate would rise.
    d. the country's exchange rate would fall.

A4. SDRs refers to
    a. Specie Draft Rights.
    b. Specie Drawing Rights.
    c. Special Drawing Rights.
    d. Special Draft Rights.

● POTENTIAL ESSAY QUESTIONS

You may also see essay questions similar to the "Problems & Applications" and "Brain Teasers" exercises.

1. How are a government's exchange rate policy and the official transactions account in the balance of payments related? Is it easier for a government to push the value of its currency up or down? Why?

2. Explain how fixed, flexible (or floating), and partially flexible exchange rates are determined. What are the advantages and the disadvantages of each? Why do most nations have a partially flexible exchange rate policy?

ANSWERS

SHORT-ANSWER QUESTIONS

1. The balance of payments is a country's record of all transactions between its residents and the residents of all foreign nations. It is divided into the current account, the capital account, and the official transactions account. The balance of trade is one part of the balance of payments— specifically that part dealing with goods. It is not all that satisfactory a measure of the country's position in international markets since it does not include services. Generally, economists pay more attention to the combined balance on goods and services account. (371-376)

2. As discussed in question 1, the balance of trade is one part of the balance of payments. Thus, if other parts of the international payments —for example, the capital account—are in deficit, the balance of trade could still be in surplus. (373-376)

3. The balance of payments records the flow of a currency in and out of a country (1) in order to buy and sell goods and services in the current account, (2) in order to buy and sell assets along with payments resulting from previous purchases of assets in the capital account, and (3) in order to affect the value of a country's currency in the official transactions account. To buy foreign goods and assets one must supply domestic currency and demand foreign currency. Therefore, the balance of payments records the demand and supply of a country's currency during a given period of time. (373-376)

4. Three fundamental determinants of the value of a country's exchange rate are (1) domestic income, (2) domestic price level and (3) domestic interest rates. (378)

5. The current account and capital account reflect private demand and supply of a country's currency. If the official transactions account were zero, then the currency's value is market determined. If a country wants to fix the value of its currency to maintain its value at the fixed value, the government must buy and sell its currency using official reserves. Buying (selling) one's own currency shows up as a positive (negative) in the official transactions account. (379-380)

6. Market exchange rates are determined by the demand and supply of a country's currency. Since not all goods, services and assets produced in a country can be traded internationally, the value of an exchange rate may not reflect the relative prices in each country. The purchasing power parity concept adjusts the value of a country's currency by determining that rate at which equivalent baskets of goods can be purchased in each country. (382-383)

7. A fixed exchange rate is an exchange rate that the government chooses and then holds at the chosen rate, by standing ready to buy and sell at that rate. (384)

8. Flexible exchange rates are exchange rates that are determined by the market without any government intervention. (385)

9. Partially flexible exchange rates are exchange rates that are determined by the market but are sometimes also affected by government intervention. (386)

10. It depends. Each has its advantages and disadvantages. Flexible exchange rates give a country more control over domestic policy, but it can experience large fluctuations in the value of its currency, hurting trade. But with fixed exchange rates, such fluctuations can be avoided. (384-387)

11. The most important international trade restrictions include tariffs, quotas, voluntary restraint agreements, and regulatory trade restrictions. (387-388)

12. Economists generally support free trade because restrictions in trade lower output, reduce international competition (raising prices to consumers), and often result in harmful trade wars that hurt everyone. (390)

ANSWERS

MATCHING

1-c; 2-k; 3-m; 4-n; 5-j; 6-f; 7-g; 8-i; 9-l; 10-e; 11-a; 12-h; 13-d; 14-b.

━━━━ **ANSWERS** ━━━━

PROBLEMS AND APPLICATIONS

1. **a.** Capital account. This is a long-term outflow. (374-375)
    b. Capital account. This is a long-term inflow. (374-375)
    c. Current account. This is merchandise imports, a short-term flow. (374-375)
    d. Neither. It is a domestic transaction. (374-375)
    e. Current account. This is merchandise exports, a short-term flow. (374-375)
    f. Current account. This is net investment income. (374-375)

2. **a.** The French person supplies francs and demands dollars because the French person sells francs to get U.S. dollars to purchase the china. (376-377)
    b. The U.S. tourist supplies dollars and demands Japanese yen because the tourist has to sell dollars to get yen. (376-377)
    c. The Italian trader will supply Italian lire and demand U.S. dollars because the trader wants to purchase that exchange that is believed to rise, the dollar. The trader must sell lire to get the dollars. (376-377)
    d. The Swiss investor will supply Swiss francs and demand German marks because the Swiss investor needs German marks to invest in Germany. (376-377)

3. A market for British pounds is shown below. Price of pounds in U.S. dollars is on the vertical axis and quantity of pounds is on the horizontal axis. Equilibrium price and quantity is determined by where they intersect. (376-377)

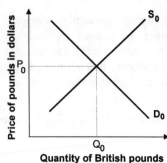

   a. If only two countries exist, the United States and Britain, the demand for dollars is the supply of pounds. (376-377)

   b. As the dollar value of the pound rises, individuals will supply more pounds. (376-377)
   c. As the dollar value of the pound declines, individuals will demand more pounds. (376-377)
   d. An increase in the demand for pounds by the British would shift the demand for pounds as shown in the graph below. The price of pounds in dollars would rise. (376-377)

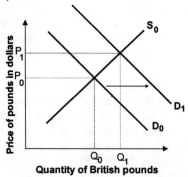

   e. An increase in the demand for dollars by the British is equivalent to an increase in the supply of pounds. The supply curve for pounds would shift to the right as shown in the graph below. The price of pounds in dollars would fall. (376-377)

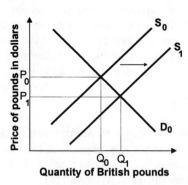

4. **a.** Demand for imports by the British rises; hence demand for dollars (supply of pounds) rises. This is shown in the graph below. (376-378)

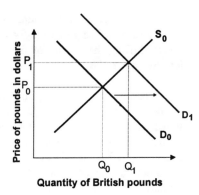

b. Demand for imports by Americans rises; hence demand for pounds rises. This is shown in the graph below. (376-378)

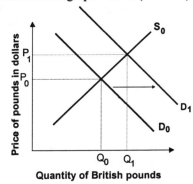

c. Demand for imports by the British falls; hence demand for dollars (supply of pounds) falls. This is shown in the graph below. (376-378)

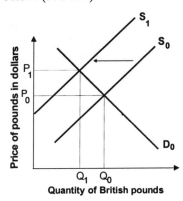

d. Demand for British assets will rise; hence the demand for the pound rises. This is shown in the graph below. (376-378)

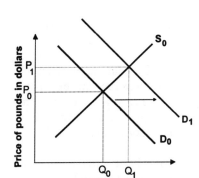

e. The demand for the pound falls. This is shown in the graph below. (376-378)

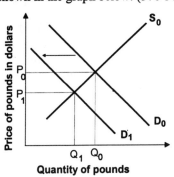

━━━━━━ ANSWERS ━━━━━━

A BRAIN TEASER

1. A decrease in the demand for the dollar and/or an increase in the supply of the dollar in international exchange rate markets will create a temporary balance of payments deficit (because the quantity of dollars supplied will exceed the quantity demanded—imports will exceed exports). The balance of payments deficit will also put downward pressure on the exchange rate value of the dollar. (376)

━━━━━━ ANSWERS ━━━━━━

MULTIPLE CHOICE

1. c   An exchange rate is the rate at which one country's currency can be exchanged for another country's currency. See pages 376-377.

2. a   With perfectly flexible exchange rates the balance of payments must sum to zero; thus the capital account must be in surplus if the current account is in deficit. The official transactions account could not be negative because if there are perfectly flexible exchange rates, there are no official transactions. See page 376.

3. a   Although net investment income might seem to many people as if it goes in the capital account, it is a return for a service and is considered part of the current account, as is discussed on page 374.

4. a   A surplus in the official transactions account means the balance of payments would otherwise be in deficit. The country is buying up its own currency. This means it is trying to hold up its exchange rate. See page 376.

5. b   See pages 373-374.

6. a   Running a capital account surplus is the other side of the balance sheet from the trade deficit. See pages 373-374.

7. a   All the others allow free exchange of currency and hence would not generate a black market. See page 380.

8. b   To purchase greater amounts of U.S. products, the French must increase the supply of their currency, pushing down its value relative to the dollar. See page 378.

9. a   To purchase greater amounts of French products, U.S. citizens must increase the supply of their currency, pushing down its value relative to the franc. That means, the value of the franc rises relative to the dollar. See pages 377-378.

10. c   If U.S. income increases, the U.S. demand for French imports will increase, shifting the demand for francs out to the right. See page 378.

11. c   An increase in French interest rates will increase the demand for French assets. As a result, the demand for French francs will

shift out to the right. In addition, the French will substitute foreign assets for domestic assets shifting the supply of francs to the left. See page 378.

12. d   An increase in French inflation will reduce the demand for French goods. Foreigners will demand fewer francs with which to buy French goods and French citizens will supply more francs as they exchange francs for other currencies to buy cheaper goods abroad. See page 378.

13. b   This is a review question from the previous chapter. Expansionary monetary policy decreases interest rates and thereby tends to decrease the exchange rate in the short run. See page 378.

14. a   At P_1, there is an excess supply of dollars. To keep the value of the dollar from falling, the U.S. will have to buy up that excess using official reserves of foreign currencies. Disallowing conversion except at an official rate would make the dollar a nonconvertible currency. See pages 379-380.

15. b   Since the purchasing power parity exchange rate is lower than the actual exchange rate, the taka is undervalued. See page 383.

16. a   Under a fixed exchange rate system countries must use their monetary policies to meet international commitments. Thus flexible exchange rate policies allow them more flexibility in their monetary policies. Flexible exchange rates *may* allow them more flexibility in their industrial policies, but flexible exchange rates *definitely* do allow them more flexibility in their monetary policy, so a is the preferred answer. See pages 384-385.

17. c   See page 387.

18. d   Trade restrictions hurt all countries. See page 390.

A1. a.   See page 395.

A2. a. When there is an imbalance of trade in the gold system, gold—which is money—flows from the deficit country to the surplus country, pushing the price level down in the deficit country and up in the surplus country. This process brings about a trade balance equilibrium, eventually. See page 395.

A3. a See page 395 about the flow of gold. The last two answers could be eliminated since the gold standard involves fixed exchange rates.

A4. c As discussed on page 396, SDRs refers to Special Drawing Rights.

ANSWERS

POTENTIAL ESSAY QUESTIONS

The following are annotated answers. They indicate the general idea behind the answer.

1. If a country is experiencing a balance of payments deficit (the quantity supplied of its currency exceeds the quantity demanded at the current exchange rate) then its currency will fall in value over time. A country's government could prevent its currency from falling (depreciating) by buying its own currency in exchange rate markets. If it does, then this shows up in the official transactions account as a plus sign and we say that the government is supporting the value of its currency. The opposite is also true. Because a country can create and then sell its own currency it is easier for a country to push the value of its currency down, than up.

2. See pages 384-386. Also, notice the "margin list" on pages 385 and 386. Most nations have opted for a partially flexible exchange rate policy in order to try to get the advantages of both a fixed and a flexible exchange rate.

INTERNATIONAL DIMENSIONS OF MONETARY AND FISCAL POLICIES

● CHAPTER AT A GLANCE

This review is based upon the learning objectives that open the chapter.

1a. There is significant debate about what U.S. international goals should be because exchange rates have conflicting effects and, depending on the state of the economy, there are arguments for high and low exchange rates. (399)

A high exchange rate (strong value of the $) helps hold down the prices of imports and therefore inflation. However, it creates a trade deficit and that has a depressing effect on aggregate demand and therefore the income level.

1b. Running a trade deficit is good in the short run but presents problems in the long run; thus there is debate about whether we should worry about a trade deficit or not. (399-400)

Trade deficit ⇒ *imports > exports.*

Short-run benefit: We are able to consume more than we would otherwise be able to.

Long-run cost: We have to sell off U.S. assets because we are consuming more than we are producing. All the future interest and profits on those assets will thus go to foreigners, not U.S. citizens.

2. A country that has fixed exchange rates is limited in its ability to use fiscal and monetary policy to address domestic policy goals. (401)

A country with fixed exchange rates must give up any attempt to target domestic interest rates to achieve domestic goals.

3a. Monetary policy affects exchange rates through the interest rate path, the income path, and the price-level path, as shown in the diagram on pages 403 and 404. (403-404)

Expansionary monetary policy (increasing the money supply) lowers exchange rates. It decreases the relative value of a country's currency. Contractionary monetary policy has the opposite effect.

Be able to explain why!

3b. Monetary policy affects the trade balance through the income path, the price level path, and the exchange rate path, as shown in the diagram on page 405. (404-405)

Expansionary monetary policy makes a trade deficit larger.

Contractionary monetary policy makes a trade deficit smaller.

Be able to explain why!

4a. Fiscal policy affects exchange rates through the income path, the interest rate path, and the price-level path, as shown in the diagram on page 407. (406-407)

The net effect of fiscal policy on exchange rates is ambiguous.

Be able to explain why!

4b. Fiscal policy affects the trade deficit though the income path and the price-level path, as shown in the diagram on page 408. (407-408)

Expansionary fiscal policy increases a trade deficit.

Contractionary fiscal policy decreases a trade deficit.

Be able to explain why!

5. Governments try to coordinate their monetary and fiscal policies because their economies are interdependent. (408-409)

   Each country will likely do what's best for the world economy as long as it is also best for itself.

6. While internationalizing a country's debt may help in the short run, in the long run it presents potential problems, since foreign ownership of a country's debts means the country must pay interest to those foreign countries and that debt may come due. (409-410)

   We have been internationalizing our debt since the early 1980s, which means that we must, at some point in the future, export more than we import (consume less than we produce) to pay for this.

● SHORT-ANSWER QUESTIONS

1. What should U.S. international goals be?

2. Why can a country achieve an interest rate target or an exchange rate target, but generally cannot achieve both at the same time?

3. W1hich dominate for a country: domestic or international goals? Why?

4. If a country runs expansionary monetary policy, what will likely happen to the exchange rate?

5. If a country runs contractionary monetary policy, what will likely happen to the trade balance?

6. If a country runs expansionary fiscal policy, what will likely happen to the exchange rate?

7. If a country runs contractionary fiscal policy, what will likely happen to the trade balance?

8. Given the difficulty of doing so, why do countries try to coordinate their monetary and fiscal policies with other countries?

9. The United States in recent years has run a large capital account deficit and has become the world's largest debtor nation. What are some of the potential problems that this presents?

● PROBLEMS AND APPLICATIONS

1. You observe that over the past decade, a country's competitiveness has improved, reducing its trade deficit.

    a. What monetary or fiscal policies might have led to such results? Why?

b. You also observe that interest rates have steadily fallen along with a fall in the exchange rate. What monetary or fiscal policies might have led to such results?

2. You have been hired as an adviser to Fantasyland, a country with perfectly flexible exchange rates. State what monetary and fiscal policies you might suggest in each of the following situations. Explain your answers.

a. You want to increase domestic income and to reduce the exchange rate.

b. You want to reduce interest rates, reduce inflation, and reduce the trade deficit.

c. You want lower unemployment, lower interest rates, a lower exchange rate, and a lower trade deficit.

● A BRAIN TEASER

1. Suppose a country has been running a significant expansionary fiscal policy for many years. Monetary policy has been neutral. What can you expect to have happened to this country's trade balance? What are the benefits and costs of this trade imbalance? If this country wishes to correct for its trade imbalance, what fiscal and monetary policies would you suggest this country pursue now? Will your recommended polices coincide or conflict with any of the country's domestic goals? If so, which goals?

● MULTIPLE CHOICE

Circle the one best answer for each of the following questions:

1. If a country has fixed exchange rates
   a. the government need not worry about the exchange rate.
   b. governments are committed to buying and selling currencies at a fixed rate.
   c. the exchange rate is set by law.
   d. the exchange rate has a fixed component and a flexible component.

2. If a country has a flexible exchange rate, the exchange rate
   a. is determined by flexible government policy.
   b. is determined by market forces.
   c. fluctuates continuously, changing by at least 1 percent per year.
   d. fluctuates continuously, changing by at least 10 percent per year.

3. Countries prefer
   a. a high exchange rate.
   b. a low exchange rate.
   c. sometimes a low and sometimes a high exchange rate.
   d. a fixed exchange rate.

4. Countries prefer
   a. a trade deficit.
   b. a trade surplus.
   c. sometimes a trade deficit and sometimes a trade surplus.
   d. a trade equilibrium.

5. If a country wants to maintain a fixed exchange rate above equilibrium, but does not have the necessary official reserves, it can:
   a. increase demand for its currency by running contractionary monetary policy.
   b. reduce the supply of its currency by running expansionary monetary policy
   c. increase demand for its currency by running contractionary fiscal policy.
   d. increase supply of its currency by running expansionary fiscal policy.

6. Expansionary monetary policy has a tendency to
   a. push interest rates up and exchange rates down.
   b. push interest rates down and exchange rates down.
   c. push income down and exchange rates down.
   d. push imports down and exchange rates down.

7. Contractionary monetary policy has a tendency to
   a. push interest rates up and exchange rates down.
   b. push interest rates down and exchange rates down.
   c. push income down and imports down.
   d. push imports down and exchange rates down.

8. If the exchange rate has gone up, it is most likely that the government ran
   a. an expansionary monetary policy.
   b. a contractionary monetary policy.
   c. an expansionary fiscal policy.
   d. a contractionary fiscal policy.

9. If the trade deficit has gone up, it is most likely that the government ran
   a. an expansionary monetary policy.
   b. a contractionary monetary policy.
   c. a contractionary fiscal policy.
   d. an expansionary monetary policy and a contractionary fiscal policy.

10. Expansionary monetary policy tends to
    a. push prices up and the trade deficit down.
    b. push prices down and the trade deficit down.
    c. push income up and the trade deficit down.
    d. push income up and the trade deficit up.

11. Expansionary fiscal policy tends to push
    a. income up and exchange rates up.
    b. income up and exchange rates down.
    c. income up and imports up.
    d. income up and imports down.

12. If the exchange rate has gone up, it is most likely that the government ran
    a. an expansionary fiscal policy.
    b. a contractionary fiscal policy.
    c. Who knows?
    d. an expansionary monetary policy.

13. Contractionary fiscal policy tends to push
    a. income down and imports up.
    b. income down and the trade deficit up.
    c. prices down and the trade deficit down.
    d. prices down and imports up.

14. Assume the United States would like to raise its exchange rate and lower its trade deficit. It would pressure Japan to run
    a. contractionary monetary policy.
    b. contractionary fiscal policy.
    c. expansionary monetary policy
    d. expansionary fiscal policy.

15. According to the textbook, generally, when international goals and domestic goals conflict
    a. the international goals win out.
    b. the domestic goals win out.
    c. sometimes it's a toss-up which will win out.
    d. international monetary goals win out but international fiscal goals lose out.

16. When a country runs a large trade deficit, the amount of crowding out that occurs because of fiscal policy is
    a. increased.
    b. decreased.
    c. unaffected.
    d. sometimes increased and sometimes decreased.

● POTENTIAL ESSAY QUESTIONS

You may also see essay questions similar to the "Problems & Applications" and "Brain Teasers" exercises.

1. If there was initially a trade balance, what kind of trade imbalance would be created by an increase in the exchange rate value of the dollar (a stronger dollar)? Why?

2. What are the benefits and costs to the U.S. of having a strong dollar–a high exchange rate value of the dollar?

3. Why do domestic economic goals usually dominate international economic goals?

ANSWERS

SHORT-ANSWER QUESTIONS

1. By "international goals" economists usually mean the exchange rate and the trade balance that policy makers should shoot for. There is significant debate in the United States about what our international goals should be, and there are arguments for both high and low exchange rates, and for both trade deficits and trade surpluses. The argument for a high exchange rate is that it lowers the cost of imports; the argument against it is that it raises the price of exports, making U.S. goods less competitive. The argument in favor of a trade deficit is that it allows a country to consume more than it produces; the argument against is that a trade deficit will have to be paid off at some point. (399-400)

2. Because monetary policy affects the value of one's currency, a country cannot target both interest rates and exchange rates simultaneously. Suppose one's currency is at its desired level, but interest rates are too high. Expansionary monetary policy would lower the interest rate, but a lower interest rate reduces foreign demand for the country's interest-bearing assets. The demand for one's currency will shift in to the left and its exchange rate will fall. Likewise, citizens of the country will invest elsewhere and the supply of one's currency will shift out to the right. The value of one's currency will be lower than its target. (401-402)

3. Generally, domestic goals dominate for two reasons. (1) International goals are often ambiguous, as discussed in answer 1 above and (2) international goals affect a country's population indirectly and, in politics, indirect effects take a back seat. (400-401)

4. Expansionary monetary policy tends to push income and prices up and interest rates down. All these phenomena tend to push the exchange rate down. Contractionary monetary policy has the opposite effect. (402-404)

5. Contractionary monetary policy tends to push income and prices down and interest rates up. The strongest effect of these phenomena on the trade balance in the short run is the effect on income, which causes a fall in imports and a fall in the trade deficit. (402-404)

6. Expansionary fiscal policy pushes interest rates, income, and prices up. The higher income and higher prices increase imports and put downward pressure on exchange rates. The higher interest rate pushes exchange rates in the opposite direction so the net effect of fiscal policy on exchange rates is unclear. (406-407)

7. Contractionary fiscal policy pushes income and prices down. This tends to decrease imports and increase competitiveness, decreasing a trade deficit. (406-407)

8. The policies of one country affect the economy of another. So it is only natural that they try to coordinate their policies. It is also only natural that since voters are concerned with their own countries, that coordination is difficult to achieve unless it is in the interest of both countries. (408-409)

9. While internationalizing a country's debt may help in the short run, in the long run it presents potential problems, since foreign ownership of a country's debts means the debtor country must pay interest to those foreign countries, and also, that debt may come due. (409-410)

ANSWERS

PROBLEMS AND APPLICATIONS

1. a. An increase in competitiveness and a decrease in the trade deficit are probably due to contractionary fiscal policy. Contractionary fiscal policy reduces inflation, improves competitiveness, and decreases income which reduces imports. Improved competitiveness and decreased income both work to reduce the trade deficit. Contractionary monetary policy would also reduce the trade deficit, but its effect on competitiveness is ambiguous. (402-408)

    b. If interest rates have also fallen, it is likely that fiscal policy has been very contractionary because contractionary monetary policy would have led to higher interest rates and a higher exchange rate value of the dollar. (402-408)

2. a. Expansionary monetary policy will reduce the exchange rate through its effect on interest rates and will increase domestic income. Expansionary fiscal policy will increase domestic income. The increase in income will increase imports, which will tend to decrease the exchange rate, but higher interest rates will tend to lead to a higher exchange rate. The effect of expansionary fiscal policy on exchange rates is ambiguous. (402-408)

    b. Contractionary fiscal policy will tend to reduce inflation and interest rates. The reduction in inflation will improve competitiveness and a reduction in income will reduce imports. Both work to reduce the trade deficit. (402-408)

    c. Expansionary monetary policy will reduce unemployment and reduce interest rates. Lower interest rates will tend to make exchange rates fall. Expansionary monetary policy, however, will make the trade deficit higher. Expansionary fiscal policy will also reduce unemployment. Interest rates, however, will rise and so will the trade deficit. This mix of goals is difficult to attain. (402-408)

ANSWERS

A BRAIN TEASER

1. Because of the expansionary fiscal policy, this country will have moved in the direction of a trade deficit. The benefit of the trade deficit is that the country has been able to consume more that it has produced. The cost, however, is that it has had to sell off some of its assets. All the future interest and profits on these assets will now go to foreigners, not the country's citizens.

    To reduce the trade deficit the country should pursue contractionary fiscal and monetary policies. This will reduce imports and increase exports and increase the country's competitiveness in the global economy. That's good. However, even though fewer imports and

greater exports should help stimulate aggregate expenditures, the effects of the contractionary fiscal and monetary policies are also simultaneously at play. Aggregate demand may fall on balance. If it does, then you may have created a recession. That's bad. Sometimes, countries can find themselves "in a pickle." (There could be other effects associated with the prescribed contractionary policies.) (399, 405, 408)

ANSWERS

MULTIPLE CHOICE

1. b To keep the exchange rate at the stated amount governments must be willing to buy and sell currencies so that the quantity supplied and quantity demanded are always equal at the fixed rate. See page 401.

2. b There are no predetermined levels of change with a flexible exchange rate. See page 399.

3. c The answer is "sometimes a low and sometimes a high exchange rate" because, as discussed on page 399, there are rationales for both.

4. c The domestic economy's needs change over time and as they do, so does the country's preferred trade situation. Both a deficit and a surplus have their advantages and disadvantages. See pages 399-400.

5. a Contractionary monetary policy will increase the demand for one's currency and increase its value. Contractionary fiscal policy will reduce the supply of one's currency and increase its value. Contractionary monetary and fiscal policy is one way to fix one's exchange rate without intervening in the exchange market. See pages 401-402.

6. b See the diagram on page 403.

7. c See the diagram on page 404.

8. b As discussed on page 404 the b answer is

definitely correct. As discussed on page 406, fiscal policy has an ambiguous effect on exchange rates.

9. a   Both expansionary monetary policy and expansionary fiscal policy increase the trade deficit. Thus, only a fits. See the discussion and charts on pages 405-408.

10. d   See the discussion on pages 404-405 and the diagram on page 405.

11. c   The effect of expansionary fiscal policy on exchange rates is ambiguous, which eliminates a and b. Increased income increases imports, not decreases them. See pages 406-407.

12. c   The effect of expansionary fiscal policy on the exchange rate is ambiguous, as shown on the diagram on page 407, eliminating a and b. As discussed on pages 403-404, an expansionary monetary policy pushes the exchange rate down, eliminating d, leaving only c.

13. c   See diagram on page 407 and the discussion on pages 407-408.

14. c   The effect of fiscal policy on the exchange rate is ambiguous, so the only sure option is c. See the box on page 409.

15. b   As discussed in the text on page 408, usually, because of political considerations, domestic goals win out.

16. b   Since the trade deficit means capital is flowing into the country, the capital usually ends up buying some government debt, which reduces crowding out, as discussed on pages 409-410.

ANSWERS

POTENTIAL ESSAY QUESTIONS

The following are annotated answers. They indicate the general idea behind the answer.

1.   A stronger dollar means that a single dollar will now buy more units of a foreign currency. This makes foreign products cheaper to Americans. The U.S. would import more. At the same time, a stronger dollar means it will now take more units of a foreign currency to buy a single dollar. This will cause U.S. goods to become more expensive to foreigners. The U.S. would export less. The combined effects of more U.S. imports and fewer U.S. exports means a trade deficit will be created or get larger in the U.S.

2.   A strong dollar holds down the price of imports and therefore inflation. However, the cost is a trade deficit that would have a depressing effect on total spending and therefore the nation's income level (there would be an especially depressing effect on the nation's exporting industries).

3.   First, there is more agreement on domestic goals. Second, domestic goals affect people within one's country more directly. Finally, pursuing domestic goals is politically more appealing.

TOOLS, RULES, AND POLICY

18

CHAPTER AT A GLANCE

This review is based upon the learning objectives that open the chapter.

1. Two important micro models for macro are the production possibility curve model (which emphasizes tradeoffs) and the supply/demand model, which serves as a building block of macro reasoning. (415-416)

    One must be careful about the fallacy of composition when applying the supply and demand model to macro issues

2a. The two central long-run models are the long-run growth model (both the Classical and the New Growth model) and the quantity theory model. (418-419)

    The Classical long-run growth model focuses on investment and saving; new growth theory focuses on technology.

    The quantity theory model (MV=PQ) assumes velocity and output (Q) constant, so money increases cause price increases. Long-run models tend to focus on supply.

    Remember: Models are not right or wrong: they are simply tools.

2b. Two important short-run macro models are the multiplier model and the AS/AD model. (419-420)

    The multiplier and AS/AD models are the same model but they emphasize different things.

    The AS/AD model emphasizes how changes in the price level affect the economy; the multiplier model emphasizes how changes in the economy can reverberate through the economy.

    Short-run models tend to focus on demand. The graphs below show both models:

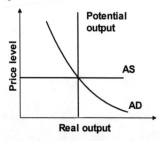

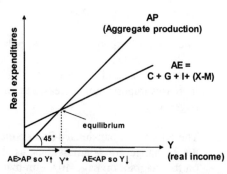

3. Classical economists tend to emphasize the long-run model and supply; Keynesian economists tend to emphasize the short-run model and demand. (424)

    Keynesians tend to be more activist and Classicals tend to be more laissez-faire.

4. The Fed conducts monetary policy primarily through buying and selling government bonds; the government conducts fiscal policy by changing taxes or expenditures. (424-427)

    Expansionary monetary or fiscal policy shifts the AD curve to the right.

    Contractionary monetary or fiscal policy shifts the AD curve to the left.

5. Policy is a process; it should not be seen as a one-time event since policy now affects people's actions in the future. To emphasize this economists emphasize policy regimes that refer to a full set of expected policies and credibility when talking about policy.(427-429)

    Rational expectations are expectations based on the best available information.

6. The New Era economy is an economy in which the old trade-offs don't apply and high growth, low inflation and low unemployment are all consistent. (429-432)

    Most economists are hesitant about conducting policy on the assumption that the New Era Economy has arrived.

SHORT-ANSWER QUESTIONS

1. What are two micro models that are relevant for macro?

2. What are the two central long-run macro models and how do they differ from short-run models?

3. What are the two central short-run macro models and how are they related?

4. How does the money multiplier differ from the income multiplier?

5. How do the Keynesian and Classical approaches to macro policy differ?

6. In the short-run model, you want to lower interest rates and increase income. Would you propose expansionary monetary or fiscal policy? What concerns would you voice about this policy

7. Why do economists generally talk about policy regimes and credibility rather than just policy?

8. How has the New Era economy undermined the economist's standard view of policy?

MATCHING THE TERMS
Match the terms to their definitions

____ **1.**	rational expectations	**a.**	a predetermined statement of the policy that will be followed in various circumstances
____ **2.**	policy regime	**b.**	forward looking expectations that use all available information
____ **3.**	new era	**c.**	a time when the economy keeps going and going

PROBLEMS AND APPLICATIONS

1. Demonstrate how a technological advance will shift the production possibility curve.

2. Demonstrate the effect of a price ceiling placed on rents.

3. What is the effect of expansionary fiscal policy in terms of the AS/AD model?

4. If the money supply rises by 30% what you predict would happen to prices and real output in the quantity theory of money?

5. If the money supply rises by 30% what would you predict would happen to prices and real output in the AS/AD model?

6. Demonstrate graphically what would happen if there is expansionary fiscal policy of 100 in the multiplier model and in the AS/AD model when the economy is far from potential income.

7. If the Fed sells $1000 worth of bonds how much will the money supply change if the reserve requirement is .1 and the cash-to-deposit ratio is .2?

8. In each of the following cases determine whether the sentence would most likely be said by a Keynesian or a Classical economist.

    a. Inflation is a combination institutional and monetary problem

    b. You should push inflation to zero following a strict monetary rule.

    c. Slow growth is probably caused by too much regulation and too-high taxes.

    d. The government should focus more on the short run than the long run.

● A BRAIN TEASER

1. Fully specified rules are always preferred to discretion, but only when there are full contingent rules. Discuss and state the relevance of this observation for macro economic policy.

● MULTIPLE CHOICE

Circle the one best answer for each of the following questions:

1. The bowed-out shape of the production possibility curve is due to:
   a. decreasing marginal opportunity cost.
   b. specialization and learning by doing.
   c. economies of scale.
   d. increasing marginal opportunity cost and comparative advantage.

2. The micro supply/demand model is best used to analyze which one of the following?
   a. Price of eggs.
   b. Unemployment.
   c. Aggregate output.
   d. World price level.

3. According to the long-run growth model, which of the following will most likely increase total income?
   a. Expansionary fiscal policy.
   b. Increased saving.
   c. Expansionary monetary policy.
   d. Increased consumption.

4. According to the quantity theory, if the money supply increases by 25 percent:
   a. the price level will increase by 25 percent and real output will remain constant.
   b. real output will rise by 25 percent and real output will remain constant.
   c. the increase in the money supply will be divided between increases in the price level and increases in real output.
   d. neither the price level nor real output will change.

5. According to the short-run AS/AD model, which of the following will most likely increase total income?
   a. An increase in the Fed funds rate.
   b. Increased saving.
   c. Higher exchange rates.
   d. Increased autonomous consumption.

6. Using the approximate, real-world money multiplier, if the reserve requirement is .3 and the cash to deposit ratio is .4 and the Fed sells $100 worth of bonds, money supply will:

   a. rise by $143.
   b. fall by $143
   c. rise by $333.
   d. fall by $333.

7. If the inflation rate is below the Fed target rate, the Fed will most likely:
   a. sell bonds to lower the fed funds rate.
   b. buy bonds to lower the fed funds rate.
   c. sell bonds to raise the fed funds rate.
   d. buy bonds to raise the fed funds rate.

8. If the mpc is .5 and the Federal government increases expenditures by $100 billion,
   a. the AD curve will shift out to the right by $100.
   b. the AD curve will shift out to the right by $200.
   c. the AD curve will not shift at all.
   d. the AS curve will shift out to the right by $100.

9. Keynesians and Classicals are *least* likely to agree that:
   a. expansionary monetary and fiscal policies have long-run stimulative effects on real income.
   b. expansionary monetary and fiscal policies have potentially long-run stimulative effects on inflation.
   c. monetary policy is politically easier to use than fiscal policy.
   d. expansionary monetary and fiscal policy tend to increase the trade deficit.

10. You have been appointed adviser to the President. He comes in and says he wants very low unemployment, zero inflation, and very high growth. You should
   a. advise him to use expansionary monetary policy.
   b. advise him to use contractionary monetary policy.
   c. tell him it is likely impossible using traditional tools.
   d. advise him to use a combination of expansionary monetary policy and contractionary fiscal policy.

11. You've been appointed adviser to the President. She wants interest rates to rise and wants unemployment to fall. You would suggest
    a. expansionary monetary policy.
    b. contractionary monetary policy.
    c. expansionary fiscal policy.
    d. contractionary fiscal policy.

12. You've been appointed adviser to the President. She wants interest rates and inflation to fall. You would suggest
    a. expansionary monetary policy.
    b. contractionary monetary policy.
    c. expansionary fiscal policy.
    d. contractionary fiscal policy.

13. Economists generally agree on all the following *except:*
    a. expansionary monetary and fiscal policies have short-run stimulative effects on income.
    b. expansionary monetary and fiscal policies have potentially long-run stimulative effects on inflation
    c. monetary policy is politically easier to use than fiscal policy.
    d. expansionary monetary and fiscal policy tend to decrease the trade deficit

14. Policy regimes are preferred to discretionary policy because:
    a. discretionary policies are more likely to affect people's expectations.
    b. regimes are more likely to be adopted by Congress.
    c. regimes provide government with more flexibility.
    d. the impact of policies are significantly affected by expectations.

15. A danger of the new era economy is that:
    a. expansionary monetary policy will lead to runaway inflation.
    b. policymakers will forget about the historic tradeoffs in the economy.
    c. the economy will never get to the long run.
    d. the currently high unemployment rate will persist for decades.

● POTENTIAL ESSAY QUESTIONS

You may also see essay questions similar to the "Problems & Applications" and "Brain Teasers" exercises.

1. Say you are a policy adviser to the government of a country that is growing at 6%, inflation is 1%, and unemployment is 2%. You are hired by the government to advise them how they can improve the economy? What advice would you give?

2. Mel Reder has stated that while there ain't no such thing as a free lunch, once in a while you can snitch a sandwich. What does he mean by this and what accounts for the possibility of doing so?

ANSWERS

SHORT-ANSWER QUESTIONS

1. Two micro models relevant for macro are the production possibility model and the supply/demand model. The production possibility model is relevant because it captures the trade-off view that is central to economists' macro policy view and the supply/demand model serves as a building block of macro reasoning. When applying the supply/demand model one must be careful, however, about the fallacy of composition. (415-416)

2. The two central long-run models are the long-run growth model, which includes both the Classical growth model and the New growth theory, and the quantity theory model (MV = PQ). These long-run models tend to focus on supply; short-run models focus on demand. (417-418)

3. The two central short-run macro models are the multiplier model and the AS/AD model. They are both models of the same phenomenon; they simply focus on different aspects; the multiplier model focuses on the repercussions of demand shifts; the AS/AD model focuses on price level changes. However, when the AD curve shifts, it shifts by an amount equal to the multiplier times the initial shift, which means that the two models are telling the same story. (419-420)

4. The money multiplier is $(1/r + c)$ and refers to the relationship between changes in bank reserves and the ultimate change in the money supply. The income multiplier is $(1/1\text{-}mpc)$ and refers to changes in income that ultimately occur after an initial change in autonomous spending. (422)

5. The Keynesian approach tends to focus on the short run and on demand policies. The Classical approach tends to focus on the long-run and supply policies. Both tend to accept the tradeoff view of macro policy. (424)

6. I would propose expansionary monetary policy. Expansionary fiscal policy would raise interest rates. I would emphasize that while the effect on income may be expansionary in the short run, in the long run, the expansionary monetary policy may simply lead to inflation. (426)

7. Policy is a process. Policies undertaken now influence expectations and actions in the future. Policy regimes take this into account whereas policies do not. Policy regimes involve rules. Those rules must be credible if they are to influence actions in the desired way. (427)

8. Economist's standard view of policy is a tradeoff view; you can get more growth and less unemployment at the cost of higher inflation. In the New Era economy, these tradeoffs have not arisen; we have had growth, low unemployment and low inflation. Most economists are happy about this, but are hesitant to base policy on the belief that the New Era will continue. Many believe that eventually the old tradeoffs will reassert themselves. (429)

ANSWERS

MATCHING

1-b; 2-a; 3-c.

ANSWERS

PROBLEMS AND APPLICATIONS

1. A technological advance will shift the production possibility curve out. (415-416)

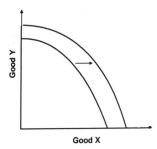

2. An effective price ceiling will cause a shortage of apartments as in the diagram on the right. (417)

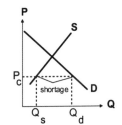

3. Expansionary fiscal policy will shift the AD curve out, increasing income. Whether the price level will rise and the AS curve shift up depends on how close the economy is to its potential income. (419)

4. I would predict that the price level would rise by 30% and real output would remain constant. This follows from the assumptions of the model (MV=PQ) where V and Q are constant. (418)

5. My prediction would depend on how close the economy is to potential income. If it is far away from potential income I would predict that real output would rise and prices would remain constant since the AS curve would be unchanged as shown in (a) below. If the economy is at potential income, I would predict that real income would remain constant (although it might temporarily rise) and prices would rise because the AS curve would shift up as shown in (b) below. (419-420)

a.

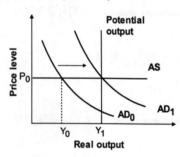

b.

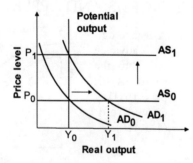

6. In both models the effect on income is the same. In the multiplier model, the AE curve shifts up by 100, and income increases by a multiple of 100, as shown below in (a). As shown below in (b), in the AS/AD model the AD curve shifts out by a multiple of 100, increasing income by the same multiple of 100 as occurred in the multiplier model. (419-420)

a.

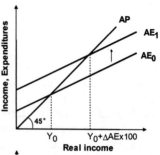

b.

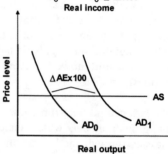

7. Using the approximate real world multiplier, (1/(r+c)) we can see that the multiplier is 3.33. Selling bonds decreases the money supply so the money supply will decrease by 3,333. (422)

8. **a.** Keynesian; **b.** Classical: **c.** Classical; **d.** Keynesian (424)

━━━━━ ANSWERS ━━━━━

A BRAIN TEASER

1. There is a long debate about the advantages of rules vs. discretion. Rules get around the problem of policies affecting expectations since they build in expectation. A full contingent rule takes into account all contingencies and therefore has pre-specified the optimal policy, including effects on expectations from the beginning and thus is better than a discretion. If one cannot specify all contingencies, then there is the possibility of an event occurring for which the rule is not optimal. In that case discretionary policy may be preferably to deal with the contingency. (428-429)

━━━━━ ANSWERS ━━━━━

MULTIPLE CHOICE

1. d   The bowed-out shape of the PPC says that as more of one good is produced ever increasing quantities of the other good must be forgone. This reflects comparative

advantage; that is, there are increasing marginal opportunity cost. See pages 415-16.

2. a   The micro supply/demand model is most appropriately applied to markets where other things can be assumed to remain constant. That is, the more micro the market, the less other things will change. See pages 416-417.

3. b   In the long-run model, investment (financed by saving) is seen as a source of growth. The others increase output only in the short run. See page 418.

4. a   According to the quantity theory, real output is determined by other factors than the money supply. Since the velocity of money is assumed to be constant, a 25 percent increase in the money supply leads to a 25 percent rise in the price level. See pages 418-419.

5. d   In the short-run model, aggregate supply is fixed. Anything that increases aggregate demand will increase output. Since consumption is a component of aggregate demand increased consumption will increase output in the short-run model. Increased saving in the short run means less consumption spending. See pages 419-420.

6. b   The approximate real-world money multiplier is $1/(.3 + .4) = 1.43$. Since the government sells $100 worth of bonds, the money supply falls by the multiplier times the amount of the sale. See page 422.

7. b   To increase actual inflation, the Fed will want to increase investment expenditures by lowering the fed funds rate. It does so by buying bonds. See pages 422.

8. b   The AD shifts to the right by the multiplier $(1/.5)$ times the increase in government expenditures. See pages 420-421.

9. a   Classicals see minimal long-run effects of policy on real income. Many Keynesians also see minimal long-run effects of policy on real income, but some see policy having measurable long-run effects. See pages 423-424.

10. c   This combination of goals, for the most part, is unattainable. See page 426.

11. c   Only expansionary fiscal policy will work since the President also wants interest rate to rise. See page 426.

12. d   Only contractionary fiscal policy will work since the President also wants interest rates to fall. See page 426.

13. d   Expansionary monetary and fiscal policy increase the trade deficit. See page 426.

14. d   Policy regimes are preferred because regimes are better able to affect people's expectations and the effect of a policy are more predictable. See page 428-429.

15. b   The new era economy is the experience of rapid growth and low unemployment without inflation. If the economy has not really entered a new era where past tradeoffs are no longer important, the reappearance of those tradeoffs may surprise policymakers and result in policy mistakes. See pages 429-430.

ANSWERS

POTENTIAL ESSAY QUESTIONS

The following are annotated answers. They indicate the general idea behind the answer.

1.   I would start by pointing out that by most western economy standards the economy is going quite well, and that perhaps they should be satisfied with what they have. If they insist on policy actions, I would try to find out more information about the economy. For example, I would be worried that with high growth and low unemployment, that inflation may soon become a problem. Thus I would be very hesitant to use any demand-based policy. With growth of 6%, I would assume that supply incentives are working, but I would consider them carefully to see if a technology or pro-savings policy may make sense.

2.   The policy focus in microeconomics is on the tendency of individuals to take up useful trading activities through voluntary exchange. This leads to the no free lunch policy conclusion. In macro there is the fallacy of composition problem and some problems are so indirectly tied to individual actions that individuals cannot take advantage of all trading opportunities. In this case, there is a potential for gain through policy action—the snitching of a sandwich. Keynesian short-run models emphasize the snitching of a sandwich possibility.

Pretest
Chapters 13 - 18

Take this test in test conditions, giving yourself a limited amount of time to complete the questions. Ideally, check with your professor to see how much time he or she allows for an average multiple choice question and multiply this by 30. This is the time limit you should set for yourself for this pretest. If you do not know how much time your teacher would allow, we suggest 1 minute per question, or 30 minutes.

1. For every financial asset
   a. there is a corresponding financial liability.
   b. there is a corresponding financial liability if the financial asset is financed.
   c. there is a real liability.
   d. there is a corresponding real asset.

2. Which of the following is not a function of money?
   a. Medium of exchange.
   b. Unit of account.
   c. Store of wealth.
   d. Equity instrument.

3. Assuming individuals hold no cash, the reserve requirement is 20 percent, and banks keep no excess reserves, an increase in an initial $100 of money will cause an increase in total money of
   a. $20.
   b. $50.
   c. $100.
   d. $500.

4. If banks hold excess reserves whereas before they did not, the relative money multiplier
   a. will become larger.
   b. will become smaller.
   c. will be unaffected.
   d. might increase or might decrease.

5. FDIC is an acronym for
   a. major banks in the United States.
   b. major banks in the world.
   c. U.S. government program that guarantees deposits.
   d. types of financial instruments.

6. The central bank of the United States is
   a. the Treasury.
   b. the Fed.
   c. the Bank of the United States.
   d. Old Lady of Threadneedle Street.

7. Tools of monetary policy include all the following *except*
   a. changing the reserve requirement.
   b. changing the discount rate.
   c. executing open market operations.
   d. running deficits.

8. When the Fed sells bonds, the money supply
   a. expands.
   b. contracts.
   c. Selling bonds does not have any effect on the money supply.
   d. sometimes rises and sometimes falls.

9. Assuming the Fed is following the Taylor Rule, if inflation exceeds the target inflation by 1 percent and output is 1 percent above potential, what would you predict would happen to the Fed funds rate?
   a. It will rise by 1 percent
   b. It will rise by 2 percent
   c. It will fall by 2.5 percent
   d. It will fall by 3 percent

10. The real interest rate is 3 percent; the nominal interest rate is 7 percent. It is likely that one could deduce an expected inflation rate of
    a. 1%.
    b. 2%.
    c. 3%.
    d. 4%.

11. In an expected inflation lenders will generally:
   a. gain relative to borrowers
   b. lose relative to borrowers
   c. neither gain nor lose relative to borrowers
   d. The effect will be totally random.

12. If productivity growth is 2 percent and inflation is 5 percent, on average nominal wage increases will be:
   a. 2 percent.
   b. 3 percent.
   c. 5 percent.
   d. 7 percent.

13. The inflation tax is
   a. a tax placed by government on inflators.
   b. a tax placed by god on inflators.
   c. a tax on the holders of cash.
   d. a tax on holders of goods whose price is inflating.

14. If an economist focuses on social pressures in his or her discussion of inflation, that economists is likely:
   a. a quantity theory advocate.
   b. an Institutionalist theory of inflation advocate.
   c. an insider theory of inflation advocate.
   d. an outsider theory of inflation advocate.

15. If the economy is at Point A in the Phillips curve graph below, what prediction would you make for inflation?

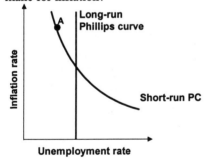

   a. It will increase
   b. It will decrease.
   c. It will remain constant.
   d. It will immediately fall to zero.

16. If a country has perfectly flexible exchange rates and is running a current account deficit, it is running
   a. a capital account surplus.
   b. a capital account deficit.
   c. an official transactions surplus.
   d. an official transactions deficit.

17. If there is a black market for a currency, the country probably has
   a. nonconvertible currency.
   b. a fixed exchange rate currency.
   c. a flexible exchange rate currency.
   d. a partially flexible exchange rate currency.

18. If a country runs expansionary monetary policy, in the short run one would expect the value of its exchange rate to
   a. rise.
   b. fall.
   c. be unaffected.
   d. sometimes rise and sometimes fall.

19. Refer to the graph below. If the U.S. government wants to fix its convertible currency at exchange rate P_1, it will have to:

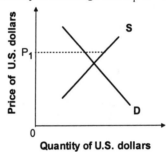

   a. supply official reserves in exchange for dollars.
   b. supply dollars in exchange for official reserves.
   c. disallow currency conversion except at the official rate P1.
   d. supply both official reserves and dollars because excess supply of dollars is so large.

20. Compared to a fixed exchange rate system, a flexible exchange rate system
   a. allows countries more flexibility in their monetary policies.
   b. allows countries less flexibility in their monetary policies.
   c. has no effect on monetary policies.
   d. allows countries more flexibility in their industrial policies.

21. If a country has a flexible exchange rate, the exchange rate
   a. is determined by flexible government policy.
   b. is determined by market forces.
   c. fluctuates continuously, changing by at least 1 percent per year.
   d. fluctuates continuously, changing by at least 10 percent per year.

22. Expansionary monetary policy has a tendency to
   a. push interest rates up and exchange rates down.
   b. push interest rates down and exchange rates down.
   c. push income down and exchange rates down.
   d. push imports down and exchange rates down.

23. If the trade deficit has gone up, it is most likely that the government ran
   a. an expansionary monetary policy.
   b. a contractionary monetary policy.
   c. a contractionary fiscal policy.
   d. an expansionary monetary policy and a contractionary fiscal policy.

24. If the exchange rate has gone up, it is most likely that the government ran
   a. an expansionary fiscal policy.
   b. a contractionary fiscal policy.
   c. Who knows?
   d. an expansionary monetary policy.

25. When a country runs a large trade deficit, the amount of crowding out that occurs because of fiscal policy is
   a. increased.
   b. decreased.
   c. unaffected.
   d. sometimes increased and sometimes decreased.

26. The micro supply/demand model is best used to analyze which one of the following?
   a. Price of eggs.
   b. Unemployment.
   c. Aggregate output.
   d. World price level.

27. According to the short-run AS/AD model, which of the following will most likely increase total income?
   a. An increase in the Fed funds rate.
   b. Increased saving.
   c. Higher exchange rates.
   d. Increased autonomous consumption.

28. If the mpc is .5 and the Federal government increases expenditures by $100 billion,
   a. the AD curve will shift out to the right by $100.
   b. the AD curve will shift out to the right by $200.
   c. the AD curve will not shift at all.
   d. the AS curve will shift out to the right by $100.

29. You've been appointed adviser to the President. She wants interest rates and inflation to fall. You would suggest
   a. expansionary monetary policy.
   b. contractionary monetary policy.
   c. expansionary fiscal policy.
   d. contractionary fiscal policy.

30. A danger of the new era economy is that:
   a. expansionary monetary policy will lead to runaway inflation.
   b. policymakers will forget about the historic tradeoffs in the economy.
   c. the economy will never get to the long run.
   d. the currently high unemployment rate will persist for decades.

━━━━━ ANSWERS ━━━━━

1.	a	(13:1)	16.	a	(16:2)
2.	d	(13:3)	17.	a	(16:7)
3.	d	(13:9)	18.	b	(16:13)
4.	b	(13:12)	19.	a	(16:14)
5.	c	(13:14)	20.	a	(16:16)
6.	b	(14:1)	21.	b	(17:2)
7.	d	(14:6)	22.	b	(17:6)
8.	b	(14:12)	23.	a	(17:9)
9.	b	(14:15)	24.	c	(17:12)
10.	d	(14:21)	25.	b	(17:16)
11.	c	(15:1)	26.	a	(18:2)
12.	b	(15:4)	27.	d	(18:5)
13.	c	(15:8)	28.	b	(18:8)
14.	b	(15:11)	13.	d	(18:12)
15.	a	(15:17)	14.	b	(18:15)

Key: The figures in parentheses refer to multiple choice question and chapter numbers. For example (1:2) is multiple choice question 2 from chapter 1.